D

DATE DUE

DATE DUE			
− 5 NOV 2008			
GAYLORD			PRINTED IN U S A

W

R

War, Culture and the Media:
Representations of the Military in 20th Century Britain

Edited by Ian Stewart
and Susan L Carruthers

Studies in War and Film · 3

FLICKS
BOOKS

British Library Cataloguing-in-Publication Data

War, culture and the media : representations of the military in
    20th century Britain. – (Studies in war and film ; 3)
    1.Mass media and war – Great Britain 2.War in mass media
    – Great Britain
    I.Stewart, Ian II.Carruthers, Susan
    355'.02

    ISBN 0-948911-86-7 (Pb)

This paperback edition first published in 1996 by

Flicks Books
29 Bradford Road
Trowbridge
Wiltshire BA14 9AN
England

Volume 3 in the series *Studies in War and Film*

A hardback edition of this book is published by Flicks Books
(ISBN 0-948911-85-9) and, in North and South America only,
by Associated University Presses (ISBN 0-8386-3702-7).

© individual contributors, 1996

Printed and bound in Great Britain.

Contents

Acknowledgements

The editors wish to thank the following: Matthew Midlane, Director of Studies RMAS, for his encouragement during this project; Sarah Alford and Marion Matthews for their help in typing sections of the manuscript; Cari Brandi for her assistance in providing software; Andrew Orgill at the Central Library, RMAS, for his continued and invaluable support; and, finally, many thanks to Lewis Smage, particularly for his comments on matters of style.

*   *   *

The views expressed in this book are those of these authors and in no way reflect the views of the Ministry of Defence.

Eight of the contributors to this collection of essays are members of the academic staff at the Royal Military Academy, Sandhurst. Stephen Badsey, Lloyd Clark, Nigel de Lee, Sean McKnight and G D Sheffield are all senior lecturers in the Department of War Studies. Edmund Yorke is a senior lecturer in the Department of Defence and International Affairs. John Allen is Head of the Communication Studies Department, where Ian Stewart also teaches. Jonathan Bignell is a lecturer in the Department of English at the University of Reading. Susan Carruthers lectures in international politics at the University of Wales, Aberystwyth. Andrew Steed is a freelance writer living in London.

Introduction
Ian Stewart and Susan L Carruthers

What is the role of the British media in our perception of warfare? How useful are the impressions which we glean from war films, television news reports and newspaper stories in helping us understand what soldiers, sailors and air force personnel do in the public's name? What are the practical and political issues involved in bringing reports of armed conflict to our television screens? Who controls the information we are given? Are British military institutions fairly represented, and how are enemy forces portrayed?

These are some of the questions addressed in this collection of specially commissioned essays. This book is intended to provide students and general readers with a concise introduction to the main arguments and issues surrounding the presentation of war and the military in 20th century Britain, with representations ranging from those contained in the moving image media and newspaper reports, to those in military history and war-toys.

Towards the end of the Vietnam War the British broadcaster, Sir Robin Day, pondered whether "in future a democracy which has uninhibited television coverage in every home will ever be able to fight a war".[1] If Sir Robin envisaged that subsequent wars would not receive "uninhibited television coverage", he was clearly correct when one considers the effort which went into media management in the Falklands and Gulf Wars. If, on the other hand, he thought television's prevalence would inhibit future wars altogether, he was clearly mistaken. At the time of writing, British troops are deployed in operational roles both in Northern Ireland, as they have been since 1969, and in Bosnia as part of the United Nations Protection Force (UNPROFOR).

If this suggests that television has had little or no effect on the frequency of wars, it certainly does not mean, however, that television has had little effect on the prosecution or presentation of war. Governments and their militaries have always considered it important how the wars and conflicts in which they have been engaged were reported and presented to the wider public. The advent of television and, in particular, live television, with its striking visuals, ever-greater immediacy and mass audience, have brought appreciation of the media near the top of the priority list of politicians and commanders. This is partly, although not wholly, explained by a conscious response to the perceived role

1

played by television coverage during the Vietnam War in destroying American public confidence.

Governments have always to some degree sought to control or influence the information about war which the public receives. The images of war that we see on our television screens or the accounts that we read in our newspapers are (and always have been) influenced to a greater or lesser extent by the military participants through, for example, control of and access to the battlefield, or the military's regulation of the release of news. Sir Robin Day's "uninhibited television" never has and probably never will exist.

Military and political leaders attempt to influence the messages carried by the media, believing that media coverage will determine the depth of national and international support on which they can hope to rely for their objectives. Stephen Badsey's essay in this collection (pages 5-21) addresses the current state of military-media relations and examines in depth the role played by a consideration of the accompanying media coverage of armed conflict in the planning and execution of a military operation. To account for and accommodate the media is a command function considered alongside the other central elements of military planning and procedure.

The arrangements that exist between the military and the media in the 1990s are the result of a relationship that has been developing since the growth of the mass media in the 19th century and the advent of the war correspondent (generally acknowledged to have occurred during the Crimean War). Indeed, early correspondents themselves often were officers writing home from the front – Winston Churchill being a famous but not uncommon example. However, as Andrew Steed's essay shows (pages 22-37), what began as informal agreements between individual editors and servicemen was formalised with the outbreak of the First World War by the setting up of a press corps, whose role was to provide newspaper coverage for the home audience.

However, at home the Great War was represented also in other ways. Lloyd Clark's essay (pages 38-53) takes as its subject the ways in which artists, poets, playwrights and filmmakers presented their own, sometimes contradictory, versions of the war. In some ways, Clark argues, it is these sources that are most important in colouring the enduring popular perception of the war. However, the cultural meanings of past wars are not static and Clark shows how understandings of the First World War changed in the decades following its termination. Bringing the analysis up-to-date, G D Sheffield (pages 54-74) examines the reputation of the First World War today, suggesting that myths about both the causes and the conduct of the war have been repeatedly reinforced and passed off as history in popular culture.

By the outbreak of the First World War the British public had witnessed the birth of a new and influential mass medium: filmmaking. Ian Stewart's essay (pages 75-90) assesses some of the ways in which war has been presented on film, focusing in particular on the cinematic codes and conventions – the "grammar" of cinema. Where Stewart is chiefly concerned with the form in which warfare has been presented, Edmund Yorke's essay (pages 91-100) examines the content of some British war films. He specifically looks at those films which deal with Britain's imperialist wars in various parts of the Empire.

In every conflict the military and policy-makers are concerned not only with how they themselves are represented, but also with how the media portray the enemy. Susan Carruthers's essay (pages 101-129) focuses on that particularly elusive enemy – the terrorist. Drawing on examples from Britain's colonial past and on more recent examples in Northern Ireland, she shows how successive British governments and their agencies have sought in times of undeclared war to ensure that the media convey the illegitimacy of terrorist opponents' methods and motives.

The portrayal of enemies is also the subject of Sean McKnight's essay (pages 130-147) on the media coverage of events leading up to the Gulf War of 1991. McKnight argues that the exaggeration of Iraq's military capabilities that typified the media coverage resulted from the insatiable demand of the media for information – even inaccurate information – combined with a fundamental and widespread misunderstanding of modern military operations, and not a concerted allied propaganda campaign, as others have suggested.

A determining factor in the reporting of any conflict is, as John Allen argues (pages 148-164), the available technologies for the production and distribution of information and images. Access to and control of these technologies are the crucial factors in determining the dynamics of the military-media relationship. Tracing the major developments in transmission technologies and their impact upon the reporting of armed conflict, Allen suggests that, while the technology available as a result of the current information explosion is new, the fears and worries of governments, media institutions and the military are certainly not.

The final two essays in this collection are concerned with the way in which ideas of war and the military are more generally assimilated into our culture. Writing from a cultural studies perspective, Jonathan Bignell (pages 165-184) looks at the phenomenon of war-toys and war-games, and assesses their significance in both social and psychological terms. Lastly, in an essay designed to stimulate debate, military historian Nigel de Lee (pages 185-190) asks if our understanding of war could be better served by adopting a postmodern approach to its study. Have the pseudo-scientific, modernist ways of traditional military history outlived their usefulness?

Given the enormous impact that war has upon society and cultural life, it is necessary to examine the intersection between war, culture and the media in an interdisciplinary fashion. To this end, the collection encompasses the work of writers, teachers and researchers from a range of academic backgrounds. They are primarily drawn from the discipline of military history, but also from political science, media studies and cultural studies.

In some cases, we have sought to harness the expertise of contributors working in their own field. In this respect, Stephen Badsey's contribution on the role of the media in recent military operations, and Susan Carruthers's essay on the developments in the reporting of terrorism reflect current research in those areas. However, for the most part we have encouraged the contributors to venture away from their usual academic domain or to adopt a different perspective on material with which they are familiar. For example, G D Sheffield is a military historian who has written extensively on the First World War, but here examines ways in which perceptions and meanings of the First World War circulate in contemporary culture and find expression in the classroom or on the television screen.

The sequence of these essays is not intended to follow or suggest any (chrono)logical system – it is hoped that the individual contributions will feed into and inform each other, rather than stand alone. There are, of course, some obvious interconnections. The contributions of Clark, Steed and Sheffield, each of which focuses on a different aspect of the representation of the First World War, are clearly related, as are Carruthers's and McKnight's examinations of portrayals of "enemies". Also related – in perhaps less obvious ways – are Allen's contribution on the technology of information gathering, Stewart's on war and cinema, and Badsey's on the military-media relationship.

None of these essays represents the final word on the subject. Not only is communications technology constantly changing – and with it the nature of the relationship between the military, politicians and the media – but also representations and readings of wars past are in a state of flux. This collection charts some of the fluctuations which have occurred. It also stresses many of the enduring concerns felt by those who prosecute wars, in terms of the media's portrayal and the public's reception of their deeds.

Note

[1]   Quoted in Philip M Taylor, *Munitions of the Mind: War propaganda from the ancient world to the nuclear age* (London: Patrick Stephens, 1990): 228.

The influence of the media on recent British military operations
Stephen Badsey

The majority of those engaged in planning British military intervention operations (a term which covers everything from peacekeeping and humanitarian relief to a major war in another country), perhaps even as late as 1990, would have regarded study of the media as a peripheral – if not downright eccentric – activity. Since then, the attention given to the impact of the world's news media on military interventions has increased dramatically. Politicians, military officials and academic members of the political élite (the "think-tanks") have all acknowledged the power of the media, while denouncing its distortion of traditional behaviour. In November 1992 Professor Lawrence Martin, Director of the Royal Institute of International Affairs at Chatham House, stated quite flatly that "[t]he days of international relations as an élite game are gone...The very fact that there are soon to be British troops in Bosnia is testimony to media influence".[1] In the same month, Brigadier Patrick Cordingley acknowledged that when he commanded 7th Armoured Brigade in the build-up to the Gulf War of 1991, "very soon media was not third on my list of priorities but first on the agenda of the daily conference".[2]

The view that has been increasingly advanced in government and military circles in Britain, the United States and other NATO countries is that the new phenomenon of global instantaneous news reporting – particularly by television – has distorted their foreign policies by forcing military intervention in such areas as former Yugoslavia, Somalia or Cambodia, while at the same time preventing that intervention becoming effective by imposing arbitrary constraints on the level of force used and on the willingness to risk both taking casualties and inflicting them. The result has been what one European diplomat in Washington has described as "the CNN Curve" of public demand for military intervention, followed by public protest when casualties are suffered.[3] In turn, the response of Western governments trapped between public demand for action and no viable military options has been what Professor Lawrence Freedman has called "symbolic security politics", whereby military operations known to be ineffectual are undertaken largely for public show.[4] An example is the EC/NATO naval force deployed to the Adriatic in July 1992, which was only allowed to conduct monitoring operations for its first four months.

Certainly, at the end of the 20th century the role of the media in military affairs cannot any longer be treated as a side-issue, except by wilful ignorance. From a military perspective, the "media war" is beginning to rank in importance with the war fought on the ground or in the air, and in many cases the behaviour of the media will help determine military success or failure.[5] However, the treatment of the importance of the media as a radical and completely unprecedented phenomenon of the 1990s is a considerable distortion of the facts. Military-media relations have an history, particularly as part of the wider issue of the role of the media in liberal democratic states, which has been traced by researchers (working in this field for over two decades now) back to the origins of both in the middle of the 19th century.[6] There is little in the complaints of diplomatists about the ability of the modern media to circumvent traditional political channels that cannot be found in similar writings of the 1920s on the consequences for diplomacy of the development of the cable wire services, while many military anxieties about the media on the battlefield predate the First World War.

Most of the problems associated with military-media relations are political, and their solutions exist only at the highest political levels. Unfortunately, at present there exists a methodological chasm – to call it a "conflict" would imply a degree of mutual recognition which does not exist – between, on the one hand, academics and others who view military-media relations as part of the much wider issue of the place of the media in society, and, on the other, military personnel who are inclined to view the problem as if the world exists for them to fight wars in, and the media are getting in the way. Even to approach the subject requires an engagement between very different academic disciplines, most notably media studies on one side, and security studies on the other (together with as many as seven other disciplines related to them both, ranging from electronic engineering to modern history), whose devotees have in the past scarcely acknowledged each other's existence and tend to be associated by stereotype with, respectively, left-wing and right-wing political positions.

The central term "media" is here taken to mean the modern, electronically-based international news media of television, radio, the wire services and the major newspapers, which report regularly and in depth on foreign and military affairs. It does not mean the fictional media, advertising, entertainment, or purely national or regional media. For reasons which will become apparent, the Western popular, tabloid or supermarket press are treated as a special case. In this definition, which would be widely accepted, there is no doubt that the media are American, in the sense that the United States and its interests dominate the

6

market, selling its product and its perspective on the world indirectly to national or local news media, and increasingly through English-language television, radio and newspapers directly to the cultural and political élites of non-Western countries. In the context of international news, this American domination is supplemented by a strong secondary British element, based on a largely shared language between the United States and Britain, the continued importance of the BBC World Service and World News, and the fact that both the Reuters news agency and Visnews (the world's largest independent supplier of news film and video) are based in London. Only Agence France Presse (AFP) in France and the Bertelsmann group in Germany represent a significant challenge to this American-British hegemony, in which the News International Group (which originated in Australia) may also be included.

This places the United States in the unusual position that its national media, which interact with the national government in matters of power and influence, are also the international media, which set the agenda to a remarkable degree for the inhabitants of other countries. It is therefore important to emphasise the uniqueness of the political culture within which the US media work, with its basis in the First Amendment to the Constitution, the 1974 Amendments to the Freedom of Information Act, and a presumed media "right of access" which has never been adequately tested in court. This should be compared with the battery of secrecy laws facing journalists in any European country, and the absence of any equivalent tradition of investigative reporting. The openness and lavish facilities which the Pentagon provides for American defence journalists are viewed with envy and incredulity by their British counterparts seeking to deal with the Ministry of Defence (MoD).[7]

In recent years Britain has engaged mostly in multinational military operations, preferably in company with the United States, rather than acting alone (the single exception being the 1982 Falklands War). In any multinational operation, an inevitable tension exists between governments seeking to stress the unity and solidarity of their positions, and the media seeking to probe the differences in policy and practice between them. It is a standard journalistic technique to build a story by exploiting small discrepancies between statements in this way. Any multinational use of force involving the United States is likely to come into conflict with the laws and customs of other countries in handling the media. However, the military experience of the Gulf War suggests that training and a mutual exchange of ideas between countries before a conflict can produce reasonable unanimity. The problem is much greater if the forces involved include those from countries with little or no tradition of media freedom, and different views on the relative social positions of the armed forces and the press. Yet, paradoxically, in the absence of any clear guidance from their own superiors, the forces of such countries may also often respond to the presence of the Western media in a completely open and helpful way. This phenomenon has been exploited by Western reporters, sometimes called "unilateralists", who from choice or necessity do not develop close links with their own national armed forces. The role of the unilateralists in the Gulf War, who are regarded as having produced some of the best reporting of the conflict, remains one of great controversy, and of sensitivity among the media themselves.

In 1990 Ted Turner, owner of Cable News Network (CNN) gave his opinion that "[t]here will not be a totalitarian state on the planet in 10 years due to communications".[8] Many other similar, very large claims have been made for the effects that exposure to the media may have on a target audience, particularly regarding military operations. It is therefore necessary to review briefly the academic theory of the subject, which will be very familiar to students of the media, but which has been largely neglected by political or military analysts.[9]

The study of the impact of the media on public opinion dates from research first conducted largely in the field of psychology in the early and mid-20th century, as part of what became known as "mass society theory". This led by the 1950s to the "stimulus/response" or "injection" model of the media, in which the public *en masse* was viewed as passive recipients for whatever message was provided for them, acting like the injection of a drug. If people were told to buy a certain product or vote in a certain way sufficiently often, they would do so. A more radical version of this was the "conversion" theory, whereby finely tuned media messages could cause an individual or a society to reverse its opinion on a given subject in a short space of time. These ideas became enormously influential, particularly in the United States, providing an apparently satisfactory explanation for the rise of the European Fascist demagogues, the appeal of Communism, and, at a more personal level, the behaviour of American collaborators in prisoner-of-war camps during the Korean War of 1950-53, all of which were seen as the results of directed propaganda and even mass brainwashing.[10] The idea of a precise, scientific method of measuring the impact of the media reached its high point in the mid-1960s in US think-tanks such as the Hudson Institute, which mooted the idea of practical "opinion control" by governments within a generation.

From about 1960 onwards, the "stimulus/response" model began to fall into disrepute, as increasing psychological and sociological research demonstrated that the impact of the media on individual opinions was very much more weak and indirect than had been thought. This led to a variety of pluralist liberal democratic theories of the media, of which the most famous is the "two step" theory (information received as a first step is modified in a second step, depending on the individual's socialisation), all based very heavily on empirical findings that the media's input was highly affected by the social context of the recipient. Rather than being injected with an idea, the individual was presented with a suggestion to accept, reject or modify, according to circumstances. The idea of "conversion" became entirely discredited, and has remained so.

In the early 1970s this liberal pluralist view of the media was in turn challenged by a broadly Marxist perspective, heavily influenced in the United States by the Frankfurt School of cultural philosophers. One feature of this tradition is its emphasis on the social and economic aspects of the media, which has been very valuable in explaining the media as an industry or as a business. While largely accepting the evidence of studies of the media, this tradition reinterpreted the data to produce the "dominant values" model, in which the media were seen to act through social and economic pressures to reinforce the prevailing ideology of their society. The effects of the media would therefore be strong when supporting the "dominant values" of society, and weak otherwise. In a bourgeois liberal democracy, for example, the capitalist media would portray violence as evil if perpetrated by a criminal, but good if perpetrated by the armed forces of the state, and the individual would respond accordingly. It is this "dominant values" perspective which lies at the heart of much academic criticism of recent British media coverage of military operations.[11] However, both research into the history of the subject and recent work on the Gulf War in particular have led to a revival of the liberal empiricist tradition in this country, and fruitful debate is now once more under way.[12]

Unfortunately, these 30 years or more of research into the influence of the media appear to have had little or no impact on the beliefs of British political and military leaders, or even on other academics working in the security studies field, in whose minds the "stimulus/response" and "conversion" theories remain alive and well. One British general observed on the deployment of troops to Bosnia in autumn 1992 that "we are going because television reporters are asking why we aren't doing something. Give us one nasty ambush and two or three dead Cheshires and the same television reporters will be asking why British soldiers are being killed in Yugoslavia".[13] This military attitude is not confined to television coverage, and a similar observation was made by Lieutenant-Colonel R A ("Bob") Stewart commanding the 1st Cheshire Regiment Battalion Group, the first British troops into Bosnia:

I noticed in the newspapers the growing press scepticism about the rationale behind a possible deployment. It was rather amusing, considering the press had demanded British involvement there in the first place. Surely these journalists need only read their own columns to discover why we were going.[14]

At least part of the responsibility for this curious state of affairs must be seen to lie with those academic theorists of media studies who have promoted a narrowly Marxist and culturally-based approach to the subject, which has had increasingly little connection with the real world of politics. As Robert Hughes of *Time* magazine observed, "[t]he world changes more deeply, widely, thrillingly than at any moment since 1917, perhaps since 1848, and the American academic Left keeps fretting about how phallocentricity is inscribed in Dickens' portrayal of Little Nell".[15]

British official attitudes towards the media in military operations have developed since the 1960s, therefore, almost in an intellectual vacuum, being heavily dependent upon the convictions of individuals and upon the most recent experience of other countries. Given the dominant position of the United States in British military thinking, it was inevitable that British views on the media would be heavily influenced by the American experience in Vietnam (the Second Indochina War, 1960-75), and in particular by the American media's coverage of the Tet Offensive of 1968. Here also a chasm of misunderstanding exists between two very firm positions. On the one side there is a solid body of research into the conduct of the American media and its impact on domestic public opinion, based on the usual accepted scholarly apparatus of evidence. Without exception, studies conducted in this way have shown that the American media behaved responsibly in their coverage of the war, and that there was no verifiable connection between the media's behaviour and shifts in American public opinion, a conclusion shared even by the relevant volume of the US Army's official history of the war.[16] On the other side, however, there is an influential and substantial group within the defence community, including many veterans of Vietnam, who are either unaware of these scholarly conclusions or reject them out of hand, expressing an absolute conviction that the Vietnam War was lost because of a betrayal of the US fighting forces by the media. What passes for evidence among this latter group is almost entirely anecdotal, where it exists at all.[17] Their viewpoint closely resembles that of right-wing Germans of the interwar years who claimed a "stab in the back" as the reason for Germany's defeat in the First World War, while at their most extreme they appear to argue that the simple fact of reporting a war, particularly by television, makes military victory impossible.

This fear of the media by the American military is closely connected with another apparent lesson of the Vietnam War – the statistical correlation showing that American public support for the war, as measured by opinion polls, fell 15% each time casualties increased by a factor of ten (that is, from 100 to 1000, from 1000 to 10 000, and so on).[18] Divorced from any form of context, this belief in an inexorable connection between casualties and public support – that, for example, the loss of 10 000 casualties in any circumstances would automatically cause public support to drop from 80% to 50% – became American military orthodoxy for the late 20th century. On more than one occasion before the Gulf War, the same figure of 10 000 American casualties was advanced by both sides as politically unacceptable to the United States, representing just 2% of the American troops finally sent to the Gulf.[19]

There are, of course, excellent moral and political grounds for any country's government to seek to hold its own casualties in a military operation to a minimum, and throughout the Gulf War American public opinion appeared to follow the same pattern of tolerance for casualties as during Vietnam.[20] Perhaps because of the very low level of US casualties suffered in the Gulf War, the military and political reaction has been that virtually any casualties suffered in a military operation would cause the collapse of public support. This theory appeared to be the basis behind the decision for American intervention in Somalia in 1992-94 to emphasise air support only at first, and leave the ground role to others, notably the Pakistanis, who suffered 23 dead in one incident in June 1993. Indeed, the loss of only a handful of American Special Forces troops in 1994 was a powerful motive behind the American withdrawal from Somalia that year. The use of surrogate forces, particularly from developing countries, may be legitimately seen as an American doctrine stretching back at least to the Korean War, but its implications proved unsettling for UN operations based on the global political consensus of the Security Council and General Assembly.

The extent of the American influence on British and other NATO military thought in recent times has been so great that the belief in a simple causal relationship between casualties, the media and public opinion has been absorbed virtually without question into British political and military thinking, despite the considerable differences between American and British society and political culture. This theory featured heavily in British reluctance to send ground troops to former Yugoslavia between September 1991 and November 1992, and also formed the background to the failure of the United States and European Community/Union powers to reach a consensus over military action in former Yugoslavia in 1993-94.

The "double-bind" of fear of the media and fear of casualties had also been influential in the strong American preference for military intervention by air rather than by ground forces, ranging from the humanitarian air-supply drops over Bosnia in 1993-94 to the aircraft and cruise missile attacks on Iraq in January and June 1993. From the perspective of a government wishing to limit involvement of the media in its military operations, air power (and, increasingly, "missile power") represents by far the best instrument. During the air campaign in the Gulf War, the military were able to dictate the story to the media (virtually depriving them of their traditional "gatekeeper" function in deciding which news was to be passed to the public and how it was to be presented) by releasing bomb or missile camera videotape, or scenes on board the aircraft, after the operation. By the very nature of such operations, the media's ability to check and verify the story, or to obtain another perspective, is severely limited. For the same reasons, however, the media can be profoundly suspicious of what they are being offered, while countries that have been subject to American air attacks have grown more politically sophisticated in providing the media with another dimension to the story. An interesting comparison may be made between the slow and ineffective Libyan media response to the American air raid on Tripoli in 1986, and the rapid Iraqi response to the cruise missile attacks of 1993, providing journalists with access to the sites attacked and putting forward their own version of events.

As the technological nature of military operations has changed in the second half of this century, the idea of a fixed division between ground warfare, air warfare and sea warfare is now seen as unrealistic by most Western military forces. Nevertheless, purely naval operations are still regarded as the lowest in political profile and therefore in attracting media attention. The record of navies in dealing with the media, on the rare occasions that a naval commander has been placed in a politically sensitive position requiring media skills during a war, has not generally been a happy or successful one. Air operations occupy a middle position, while the sending of ground forces to another country undoubtedly attracts the highest political and media profile. Any government engaged in military intervention operations involving ground forces is at present faced with the terrible dilemma that the only way to test the theory that casualties cause the collapse of public support is to risk taking those casualties, a mode of behaviour that has little appeal.

This unpleasant subject is far removed from the areas of social and cultural investigation traditionally associated with "media studies", but it is nevertheless of great political and social significance. On the one hand, the view that the lives of professional soldiers are entirely at the service of the state seems too politically and morally cynical for most people to accept it. On the other hand, there is the undeniable fact that fear of public reaction to losses, transmitted through the media, has restricted both the political will and the military ability of Western nations to intervene effectively in other countries, even when such intervention might have been morally justified (for example, to prevent the genocide in Rwanda in 1994). Moreover, the most that can be said for the theory that casualties cause the collapse of public support is that it may have some validity when applied only to the United States. The French suffered most of the UN's 39 dead in former Yugoslavia in the year to April 1993, but were still prepared to deploy troops to Somalia and Zaïre (although some of these, being from the Foreign Legion, were not French citizens). As for the British, it is perhaps stating the obvious that if the theory were true, their military operations in Northern Ireland between 1969 and 1994 would have been impossible, although this is not an exact parallel. It is in this deeply unsatisfactory position that the issue presently rests.

In August 1992 one British newspaper claimed of an Independent Television News (ITN) report, showing pictures of Serbian prison camps in Bosnia, that "twenty minutes after this report was broadcast on American television, President Bush changed his policy towards Serbia".[21] Evidence for this type of media impact on decision-making at the highest level is, by its very nature, fragmentary, anecdotal and usually unverifiable. Nevertheless, it is also remarkably consistent over the last three decades, suggesting that in both the United States and Western Europe media coverage of foreign affairs not only makes an impact through the occasional crisis, but also consistently sets the political agenda. It is not unusual for the main daily meeting between a Cabinet Minister and his deputies to consist of nothing but a review of that morning's press cuttings and television news. The greatly increased speed and volume of modern media communications have therefore meant that, particularly in the case of military operations, governments have begun to lose the initiative and simply react to the media. In 1993 Britain experienced – certainly for the first time in recent years – the unusual phenomenon of several experienced journalists complaining that they had too much influence. As that eminent establishment figure, the Editor of *The Economist*, Rupert Pennant-Rea, put it, "[i]f the press and the broadcasters take the side of a special interest the politicians will give in. Indeed, they will not even think of themselves as 'giving in'. They will pride themselves on having reached a judicious decision, one that is supported by the evidence and the views of intelligent people."[22]

Reaction to the media in political terms, which has a considerable effect on military grand strategy, is most often expressed as concern for "public opinion", which is itself a very imprecise term used with great laxity. Public opinion in its common sense meaning – i.e. the opinion of the public – is virtually impossible to measure in the short term, except by the very haphazard method of the opinion poll (called rather appropriately by the Germans a "Blitzumfragen"). However, there is considerable evidence that in most democracies this form of public opinion is largely indifferent to foreign affairs. In Britain, opinion polls suggest that only 2% of people regard foreign policy as significant, other than during crises. Although it is often argued that a military disaster or great loss of life might cause some form of mass reaction at home, it is noticeable that during the Falklands War public opinion in Britain was hardened towards the war by the loss of the warship HMS *Sheffield*, and during the Gulf War American public opinion also hardened towards the war after the Amiriyah bunker episode. In short, the available evidence simply does not support the currently prevailing theory. The significant questions as to just how exactly public support for a military operation might be expected to collapse, and how this collapse might manifest itself, remain entirely unanswered.

To a large extent, this is because of a tendency of governments (as the veteran German academic, Professor Hans-Joachim Schmidt, has rather neatly expressed it) to confuse *public* opinion with *published* opinion, the opinions which the media themselves express.[23] In this respect, it is useful to distinguish between the media and the press, particularly as military accounts critical of both tend to use the terms almost interchangeably, and because of significant changes in the role of newspapers in recent years. The original newspapers of Europe were, for almost two centuries, chiefly purveyors of party political opinion, advertising and lightweight society entertainment; it was the development of the electric telegraph in the early 19th century that enabled them to supply news on a regular basis. In this respect, newspapers have been progressively overtaken by television and the electronic news media since the 1960s, and as a result they are now clearly reverting to their original function. Lightweight entertainment and advertising have become the province of the popular press, while "quality" newspapers have become almost entirely a method by which the political élite seeks to communicate with itself, a function which in the United States is already being to some extent usurped by CNN. The "public opinion" which allegedly contributed to the British decision to deploy troops to Bosnia in summer 1992 consisted of a very small and distinctly transatlantic public. Indeed, a casual reader of British quality newspaper leader columns at the time would have been forgiven for concluding that *The New York Times* was a British mass-circulation daily.

The progressive replacement of newspapers by television as

the dominant news medium has been entirely bad for the reporting of military operations, and not only because it has produced a decline in factual newspaper reporting. Television is impressionistic, selective, superficial and sensationalist, and very poor at conveying the complexities of any situation. This is not a criticism of television, but simply a description of a medium in which an "in-depth" item lasts for 150 seconds. An even larger limitation is placed upon television as a news medium by its economic structure as a business, which is heavily based on entertainment with extremely high entry costs, and a correspondingly low threshold for audience understanding – a problem that grew throughout the 1980s, with television deregulation and an increased emphasis on market forces, rather than public service, as the determining factor for broadcasters. While television journalists acknowledge these problems, they nevertheless claim that their dominance of the news market should give them absolute precedence over newspaper journalists. In practice, the presence of newspaper journalists with British forces at war may depend on the degree of political influence that they can wield. The extreme case of this was the Falklands War, in which the number and members of an improvised press pool were determined entirely by political lobbying under frantic circumstances at the start of the campaign.[24]

Just as a sketch of prevailing media theories may have seemed elementary to some readers, so the habit in popular British culture of referring to the Second World War as "the last war" (or of subsequent events as "since the war") remains so strong that what is a commonplace of security studies may come as a genuine shock to others: depending on the exact choice of definition, there have been over 150 wars since 1945, costing between them in excess of twenty million lives, of which about 30 have been waged at any one time, a figure which remains broadly constant today.[25] Again, the degree of British involvement in such wars may startle those outside the defence community: British troops are believed to have been killed in action somewhere in the world in every year but one since 1945 (appropriately, the year of peace was 1968).

The international television networks (which in practice means the American networks augmented by the British and the French) can afford to cover two or three of these wars at the most, often sharing facilities and bringing the print media in their wake. The issue of which wars become international news is determined by complex and not always entirely predictable factors, of which cost and the ability of reporters to reach the story are often the most important. The presence of US troops will usually bring international news coverage. Beyond that, in each country which wars will receive attention is usually dictated by whether its own troops are involved, although in 1993 British television gave considerable attention to American involvement in Somalia and almost none to the small British contingent in Cambodia. A similar lack of British media attention accompanied a humanitarian operation in Rwanda in 1994. Given the limitations of the international media, it is possible for quite major wars to take place below the media threshold of attention: that they are happening is neither a secret, nor news in the global context. Perhaps the most extreme example of this is the war fought by the Republic of South Africa against the "front line" states in the early 1980s, which claimed an estimated 100 000 lives but received virtually no global media attention.[26]

The sometimes apparently arbitrary choice of newsworthy crisis areas, and the ability of television communications to beam pictures through by satellite link "live" (in practice, recorded a few minutes beforehand) are often cited as a major factor in distorting crisis management. British Foreign Secretary Douglas Hurd stated in January 1993 that:

> When it comes to distant but important events, even all the Foreign Office cables do not have the same impact as a couple of minutes of news video. Before the days of [lightweight] video cameras people might have heard about atrocities, but accounts were often old and disputed. The cameras are not everywhere. But where the cameras operate, the facts are brutally clear.[27]

In fact, the practical pace of television news has altered less since the Vietnam era than is often supposed. The instantaneous transmission of pictures from a war zone onto television screens remains very rare, and its impact on government policies extremely hard to demonstrate. Perhaps the single most credible and well-documented example of a television broadcast causing a British government to use troops is Prime Minister John Major's proposal for "safe havens" for Kurds in northern Iraq in March 1991.[28] However, it seems undeniable that 24-hour global television has significantly shortened the time within which governments sensitive to media coverage feel able to make decisions. Whether this sensitivity is justified is altogether another issue.

Given the fact of a media presence, some form of accommodation between the military and the media is inevitable. Direct censorship of the national media is commonplace in many parts of the world, and in multinational operations it has become standard practice to leave the host government to regulate its own media. But direct censorship was last used by the British in the Korean War, and its reintroduction during a humanitarian or intervention operation would send a very powerful and almost certainly inappropriate political signal. In a sensitive military situation, the most successful forms of control of the media are based on informal and delicate agreements between governments and the media at the highest level. It is a cliché of the subject, dating back at least to the Crimean War of 1853-56, that no journalist will file a story or take a picture if he knows that it will never be used. Élite journalists even pride themselves on what they call their "news sense", by which is meant a knowledge of the political and commercial tolerances within which they work, and of which stories will be acceptable. Naturally, such behaviour reinforces the claims of critics that the international media collaborate with Western governments, and that within Western countries themselves the media support, rather than challenge, the "dominant values" provided by governments. These subjects are a matter for some debate within the media themselves.

An alternative to direct censorship is some form of voluntary restraint on the part of the media, as with the improvised "press pool" in the Falklands War, which submitted to a vetting system. This pool system was reintroduced in the Gulf War, and has now been formalised by the British for their own media in any future major conflict. Indeed, the advantages of the pool are sufficiently recognised that the media organised their own informal pool in former Yugoslavia in 1992 when the military were unable to do so officially. During the century, a largely unwritten contract has developed with the British media as to what constitutes acceptable military behaviour in return for their cooperation, offered here as a list of "Principles of Military-Media Relations". The quotations which head each section are phrases (or, in some cases, paraphrases) which occur frequently in British official documents dating back to the First World War.

PRINCIPLES OF MILITARY-MEDIA RELATIONS

1. "The Propaganda of Facts". An official statement should never contain a conscious lie. But there is no obligation to volunteer specific information unless asked, nor to correct errors of press interpretation.

2. "Information must wait upon policy". Information strategy is dictated by broader political and military strategy. It cannot rescue a political or military strategy which is itself misconceived.

3. "PR is a command function". Commanders must keep their media relations staff fully aware of what is happening, and must themselves be aware of the media implications of their actions.

4. "Co-operate rather than censor". Media relations work better by treating the media as allies rather than as enemies, and by trust rather than by restriction.

5. "Silence breeds speculation". Cutting off information will not restrict the news flow. Telling the media nothing only forces them to guess, and they will often guess right.

6. "Propaganda destroys credibility". The "dirty tricks" of psychological warfare, such as black propaganda, should be kept entirely separate from any agency responsible for official contacts with the media.

To those outside the field of security studies, these "principles" may appear as an attempt to restrict the media on military operations. In fact, their intention is exactly the opposite: to enable the media to function in conjunction with military operations with the minimum of friction.

The traditional military attitude towards the media has been one of hostility. In the past it has been a cliché of military-media relations that "the essence of successful journalism is publicity, while the essence of successful military operations is secrecy", and that the objectives of the two sides are fundamentally opposed. However, while this necessary opposition may have been a fact of war as recently as even a decade ago, it is manifestly untrue of many modern forms of military operations, in which the objectives of the military and of the media frequently run in parallel and may often converge. Particularly in peacekeeping and humanitarian operations, the international media can play a valuable role in influencing the local political and military authorities. The Canadian Major-General Lewis Mackenzie, who commanded the UN forces in Sarajevo in 1992, has said that "[t]he media was the only major weapons system that I had. In a number of cases the media had more impact on keeping the peace and reducing atrocities than the peacekeeping personnel."[29] Experienced members of the news media realise this, and will often enter into temporary alliances with military authorities as part of the peacekeeping process. The remarkable, if still controversial, use of British television broadcasts by Lieutenant-Colonel Stewart in Bosnia in 1993 is a good example of how international publicity can be exploited during a humanitarian operation. Stewart himself summed up his experience: he felt that "in UN operations the press must be considered as part of the action", and that "[t]he mere presence of cameras was also sometimes enough to change the situation".[30]

In conclusion, the decision of a country to send its armed

forces abroad is a political one, and nothing short of a complete revolution in British political thinking could reverse the current trend of British troops being sent overseas on various missions at frequent intervals. The impact of the media on these operations and the relationship between the military and the media are likewise political subjects, to be approached from the perspective of both "media studies" and "security studies". There is still a great amount of work to be done, particularly in the academic and theoretical aspects of the field.

* * *

A preliminary version of this essay was given to the International Conference on "Low Intensity Conflict in the 1990s", held at RMA Sandhurst in July 1993. An expanded version, intended principally for military officers, was published by the Strategic and Combat Studies Institute (SCSI) at Camberley in 1994 as Number 8 in their series *The Occasional*, under the title *Modern Military Operations and the Media*. The version which appears here is shorter, incorporates a number of changes, and is intended for the more general reader. The ideas expressed in this essay have been developed by the author over more than a decade of research and experience at the Imperial War Museum, the BBC, and the Department of War Studies, RMA Sandhurst. The author is particularly grateful to John Pimlott, Head of War Studies, and to Duncan Anderson for their help.

Notes

[1]   Quoted in *The Times Higher Education Supplement* 20 November 1992.

[2]   Brigadier [now Major-General] Patrick Cordingley DSO, "Future Commanders – be warned!", *Despatches* 3 (1992): 16.

[3]   *The International Herald Tribune* 26 October 1992.

[4]   Quoted in ibid.

[5]   Stephen Badsey, "The Media War", in John Pimlott and Stephen Badsey (eds), *The Gulf War Assessed* (London: Arms and Armour Press, 1992): 219.

[6]   See, in particular, Philip M Taylor, *Munitions of the Mind: War propaganda from the ancient world to the nuclear age* (London: Patrick Stephens, 1990).

[7]   Lionel Barber, "U.S. Defense Reporting: A British Perspective",

in Loren B Thompson (ed), *Defense Beat: The Dilemmas of Defense Coverage* (New York: Lexington Books, 1991): 135-147.

[8]   Quoted in Don M Flournoy, *CNN World Report: Ted Turner's International News Coup* (London: John Libbey, 1992): 2.

[9]   For a further discussion of these various theories, see, in particular, James Curran, Michael Gurevitch and Janet Woollacott, "The Study of the Media: Theoretical Approaches", in Oliver Boyd-Barrett and Peter Braham (eds), *Media, Knowledge and Power* (Beckenham: Croom Helm, in association with the Open University, 1987): 57-79.

[10]   John Marks, *The Search for the "Manchurian Candidate": The CIA and Mind Control* (London: Allen Lane; New York: Times Books; 1979): 21-33, 125-146.

[11]   See, for example, John Eldridge (ed), *Getting the Message: News truth and power* (London: Routledge, 1993) and the Glasgow University Media Group, *War and Peace News* (Milton Keynes: Open University Press, 1985).

[12]   See, for example, David E Morrison, *Television and the Gulf War* (London: John Libbey, 1992) and Philip M Taylor, *War and the media: Propaganda and persuasion in the Gulf War* (Manchester: Manchester University Press, 1992).

[13]   Quoted in *The Daily Telegraph* 11 September 1992.

[14]   Lieutenant-Colonel Bob Stewart, *Broken Lives: A Personal View of the Bosnian Conflict* (London: HarperCollins, 1993): 59.

[15]   Quoted in *The Times Higher Educational Supplement* 9 July 1993.

[16]   For a good summary of the recent evidence, see Professor Carlyle A Thayer, "Vietnam: A Critical Analysis", in Peter R Young (ed), *Defence and the Media in Time of Limited War* (London: Frank Cass, 1992): 89-115. See also William M Hammond, *Public Affairs: The Military and the Media 1962-1968* (Washington: Center of Military History, United States Army, 1988): 385-388.

[17]   See Claude C Sturgill, *Low Intensity Conflict in American History* (Westport, CN: Praeger Publishers, 1993): 94-96.

[18]   See Hammond: 262.

[19]   See Lawrence Freedman and Efraim Karsh, *The Gulf Conflict 1990-1991: Diplomacy and War in the New World Order*, second edition (London: Faber and Faber, 1993): 52, and H Norman Schwarzkopf with Peter Petre, *It Doesn't Take a Hero* (London; New

York: Bantam, 1990): 356.

[20]   John Mueller, *Policy and Opinion in the Gulf War* (Chicago: Chicago University Press, 1994): 77.

[21]   *The Sunday Times* 9 August 1992.

[22]   "An Editor's Farewell", *The Economist* 27 March 1993.

[23]   Hans-Joachim Schmidt, "The role and realities of public opinion", in Gérard Duprat and Alain-Marc Rieu (eds), *European Democratic Culture* (Milton Keynes: Open University; London: Routledge, 1993): 154.

[24]   Robert Harris, *Gotcha!* (reprinted as part of *The Media Trilogy* [London: Faber and Faber, 1994]: 10-24).

[25]   Richard Connaughton, *Military Intervention in the 1990s: A new logic of war* (London: Routledge, 1992): 4.

[26]   Joseph Hanlon, *Apartheid's Second Front: South Africa's War against Its Neighbours* (Harmondsworth: Penguin Books, 1986): 1.

[27]   Quoted in Nicholas Hopkinson, "The Media and International Affairs After the Cold War", *Wilton Park Paper* 74 (London: HMSO, 1993): 11.

[28]   See John Pimlott, "The International Ramifications", in Pimlott and Badsey (eds): 200-202.

[29]   Quoted in Hopkinson: 17-18.

[30]   Stewart: 323.

British propaganda and the First World War
Andrew Steed

> Cinema had the ability to reach the intelligence of the least
> intelligent. (Lord Balfour)[1]

The British government's attitude to propaganda in the First
World War was similar in many ways to their response to other
aspects of state intervention. Talented individuals, who had
worked in related areas prior to the war, were directed to set up
committees and departments. By a process of trial and error,
increasingly professional and effective approaches were adopted,
so that by 1918 British propagandists could claim a triumph in
the recruiting of allies, including the United States, Italy,
Romania and Greece. They could also point to the successful
propaganda directed against the German Army and the German
people, and highlight the effectiveness of the propaganda directed
at the disparate components of the Habsburg Empire which
began to disintegrate in October/November 1918.

However, the progress made in these years was not entirely
smooth, and, in describing the story of British propaganda
between 1914 and 1918, we shall see that it is impossible to
provide a purely narrative history, devoid of the conflict between
government departments, and indeed, without some mention of
the black arts of high politics. This further analysis is crucial to
an understanding of the period and especially to an appreciation
of the problems borne by the propagandists. No doubt, some of
the bickering that took place between the Foreign Office and the
War Office and the Admiralty can be put down to typical
departmental rivalries and point-scoring. Yet, there were more
serious disagreements over how the propaganda war should be
fought – even if it should be fought at all. Of particular interest
is the reaction of the service chiefs, when propaganda began to be
directed at the Home Front. To rekindle flagging enthusiasm for
the war, the propagandists decided to make use of the new and
hugely popular medium of film. In addition to the practical
problems encountered by cameramen, the propagandists had
initially to counter the formidable opposition of the War Office
and the Admiralty, who seemed excessively cautious and loath to
acknowledge any possible benefits that might result. In fact, by
1918 over 200 films had been commissioned and a twice-weekly
official newsreel had been released. This manipulation of public

opinion was itself an historic recognition that the opinion and morale of the masses were important if the war was to be brought to a successful conclusion.

In the past there has been much criticism of the early propagandists based around the very idea that they did not know how to reach the masses, and that "experts" in the field of advertising/communication should have been allowed to run the propaganda war in a more professional and businesslike manner. The arrival of Lord Beaverbrook to take charge of the new Ministry of Information (MoI), and of Lord Northcliffe to head the Directorate of Enemy Propaganda, have subsequently been taken as a significant development – not least by the two individuals themselves! Finally, it was argued, the organisation of war was being taken out of the hands of amateurs and given to ruthless but efficient professionals. Accordingly, there was a marked improvement in efficiency and effectiveness.

In fact, although the tone of some propaganda may have changed, the majority of propaganda remained the same, and there is little evidence to suggest that it improved in quantity or quality. In effect, the reorganisation and creation of the new ministry undermined staff morale and resulted in key individuals leaving the service. In addition, these political appointments only attracted attention to a part of government which did not necessarily welcome publicity, and also caused embarrassing questions to be raised in Parliament.

In his memoirs, Lord Beaverbrook went out of his way to promote the myth that, prior to his appointment as Minister of Information, very little had been achieved in the way of propaganda:

> There was no blueprint to work on. No experience to guide the new department. There was no office, no staff. There was nothing but a decision of the War Cabinet decreeing that such a Ministry should be created and that I should be Minister.[2]

In fact, Asquith's Cabinet had decided to initiate official propaganda at the end of August 1914 in response to German propaganda materials appearing in many neutral countries. Charles Masterman, a Liberal MP and Cabinet Member, was approached to set up a department, which he ran from offices in Wellington House, where he resided as Chairman of the National Health Commission. He maintained these offices and soon Wellington House was synonymous with official propaganda.

Masterman was from a lower-middle-class background and had obtained a place at Christ's College, Cambridge, where he had excelled. He was an outstanding speaker in the Cambridge Union, of which he was President in 1896; four years later, he was elected a Fellow and mixed with a circle of up-and-coming Liberals and progressives. Elected a MP in the Liberal landslide General Election victory of 1906, he quickly came to the attention of Asquith, becoming an Under-Secretary of the Local Government Board in 1908, and Financial Secretary to the Treasury in 1912.[3]

It would be convenient to paint Masterman as an inexperienced amateur in the art of communications, but it would be only half-true. He had contributed articles to numerous newspapers, becoming literary editor and a leader writer for *The Daily News*. Moreover, he had produced two commentaries on social conditions in the slums of Lambeth. It would be fair to say that his background and experience resulted in his propaganda efforts having a literary emphasis. But this should not surprise us, and nor in the early years of the war was it wrong. He may have had little experience of communicating with or to the masses, but, to his credit, Masterman was quick to appreciate that literary propaganda had most influence with "opinion formers" – to appeal to the ordinary man and to attract popular sentiment, other means of communication would have to be found.

Also to Masterman's credit was the speed with which he addressed the problem and the way in which he was able to formulate general principles to his work which largely endured until the war's end and, indeed, have a timeless relevance to those who wish to sway opinions and influence events even today.

Within a matter of weeks, Masterman had established a policy for official propaganda which was to last for much of the war, concentrating on Allied and neutral opinion, including the Dominions. At this stage in the war it was justifiably perceived that there was no need to embark upon a campaign of domestic propaganda. The mobilisation of opinion behind the war effort was left to the voluntary sector, with the activities of well-intentioned individuals and groups coordinated by the Central Committee of National Patriotic Organisations.[4] In September Masterman had two important meetings which made use of his contacts in the fields of literature and journalism, the first attended by authors, and the second by publicists and representatives of the press. The list of novelists, poets, short-story writers, critics and dramatists at the first meeting reads like a roll-call of Edwardian literature and included Sir J M Barrie, Arnold Bennett, A C Benson, G K Chesterton, Sir Arthur Conan Doyle, John Galsworthy, Thomas Hardy, John Masefield, Gilbert Murray and H G Wells. (Rudyard Kipling sent his apologies for absence!) Masterman's aim was to organise a manifesto of support in response to that signed by a group of prominent German scholars defending the attack on Belgium. The statement duly appeared in *The Times* on 18 September, calling upon

Britain and "all the English-speaking race" to defend "the ideals of Western Europe against the rule of 'Blood and Iron'".[5] The second meeting contained an equally impressive array of newspaper writers and editors, and agreed on four resolutions regarding the conduct of propaganda: that censorship should be minimal; that there should be a government coordinator for giving out government news; that the government should help journalists to report on the Dominions and neutral countries; and that British diplomats should enlist the help of journalists to correct errors in foreign news-reporting. These resolutions, together with a more detailed plan, were agreed by the Cabinet.[6]

Masterman operated on the basis of three principles, the first of which was to keep the origins of propaganda secret. He believed that manipulation directed at opinion-leaders would not succeed if they knew the source of the information they were receiving. One need only cite the German book distributor who advertised some 50 Wellington House publications and the reviews of Wellington House pamphlets in the German press as an indicator of the success of this strategy. The only problem was that, unless one was fully appraised of the work of Wellington House, one could be forgiven for believing that Britain was doing nothing to counter the less subtle German propaganda. It is hardly surprising therefore that, compared to self-publicists such as Beaverbrook, Masterman has received so little recognition, and that only recently has he become regarded as "the most important governmental propagandist in Britain during the entire war".[7]

The second guiding principle that Masterman outlined was that propaganda was to be factually-based, an ideal that would not prove easy to uphold in the climate of the times. This is best illustrated by Masterman's reaction to continued reports of German atrocities. His refusal to use such accounts unless he could satisfy himself as to their veracity only resulted in his being labelled as unpatriotic.[8] Eventually, a reluctant Masterman did produce a leaflet, and a pamphlet on the German corpse conversion factory was translated into four languages. Another notorious piece of propaganda was the Bryce Report, or the Report of the Committee on Alleged German Atrocities. Bryce was a respected Professor of Jurisprudence, a member of the House of Lords, an ex-British Ambassador to the United States, and had received the Pour le Mérite from the Kaiser. His report concluded that the Germans had been guilty of excesses and had adopted a strategy of using terror to paralyse civilian populations and demoralise enemy troops.[9] Despite the less than scrupulous methods of collating the report, Masterman seems to have had little problem in exploiting the report to the full, ordering translations into 30 languages and shipping 41 000 copies to the United States, where it received extensive coverage. It is debatable as to the extent to which one should censure Masterman, who may have been genuinely convinced by the evidence of the report. Bryce probably deserves greater criticism, but neither individual can have been unaffected both by the events of the war and by the likely impact of the report itself.

Masterman's third principle was the selective distribution of propaganda, and accordingly his office was subdivided with stations or desks for different areas or countries; there was a sub-office for Scandinavia, one for the Netherlands, and another office dealt with Italy and Switzerland. By far the most important office looked after the United States and was headed by Sir Gilbert Parker, a well-known Canadian novelist and Conservative MP for Gravesend. Parker worked for no salary and exemplified the British tradition of the talented amateur. He went about his business in an extremely professional manner. His analysis of the American press resulted in weekly reports on the most parochial of American newspapers and served as a gauge of US opinion. His staff – he started with nine and eventually employed 54 – surveyed "opinion formers" at American universities and colleges and swiftly compiled a list of influential Americans sorted by category. By the end of the war, this list numbered some 260 000. Parker also kept in contact with American correspondents stationed in London, and set up interviews with prominent British or Allied personalities. He arranged for American correspondents to be among the first to visit the Front, and by 1917 two of the four country houses in France used by foreign journalists were reserved for Americans. By various means, Parker "was able to provide news stories and other materials generated by Wellington House to some 555 American newspapers".[10] Significantly, Parker sent all his information from a private address, giving the impression that he was a disinterested supporter of the British cause, his inclusion of personalised enclosure cards further concealed this subtle manipulation of American opinion.

In the meantime, efforts were made to restrict the material produced by the Union of Democratic Control (UDC), a pressure group set up in August 1914 and opposed to the secret contacts that had taken place between British and French military chiefs, which constituted a commitment in advance to join in the war against Germany. The pamphlet by E D Morel, entitled "How the War Began", went further by arguing that Germany was fighting a defensive war. Obviously, distribution of these views complicated the official message; with Foreign Office help, Masterman prohibited all UDC publications from being sent overseas, and arranged for Gilbert Murray to write a riposte to the charge of secret diplomacy in *The Foreign Policy of Sir Edward Grey 1906-15*, which was widely distributed by Wellington House.

Ultimately, the United States entered the war on the side of the Allies, and shortly afterwards, Parker resigned from his post.

One should not overstate the role of Parker, but there is a general consensus that the Allies, and especially Britain, got the better of the Germans in the propaganda war to win the support of the American people. The British campaign was more subtle and, with the exception of British policy over the stopping of neutral shipping, there were few episodes which could be exploited by the Germans or used by sections of the American press that were sympathetic to the German cause, such as those newspapers controlled by William Hearst.

In contrast, German military actions made the task of achieving favourable publicity difficult. From the initial invasion of Belgium to the execution of Nurse Cavell, the sinking of the *Lusitania* and the contents of the Zimmerman telegram, events conspired against Germany. The inability of the Germans to counter British propaganda can be attested to by the comments of Count Bernstorff, German Ambassador in Washington, after the war:

> The [German] Press-service...never succeeded in adapting itself to American requirements. The same may be said of most of the German propaganda...This...showed a complete lack of understanding of American national psychology.[11]

He complains that Berlin missed several opportunities to publicise the effect of the Allied blockade on the German civil population which "they have made no attempt to bring to the notice of the world".

The propaganda directed against the United States demonstrates very conveniently Masterman's basic principles of keeping propaganda factual and its origins secret, and being selective about towards whom it was directed. The principles were applied elsewhere; literature was never distributed in the name of the British government, but was either sold through normal commercial channels or distributed free through a local organisation. By June 1915, Wellington House had distributed a total of 2.5 million copies of books, official publications, pamphlets and speeches, in some seventeen different languages.[12]

1916 proved to be an important year, with changes in the management of news and the beginning of the move away from reliance on literary propaganda. Firstly, the Neutral Press Committee – formed within the Home Office – and the Foreign Office News Department were amalgamated and began to concentrate on the dissemination of news in partnership with Wellington House, thus abandoning the original distinction between propaganda and the provision of news. In the meantime, censorship remained the responsibility of the Press Bureau, although both the War Office and the Admiralty had a major input. By the end of 1915, the first official propaganda film, *Britain Prepared*, had been completed and was to prove a major success, enjoying extensive distribution. Moreover, the production of pictures and photographs was well-established, with over 4000 photographs being distributed weekly by the autumn of 1916, and one million copies of six illustrated newspapers being produced every month. As Reeves points out, new forms of propaganda were being employed, including lantern slides, postcards, Gramophone records and cigarette cards.[13]

Attitudes within the great ministries of state were beginning to change – within the Foreign Office, War Office and the Admiralty, officials who originally found the whole notion of propaganda so distasteful were beginning to appreciate its importance. Both the service departments had originally banned the taking of photographs at the Front and severely restricted visits of war correspondents.[14] Undoubtedly, opinions within the War Office were coloured by the attitudes of Kitchener, who was violently anti-press. Even so, MO7, a branch of the War Office, had been formed in early 1915 to deal with press publicity, and it was MO7 who gave permission for the first war correspondents to visit the Front in May 1915. In January 1916, as part of a wider reorganisation of the Imperial General Staff, a new Directorate of Military Intelligence was created and MO7 became MI7. The death of Kitchener in June 1916 and his replacement by Lloyd George as Secretary of State for War marked a further significant change, and the War Office became increasingly critical of the civilian propagandists, calling ultimately for a separate department of propaganda. Throughout 1916 the War Office challenged the role of the Foreign Office, and claimed that it was constantly receiving complaints about the failure of British propaganda. Brigadier General Charteris, Chief of Intelligence at GHQ argued that "[w]e should employ the expert not the amateur. The expert is either a newspaper man, the company promoter or the organiser of some of our big amusements."[15] Not surprisingly, the War Office received support from the press itself, who also called for changes in organisation and content of propaganda. These two strange bedfellows found an additional ally in Lloyd George, and his rise to the premiership in December 1916 heralded change.

Within a month, Lloyd George had asked an old friend, Robert Donald, editor of *The Daily Chronicle*, to investigate the existing propaganda arrangements. His report, produced within a few weeks, was heavily influenced by the War Office and – hardly surprisingly, therefore – recommended a separate department of propaganda, controlled by one person with greater press cooperation. In fact, as Reeves has made clear, it does seem that Lloyd George had already made up his mind, and that Donald's report provided "independent" ammunition.

The new Department of Information (DOI) which came into existence was still to be based at the Foreign Office, and the man chosen to head the Department was John Buchan. Masterman's Wellington House organisation was incorporated into the new administrative structure, with Masterman himself overseeing the literary propaganda, i.e. books, pamphlets, journals and pictures. The DOI was certainly more streamlined and thus it reduced the areas of overlapping responsibility that had contributed towards the departmental conflicts. There seems little doubt that Buchan, who had risen to the rank of Major while serving with the Intelligence Corps on the Western Front, experienced much better relations with the War Office and the Admiralty, and his previous experience of writing first-hand accounts for the Foreign Office News Department and working as a liaison officer between GHQ and the civilian propagandists meant he had a foot in both camps. The fact that the DOI now had a clearly defined, separate existence, independent of the Foreign Office, enabled it to establish much better relationships with other government departments involved in propaganda.

The extent to which any changes in propaganda were due to Buchan is open to question, for it could be argued that such changes which did occur were inevitable, no matter who headed the new DOI. In many ways, Buchan remained loyal to the principles established by Masterman, and the fact that the two individuals liked and respected each other indicates that Masterman did not find the new department producing material or adopting a strategy which was so unpalatable. That the new department expanded in staff, with much greater overseas activity, was to be expected; the new Press Bureau set up in Paris and the British Information Bureau opened in New York were logical developments of the strategy of devolving the organisation and the production of propaganda to the country at which it was targeted.

There were, however, more significant changes. Buchan received a salary of £1000 per annum – thus ending the amateur tradition – and, unlike Masterman, he reported directly to the Prime Minister. There is an argument that he was instructed to be more open about the existence of a government propaganda department, and certainly he had a higher public profile than Masterman; he founded an informal Anglo-American society in London, and served as host for American newspaper editors.[16] There is a more contentious accusation that, under Buchan, propaganda became baser and more lurid – his decision to subsidise massive circulation of the hate-inspiring cartoons of Louis Raemakers is cited as evidence. Certainly by 1917 the romantic glory of war was a somewhat tarnished idea, and it is no great surprise that propaganda should have become more vicious. In any prolonged struggle, combatants resort to ever more intense means of ensuring survival and defeating the opponent; a debasing of propaganda is atypical.

The two major innovations which occurred in 1917 are again associated with Buchan: the introduction both of the first propaganda in enemy countries, and of domestic propaganda. The first was achieved by the placing of articles and cables in the newspapers of neutral states, and by the smuggling of materials through neutral Switzerland and the Netherlands, or by distributing material via aeroplane or balloon from the British front over to the German lines. This last method – of demoralising the enemy – was instigated in 1916, and suffered various setbacks, until by 1918 the Allies were distributing material over a zone 150 miles deep, behind the German Front. By August 1918, 100 000 leaflets a day were being distributed.[17]

Buchan had recognised the need for some domestic propaganda as early as February 1917, and eventually the National War Aims Committee (NWAC) emerged. Buchan sat on the Executive Committee, but it was actually administrated as an entirely separate organisation. It absorbed the Central Committee of National Patriotic Organisations and the constituency organisations of the political parties were also obliged to cooperate, ensuring that the NWAC message could be carried throughout the land. Unlike the DOI, NWAC, launched by Lloyd George in August 1917, was a very public body. Propaganda offensives were organised in the manner of election campaigns with rallies and speeches. One of the most successful speakers was Horatio Bottomley, the infamous entrepreneur and one-time Liberal MP.

Bottomley originally had been asked to make a recruiting speech at the London Opera House, Kingsway, in September 1914, probably on the strength of the popularity of his weekly newspaper, *John Bull*, which had a circulation of 1.5 million. He proved to be a success, and by 1915 he was the most popular speaker in the country, drawing crowds which far surpassed those gathered to hear Cabinet Ministers. Bottomley gave a total of 340 lectures over a three-year period, over 90% of which were "all-purpose patriotic orations".[18] Soon the government was asking Bottomley to visit munitions workers, coalminers and railway workers – he was even despatched to placate striking shipworkers on the Clyde. It was not long before he had his own column in sections of the Northcliffe press, which very obviously was aimed at the common man. Indeed, in *The Sunday Pictorial* as early as February 1916, he argued that the war was "a People's War which needed leaders of government who could understand 'the mind of the Man-in-the-Street'...One man in the Cabinet who really understood the heart and mind of the British democracy would be worth three army corps to the cause of the Allies".[19] A year later, he had persuaded the DOI to allow him to visit the Front, and in December 1917 he made an equally successful visit to the Grand Fleet. Strictly speaking, Bottomley was working in an unofficial role. In fact, he was working for the Parliamentary Recruiting Committee (PRC) initially and then the NWAC from 1917, and he had direct contact with Northcliffe and other government agents. That such a demagogue – who had been declared a bankrupt in 1912, and was to be convicted of fraud in 1922 – should receive such government backing is surely an indication of the changing attitudes of those who directed the war effort, and a recognition that, to win the war, a different attitude to the whole population was required.

Reference has already been made to the role of film, and how use of this medium symbolised a shift in thinking as to how the war was to be won. That it took until December 1915 for the first British propaganda film to be released requires some explaining, for the cinema trade were keen to prove that film had a role in the war, and that it had an ability to record the actual likeness of events. Already the Canadian government had arranged cameramen to accompany their troops, and both the Germans and French permitted cameramen near the Front. The showing of these films abroad convinced many British diplomats that Britain should follow suit. As Reeves points out, there had been cooperation between the cinema and the service departments before the war, which makes it even more difficult to comprehend the negative, dismissive attitude of the War Office and the Admiralty, once war broke out in 1914. Kitchener must bear some responsibility; he was influenced by his poor perception of the press in the Boer War, and he was determined to achieve the most rigorous management of news. Masterman, in charge of Wellington House, did see the potential of film, but as his wife wrote after the war:

> Both the services were completely convinced that every sort of secret would escape and felt it *infra dig* for this country to allow its forces to be portrayed for the delectation of foreigners. The cinema was still regarded by many as a kind of music-hall turn, probably vulgar and without serious importance.[20]

Once permission had been given for film to be shot in France, negotiations over payment and distribution rights became protracted, with the cinema trade organisation believing that it was being asked to contribute excessive amounts to the various service charities. Eventually, on 2 November 1915, Edward G Tong and Geoffrey H Malins set off for France, the first two official cameramen with official permission to film on the Western Front. A separate agreement was concluded between Wellington House, the Admiralty and the Cinema Committee, which resulted in the filming of the Grand Fleet. It was this film, *Britain Prepared*, which was the first official propaganda film; it was an immediate success and was subsequently distributed worldwide. Unfortunately, the first films from the Western Front were less popular and this led to a deterioration in relations between Wellington House, the War Office and the cinema trade, with the War Office accusing the trade of giving preferential treatment to *Britain Prepared* because they received a greater share of the profits. A new agreement was made for the next film, *The Battle of the Somme* (1916). This remarkable film, which contained scenes of actual fighting, including British dead and wounded, is now viewed as portraying war as brutal and destructive – i.e. the message seems very unlike propaganda. At the time, however, the film was a major success. Subsequent feature-length films followed, such as *The Battle of the Ancre and the Advance of the Tanks* and *The German Retreat and the Battle of Arras* (both 1917).

These last two films were both produced by the War Office Cinematograph Committee (WOCC) which continued to rival the production of the DOI Cinematograph Branch until 1918 when all official film propaganda came under one roof in the form of the MoI. Both government agencies expanded film production in 1917 and began to diversify; thus, in April 1917 the WOCC released *Sons of Our Empire* in five weekly parts, then official newsreels were produced, together with a series of films issued at weekly intervals with titles such as *Famous Regiments in France*. In the meantime, the DOI contacted all independent British production companies asking for

> a list of any films you may have made or are producing, whether of drama or purely interest pictures, that might in any way prove useful for propaganda or as records relating to Food Production, Shipbuilding, Merchant Marine Service, Railroads, other essential industries...Patriotism. War Workers, National Games and Sports.[21]

In conjunction with the NWAC, the DOI also produced the "cinemotor", an entirely self-contained, mobile film projection unit which toured the country showing free films where facilities for film showing did not exist. Gradually – and the impetus came from the DOI – there was a willingness to consider using the fiction film, seen in the DOI's support of *Hearts of the World*, a major fiction film made by the American director, D W Griffith. At the same time, other government agencies not directly related to propaganda were producing films: in April 1916 the Treasury released the film, *For the Empire*, promoting War Bonds, and the Ministry of Food released *Everybody's Business* in June 1917. All this pointed to a considerable expansion in the production of official films, but it was expansion in a very haphazard fashion. There was no single committee or government agency coordinating all cinema work until June 1918 with the formation of the Ministry of Information Cinematograph Section.

Overall, in the period between February 1917 and February 1918 the DOI made quiet but effective progress, and Buchan "had enabled official propaganda to reach its maturity".[22] But there were still areas which remained unresolved. In theory, Buchan had direct access to the Prime Minister, giving official propaganda both status and a degree of independence. Unfortunately, Buchan and Lloyd George did not "get on"; Buchan did not have access to the Prime Minister, and came to the conclusion that the only solution was to put the DOI under someone who would have access. In September 1917 it was announced that Sir Edward Carson was to be given overall responsibility of the DOI.

The actual story behind this appointment provides a good example of the machiavellian way in which Lloyd George operated. At that time, Carson was First Lord of the Admiralty and a supporter of Jellicoe, First Sea Lord. It was Jellicoe whom Lloyd George wished to replace; to facilitate the move Carson had to be sidetracked. Accordingly, he was "promoted" to the War Cabinet and given something to do – i.e. the supervision of the DOI. In fact, within three months Carson had resigned over government policy towards Ireland; in the meantime, Lloyd George got his new First Sea Lord. For Buchan, the problem of access remained, exacerbated by the presence of Robert Donald on the small Advisory Committee. Donald had written the investigative report into propaganda a year earlier, and in December 1917 Lloyd George asked him to prepare a second report. This proved equally critical and, despite the report's containing wild generalisations and inaccuracies, Lloyd George took the opportunity of Carson's resignation in January 1918 to restructure propaganda. The motives of Lloyd George seem twofold; firstly, to reduce further Foreign Office influence, and secondly, to deflect press criticism of the conduct of the war. 1917 had not been a year of conspicuous military success and Lloyd George wanted to be rid of Haig, Commander in Chief of the British Army, or Robertson, Chief of the Imperial General Staff – or preferably both. As it was, he would need the support of the press if he was to accomplish his plan. Robertson resigned in 1918 and the press owned by Northcliffe and Beaverbrook asked no awkward questions. The new MoI came into existence in February 1918, Beaverbrook became Britain's first Minister of Information, while Northcliffe was made Director of Propaganda in Enemy Countries.

Whatever the motives of Lloyd George, it is difficult to come to any conclusion other than that Buchan was wronged, and that the advent of Beaverbrook and Northcliffe contributed little that was positive to British propaganda in the last nine months of the war. Indeed, much of the good work achieved by Buchan was undone, with renewed distrust appearing between the new MoI and other government departments. Established ministers whose authority had already been undermined by the creation of the War Cabinet were deeply suspicious of a ministry run by newspapermen, which apparently had ambitions to affect almost every aspect of government policy. Beaverbrook was to comment later: "I encountered organized, vigorous and determined opposition...the War Office, Admiralty and Foreign Office joined together in determined resistance".[23] More damaging still was the resulting loss of enthusiasm and lowering of staff morale caused by the reorganisation with numerous requests by civil servants to be transferred back to the Foreign Office.[24]

Ironically, Beaverbrook himself found the continuous opposition demoralising, and eventually in September Lloyd George was forced to issue a statement defining the proper powers of the MoI. As has already been indicated, in the last months of the war little that was new or innovative occurred, although there was a final abandonment of the original emphasis with intellectual propaganda directed at opinion formers, as opposed to the "vast and uninstructed masses". The formation of Northcliffe's department at Crewe House saw for the first time a department concerned exclusively with propaganda directed at the enemy, although obviously the work was building on foundations established earlier by both the DOI and MI7. Most studies highlight the propaganda directed against the Austro-Hungarian Empire, propaganda which was largely organised by two individuals very much in the mould of the talented amateur – namely the scholar, R W Seton-Watson, and the writer and journalist, Henry Wickham-Steed.[25]

By the summer of 1918, the appointments of Beaverbrook and Northcliffe were having further political repercussions; in June, Robert Donald, so long a thorn in the flesh of both Masterman and Buchan, resigned from the MoI and began to write a series of attacks against Beaverbrook, alleging that his appointment was purely a political pay-off for conspiring with Lloyd George to bring about Asquith's fall from the premiership in late 1916. In a debate in the House of Commons in February 1918, Lloyd George was attacked by followers of Asquith, and Joseph King, a Liberal MP, suggested that Beaverbrook and Northcliffe had been appointed controllers of propaganda merely as "rewards for services", while the Scottish radical, William Pringle, "burst out with the accusation that Lloyd George was engaging in 'Improperganda'".[26]

The debates of August and November 1918 raised similar concerns and, as Messinger argues, they both deserve analysis for the themes or issues which they raised: fear of the entry of commercial values into government; fears that the propagandists might turn against their own citizens; fear that new structures of government were being created without accountability to Parliament; and, against all these concerns, a belief among many that propaganda not only was justified in wartime, but also might serve important peacetime uses.

The August debate was concerned with the allocation of funds for the MoI and was to be the only major parliamentary debate on propaganda during the entire war. The leader of the attack was Leif Jones, a Liberal MP, who proclaimed that, although the MoI was funded by government, it was "not the creation of Parliament" and "we have been kept in the dark as to its constitution, its purposes, its methods, and its relation to other Departments of the State". Jones in fact was not extreme in criticism and saw the need for an organisation to rebut the misstatements of the enemy in war. He agreed that the propagandists had done some good work, but regarded the News Department of the MoI as dangerous, "the body which dresses up facts for presentment to the public". He cited the failings of propaganda in Russia and South America, and attributed success in the United States to German failings. He then turned to the broad question of accountability and noted the commercial links of many of the individuals whom Beaverbrook had recruited: "it was dangerous to allow such commercial bias into the making of foreign policy". He concluded by accusing Beaverbrook of having global ambitions concerning the distribution of news: "He wants to control the news to be flashed all over the world".

The November debate was concerned with the Civil Service supplementary estimates for 1918-19, which included £1000 in salaries and expenses for the MoI. On this occasion, the debate centred on Northcliffe and on an article entitled "From War to Peace", which had appeared in Northcliffe's *The Daily Mail* and *The Times*. The chief antagonist this time was William Pringle, who wanted to know whether the article expressed the official view of the British government or was merely personal propaganda by a powerful press Lord whose relation to the government was far too vaguely defined. Allowing Northcliffe to issue "semi-official statements gave an enhanced value to the whole of the Press which he controls" and put him in "a special preferential and privileged position in relation to the whole of journalism of the country". Other Liberal MPs lamented the fact that "so many English newspapers are in the secret service of the Government of the day". John Whitehouse believed that, unless the MoI was abolished soon, the resources of the Ministry would be "used in order to influence public opinion in favour of one political party" in the next General Election.[27]

There are two points to be made here. Opponents of Lloyd George were quite prepared to use the appointments of

Beaverbrook and Northcliffe as an issue to cause embarrassment to the Prime Minister. Equally, the rapid rise of the two individuals did undoubtedly cause offence, and the fact that they were members of the fourth estate only made their promotion all the more unpalatable. The other striking feature of the debate is that, with a few changes in name, the arguments and accusations have a very contemporary relevance and, although there may have been some opposition to Lloyd George, for opposition's sake, the issues raised have importance in any democratic society.

Beaverbrook resigned his position as Minister of Information on 21 October 1918, giving poor health as the reason. His position was taken by the novelist, Arnold Bennett. Northcliffe resigned on the day after the Armistice. There were proposals that the MoI should continue in existence until the signing of the Peace Treaty, but the War Cabinet decided otherwise, and Lloyd George appointed his friend, Sir George (later Lord) Riddell, to be in charge of publicity during the negotiations. The propagandists were closed down, and through the interwar years little was done to counter the anti-Liberal propaganda spread by the dictators. The result of this was that when Britain went to war in 1939, a new MoI had to relearn the principles of managing official propaganda that had already been discovered by an earlier generation.

Notes

[1]   Quoted in Nicholas Reeves, *Official British Film Propaganda During The First World War* (Beckenham: Croom Helm, in association with the Imperial War Museum, 1986): 54.

[2]   Lord Beaverbrook, *Men and Power 1917-1918* (London: Hutchinson, 1956): 267.

[3]   Biographical material on Masterman is obtained from Gary S Messinger, *British propaganda and the state in the First World War* (Manchester; New York: Manchester University Press, 1992): 24-53.

[4]   For a more detailed analysis of the various government agencies, see M L Sanders and Philip M Taylor, *British Propaganda during the First World War, 1914-18* (London; Basingstoke: Macmillan, 1982).

[5]   Quoted in Messinger: 36. It is interesting to note how many of these literary figures later became employed, in one capacity or another, by the government.

[6]   Ibid: 37.

[7]   Ibid: 25.

8   Reeves: 11.

9   Messinger: 73.

10   Ibid: 61-62.

11   Quoted in Harold D Lasswell, *Propaganda Technique in World War I* (London: Kegan Paul, 1927): 34.

12   Reeves: 12.

13   Ibid: 15.

14   For an interesting account of how the British Army looked after the press at the Front, see Neville Lytton, *The Press and the General Staff* (London: W Collins & Sons, 1921).

15   Reeves: 19.

16   Claimed by Messinger: 91.

17   For more detail, see Lasswell: 180. Also Michael Occleshaw, *Armour Against Fate: British Military Intelligence in the First World War* (London: Columbus Books, 1989).

18   Messinger: 209. For these patriotic lectures, Bottomley took 65-85% of the proceeds.

19   Ibid: 210.

20   Lucy Masterman, *C F G Masterman: A Biography* (London: Frank Cass & Company, 1939): 283. Emphasis in original.

21   Quoted in Reeves: 67-68.

22   Ibid: 28.

23   Ibid: 33.

24   See Messinger: 162-183.

25   Beaverbrook saw propaganda as the popular arm of diplomacy, and insisted upon providing final clearance of all military and Foreign Office despatches, a move Balfour as Foreign Secretary resisted.

26   Messinger: 133.

27   Based on ibid: 134-138, 156-159.

"Civilians entrenched": the British home front and attitudes to the First World War, 1914-18
Lloyd Clark

The First World War was a great British victory but also a national tragedy, a cataclysmic event that shattered Britain and changed it forever.[1] The war inflicted terrible wounds. Much of Britain's economic strength was lost and many psychological injuries healed poorly, leaving ugly and persistent scars. After 1918 Britain struggled to come to terms with the experience, and a common perception emerged which has endured to this day. The First World War is seen as a horrible mistake, a débâcle in which brave young men sacrificed themselves in the mud and blood of the Western Front's no man's land during futile offensives conducted by incompetent and inhumane generals – a war that achieved nothing of lasting value.[2] For the British, the First World War has become the greatest anti-war war in history.

To understand why British attitudes towards the First World War have been dominated by repugnance, there is a need for a wide-ranging academic study into the subject.[3] This essay is certainly not that study, but it does hope to provide a brief survey of British home front attitudes towards the war while it was being fought. The aim, in short, is to analyse a phenomenon that does not seem to fit neatly into the "revulsion" perception, the fact that the majority of British people on the home front during the First World War actively supported British participation in the conflict.

The years leading up to 1914 were absolutely crucial in Britain's mental preparation for war – even though the nation prepared for a rather different war to the one that actually took place. This preparation was not led by the government, for the political élite did not regard it as their job to lead public opinion; the nation instead was moulded by indirect forces. These forces included the social, political and economic "progress" that the working class made during the approach to war, and a process of cultural conditioning that imbued the nation with a certain mind-set. Although these two forces cannot be seen as the only reasons behind British home front support for the war between 1914 and 1918, it must be recognised that they did lay solid foundations for a support so strong that the government did not have actively to strengthen it until late 1916.

The spirit and disposition of Britain's working class were of crucial importance to the nation's ability to sustain a protracted total war effort during the First World War.[4] In a total war, a nation mobilises all its human, economic and technical resources in an attempt to destroy the enemy.[5] With the working class comprising 80% of the population in early 20th century Britain, it was the support of these prospective soldiers and wartime factory workers that would have to be won by any government wishing to fight such a war.[6] One of the reasons why the government eventually planned for a short limited war in the years immediately prior to 1914 was because they thought – wrongly, as it turned out – that the proletariat would not support any other type of war.[7]

Government assumptions about the working class were born out of ignorance. The fact that workers were strike-prone and careful to fight for their own interests did not mean, as perhaps the government thought, that they were a great heaving mass on the verge of revolt. Nevertheless, the class to which the majority of the population belonged could not be neglected, and pre-war concessions granted to the proletariat certainly helped to keep them within the national fold. Working-class "appeasement" came in many different forms and was boosted by the presence of 36 Labour MPs in the House of Commons by August 1914. Lloyd George's 1906 "New Liberal" Social Reform Budget was a major step towards the development of a welfare state and, together with the onset of wage rises, a sharp decline in the infant mortality rate and a general increase in life expectancy, made for a more placid working class.

The working class was also subjected to a process of cultural conditioning which, together with the rest of the population, made it more likely to support a future war. Conditioning occurs in all countries and is part of what gives the population its own peculiar national characteristics. In Britain during the approach to the First World War, this "indoctrination" was partly responsible for creating attitudes that were to have important implications for the nation's mental preparation for war. The result was a population filled with a great patriotic fervour, a feeling of racial superiority and an understanding that to lay down one's life for "King and Country", to make the ultimate sacrifice, was the manly thing to do.

This conditioning came from a variety of sources. The press was filled with jingoistic and Germanophobic articles, while creative writers frightened many into contemplating the consequences of a German invasion of Britain.[8] It was in this atmosphere, especially after the turn of the century, that quasi-military organisations became more popular. The National Service League was founded in 1902 to counter the perceived military and national weakness that had been revealed so starkly by the Boer War, and to push for conscription in peacetime. By 1914 the League had over 200 000 members. The membership of the Boy Scouts, formed in 1907, had risen to 150 000 by 1913 and, with

39

groups such as the Boys' Brigade and the Lads' Drill Association, served to stress the need for young males to defer to military discipline and love their country.[9] It was groups such as these that inculcated a whole generation of young men, irrespective of class, with a certain set of values that were to be important to the strength of British support for the coming war.[10] Indeed, Lieutenant General Baden-Powell, the founder of the Boy Scout Movement, advised his uniformed charges to "BE PREPARED to die for your country...so that when the time comes you may charge home with confidence, not caring whether you are to be killed or not".[11]

The nation was subconsciously being prepared to fight; although the population did not lust after a European war, it did not balk at the prospect of defending itself in a short, sharp and glorious war.[12] The attraction was there for all men with dull and monotonous lives, as well as for idealistic boys yearning to prove themselves in a great adventure.[13] War was seen by various groups as a way of achieving different things. Further to the defeat of Germany and its allies, poets believed that war was an opportunity for personal fulfilment; Milnerites hoped that war would lead to an increase in the strength of the state; and Liberals thought that war would help facilitate further social and political reform. In short it was thought that victory in war not only would underline Britain's greatness, but also might act as a panacea to cure Britain of various ills.[14]

As one would expect, there were those who were virulently opposed to war and the increasing bellicosity of the nation. Some Liberal MPs spoke out against what they perceived to be the government's belief that war was inevitable, while sections of the Labour movement prided themselves on their pacifism. However, despite the best efforts of a section of the press which aligned itself to anti-war sentiment (including *The Daily News* and *The Manchester Guardian*), such views can be said to represent only a small percentage of the population. The overwhelming majority of Britons had been attuned to the idea of armed conflict, and it was just a small step for the population to move from this position to one of supporting British participation in a war against Germany, a position that underwent only minor changes through three distinct phases of the war between August 1914 and November 1918.

When war eventually came, the nation had lived for so long with the prospect of war that the real thing was something of a shock. During the last days of peace, the nation panicked; while the government drew up emergency legislation, there was a run on the banks, people hoarded bulk food purchases, and prices increased sharply. But the panic was tempered by a great feeling of excitement, captured after the war by Caroline Playne:

And they felt, in their hearts, intense relief that there was to be no more negotiating, no more thinking, no more heeding, only rushing on, on, gloriously, splendidly on, all traces kicked over, all bridles thrown away![15]

On 4 August 1914 a Union flag-festooned crowd gathered in Trafalgar Square and cheered loudly when it was announced that Britain had declared war on Germany. A demonstration against the war in London that evening was well-attended, but opposition to the war faded quickly. After the German invasion of neutral Belgium, even newspapers who had formerly taken an anti-war stance began to change their tune. On 5 August *The Daily News*, while continuing to argue that the war should never have been allowed to break out, argued that, now that Britain was involved, the most important thing to do was to win.[16]

Such conversions had much to do with the fact that British people felt that they were engaging in a legitimate act of defence and that their cause was just. In the words of Reverend Dr John Clifford, a man who had formerly argued against British participation in the war, the British government had "done everything that could be done to allay the storm and preserve the peace of the world", whereas Germany had "flouted public law, and trampled under foot with ineffable scorn the rights of small nationalities as not even the small dust of the balance".[17] It was this type of attitude that underpinned British support for the war right up until November 1918. The war became the war that would help save European civilisation, that would make the world a better and more peaceful place – "The War", in the words of the Socialist H G Wells, writing in August 1914, "That Will End War".[18]

The British people were adamant that they held the moral high ground, and it was in this sentimental atmosphere that 1.1 million men volunteered for service between August and December 1914.[19] Indeed, as a result of this remarkable response to the "call to arms", the government decided that it was not worth spending time and energy on domestic propaganda, as the nation's mind was already made up in favour of the war. As a consequence, it was left to private bodies such as the Central Committee of National Patriotic Organisations to further influence the population.[20]

By mid-August the novelty of war and the massive excitement engendered by its declaration had begun to fade and the nation began to revert to "business as usual".[21] This was not a period of massive government interference into national life, for the nation assumed a swift and victorious conclusion to the war. Such was the confidence of the government that the first Budget of the war, presented by Lloyd George on 16 November 1914, did not make provision for any new taxes, and raised existing taxes only a little in certain cases. The nation was lulled into a false sense of security, and a semblance of normality reigned while the war raged and support of the war continued to run high. By the end of August, white feathers were being presented to men in civilian dress, self-indulgent luxuries such as drink, gambling and football were castigated, and anything that looked or sounded even vaguely German, including dachshunds, was attacked. Newspapers certainly helped to keep the nation in a patriotic frenzy. The shelling of the north-east coast of England by a German cruiser in December 1914 left over 100 people dead and was widely reported in the press, with stories being accompanied by photographs of those who perished. The result was a rush to the recruiting stations, the like of which had not been seen since August. However, while censorship of home news was remarkably lax, initial government censorship of war news was clumsily harsh and led to the creation of atrocity stories by copy-hungry journalists.[22] Siegfried Sassoon wrote in his semi-autobiographical *Memoirs of a Fox-Hunting Man* (1928) that "[t]he newspapers informed us that German soldiers crucified Belgian babies. Stories of that kind were taken for granted; to have disbelieved them would have been unpatriotic."[23]

The mass-circulation press required no pressure from the government to support the war and, while helpfully lashing out at pacifists, conscientious objectors, Socialists, strikers, aliens and "shirkers", also continually praised the British military. Through newspapers the British public was fed a certain view of the war that came, thanks to strict censorship, directly from GHQ communiqués. Thus, while in October 1914 the fighting was turning into the type of deadlock for which neither the military nor the politicians had prepared, the population was reading positively confident reports about the fighting in France and Belgium. In the words of John Bourne, "[a] curtain of unreality descended between the war and the public perception of it".[24]

"Business as usual" ended with the Battle of Neuve Chapelle in March 1915, a battle that revealed that the war was not going to be short and would therefore require the total effort of the nation to sustain it successfully. In Arthur Marwick's words, Neuve Chapelle "jerked society to an awareness of what was involved in this most beastly of wars".[25] The government responded and cautiously began to take up the slack in the nation's reins.[26]

British attitudes to the war became somewhat more complicated after the spring of 1915, as new factors that affected the way in which the home front perceived the conflict began to come into play. The unintentional benefits brought about by the fighting played a significant role in shaping vital working-class attitudes to the war. These benefits stemmed from the fact that, to sustain the war effort, the government required not only people in uniform to fight, but also people in industry to produce. This delicate soldier-civilian balancing act required increased government control over British manpower resources – as increasing numbers of men were required at the front, so replacements had to be found for them in the workplace. By the end of 1915, with some 2.5 million men having volunteered for service, industry was having difficulty in finding suitable replacements, a situation which became no easier when universal conscription was introduced in May 1916.[27] The Munitions of War Act was passed in July 1915 in a desperate attempt to tackle these problems formally.

Although the Defence of the Realm Act had been in place since August 1914 and enabled the state to assume wide powers, the Munitions of War Act aimed to ensure that Britain had the quantity of munitions required to fight the war successfully.[28] The Act formally ensured that unions engaged in war work could no longer legally disrupt the war effort by strike action or by the enforcement of restrictive practices. This meant that disputes were to be settled by arbitration and skilled jobs to be opened up to the semi-skilled, the unskilled and to women – a situation that the unions did not like. As a means of compensation for these sacrifices, the labour force decided to fight to gain benefits in other areas, benefits which employers and the government were careful to grant in the circumstances. Some gains were achieved as the result of strikes which were caused by existing grievances being exacerbated by the Munitions of War Act during 1915. In Clydeside, for example, 5000 engineers, who were playing a vital role in the war effort, went on strike as the result of a wage claim and forced their employers to make concessions. Miners in South Wales also went on strike: they too found that after five days their demands were met in full, due to the disastrous effect that they were having on coal production. The working class also gained in other, less tangible ways. In November 1916, for example, a strike was provoked by the enlistment of a skilled man, and the trade unions eventually took over the role from the Manpower Boards of deciding who was and was not essential to industry. The gains made by the trade unions were mirrored by the advances of the Labour Party, whose Chairman, Arthur Henderson, first was made President of the Board of Trade in Asquith's Coalition government, and later gained a seat on Lloyd George's small War Cabinet. "Labour" was taken into junior partnership for the duration as part of the total war effort.

The war also brought increased wealth to certain sections of society, a state of affairs which front line soldiers despised. In the words of one of Kitchener's men, a volunteer who had served in the trenches, "[b]roadly speaking, the English either volunteer for this hell or else sit down and grow fat on big money at home. The contrast between the two fates is too great."[29] For those seeking employment, jobs could be found more easily during the war years and, thanks to longer hours and war bonuses, pay-packets were fatter than usual. The result of this increased wealth, together with the fact that the government lowered the income tax threshold, was that by 1916 more people than ever before were being taxed on their income. However, despite this and a dramatic rise in prices,[30] there was a diminution in the gap between the disposable incomes of the working and middle classes.[31] The results of increased working-class wealth were marked. Leaving aside newspaper articles about proletariat spending sprees on luxury items such as pianos, the war years saw a decline in pauperism, a decrease in cases of nutrition-related disease, fewer maternal deaths during childbirth, and an increase in the life expectancy of working-class men who remained in civilian employment. There is no doubt that, in the words of J M Winter, "[t]he war years were undoubtedly a period of significant gains in civilian health...for the industrial labour force".[32]

Women also made some notable gains during the war years, thanks to their ability to adapt.[33] In 1914 skilled male workers in munitions and ordnance factories began to leave for the trenches, and these men were slowly replaced by non-skilled female "dilutees". These women were drawn mainly from the working class, but also included some middle-class and even a few upper-class women determined to do "their bit". By the late summer of 1915, women began to work in a wide variety of industries; by the following year, they found that they were in even greater demand due to the advent of conscription.[34] The important work in which women were involved should not be ignored, and increasingly women were seen as an essential part of the British war effort. This recognition gave women not only increased self-confidence, but also evidence to support the argument that they should be enfranchised. Lloyd George gave the female suffrage movement hope when in July 1915 he said that "[w]ithout women victory will tarry and the victory which tarries means a victory whose footprints are footprints of blood".[35] Other influential voices such as those of Winston Churchill, Sir Arthur Conan Doyle, *The Times*, *The Observer* and *The Daily Mail* were soon to be heard supporting the female suffrage cause. Eventually, on 6 February 1918, an Act was passed that enfranchised all women aged thirty and above who were married to registered voters.[36]

The unintentional benefits brought about by the war undoubtedly helped to sugar-coat the bitter pill of war for the British population, just as a number of key events continued to convince it of the righteousness of the Allied cause. German "atrocities", such as the sinking of the Cunard liner, *Lusitania*, on 7 May 1915, inspired public outrage after pictures of the dead, including children, were published in the press. The execution of nurse Edith Cavell and the death of Lord Kitchener in June 1916, drowned after the ship carrying him to Russia was sunk in Scapa Flow, helped to reinforce the public belief that they were waging a just war. However, by mid-1916, with casualties mounting and no obvious end to the war in sight, the need for domestic propaganda was seen as increasingly necessary to counter flagging morale. The Secret War Propaganda Department at Wellington House, led by Charles Masterman, sponsored filmmakers with increasing regularity from 1916. *The Battle of the Somme*, released in August 1916, was a tremendous success and played to packed houses.[37] The film presented waving and grinning soldiers happily fighting for "King and Country", while at the same time showing British casualties and thereby drawing the audience's attention to the sacrifice that these men were making. *The Battle of the Somme* thus presented a hard-hitting and yet subtly sanitised version of events. This consequently raises an interesting question: to what extent were home front attitudes towards the war rooted in ignorance of what was happening at the front?

It would be easy to argue that, due to wartime censorship, the home front had little idea as to what was really happening in the war, but in fact this was not the case.[38] By the end of 1916 there were few families in Britain who had not grieved for a loved one. Major railway stations received trains of wounded soldiers and such men, dressed in distinctive blue uniforms, became a common sight on Britain's streets. Newspapers carried lists of about 4000 casualties daily.[39] It was also easy to read about casualties in the provincial press which published not only casualty lists, but also photographs of local men who had been killed, together with a short obituary. These newspapers seem not to have been as rigorously censored as their national counterparts. Generally, local newspapers carried more truthful material than the reports in the national press: during the Battle of Loos (1915) the *Northampton Daily Chronicle* ran the headline, "7TH NORTHAMPTONS CUT UP".[40] Of course, the civilians on the home front could never truly understand what it was like to serve in the front line, but the population did not lack information about the human cost of the war, which was undoubtedly high, but which the British people thought worth paying to ensure victory. At first, heavy casualties were a great shock but soon the population adjusted to the demands of trench warfare. R D Blumenfeld, editor of *The Daily Express*, noted in his diary as early as 24 October 1914:

> One would have thought, before the war began, that the single report of the killing or disablement of any friend or acquaintance would be terribly disconcerting. So it was, at the beginning. The first eight or ten casualties had as much

publicity as all the rest put together...Gradually the familiarity of the thing became apparent. You receive the news of the death of your friends as a matter of fact.[41]

Thus, by the end of 1916, despite the terrible losses incurred during the Battle of the Somme, the nation remained united in support of the war, although increasingly weary of it. This increasing lassitude was to show itself clearly during an upsurge in working-class discontent during 1917. The reasons for this dissatisfaction varied from place to place, but often included the overzealous application of the Conscription Act; the provisions of the Munitions of War Act; the difficulties in changing jobs brought about by the need for "leaving certificates"; attempts by employers to extend dilution to industries manufacturing products other than war materials; higher prices; bad housing; and the resentment felt by skilled workers who found themselves overtaken in the earnings-increase race by the unskilled. A strike over extended dilution occurred in Rochdale in May 1917 and led to a wave of other unofficial strikes throughout the country. The strikes lasted for a couple of weeks and ended only when the government agreed that all future grievances would be solved through negotiations between themselves and the trade union leadership. Eventually, proposals for further dilution were dropped, and leaving certificates were abolished as the government endeavoured keep the working class contented. National morale became a distinct problem during the third year of the war.

In 1917 a war-weary nation saw no let-up in the casualty rate and only more air-raids, further price rises and the first real shortages of the war. Although there was never any widespread privation in Britain during the First World War, submarine warfare did mean that there was a shortage of some basic commodities (including sugar, coal, potatoes and margarine) which led to the inevitable queues.[42] On 8 April 1917 *The Observer* reported:

> The usual week-end potato and coal scenes took place in London yesterday. At Edmonton 131 vehicles were lined up at the gates of a coal depot at nine o'clock in the morning, while the crowd numbered several hundreds. There were also bread and potato queues of such a length that the police had to regulate them, and newcomers had to inquire which was the particular queue that they wanted.[43]

Such circumstances led to increased government intervention during this period to minimise the suffering. The establishment of a Food Controller, a Food Ministry, rationing and price controls were all the result of this difficult period, when the civilian population was being asked to make more sacrifices than at any other time since the outbreak of hostilities. It was in this atmosphere that domestic propaganda was to play a vital role in boosting home front morale.

It was the task of the Department of Information, established in February 1917, to coordinate the propaganda effort. Propaganda offensives were launched across the land with special treatment being given to areas where it was believed that morale was suspect. The idea was to restate as often as possible the reasons why the war was being fought, to show workers contributing to the war effort that their input was appreciated, and to shame those who were not making sacrifices into doing so.

It was in the spring of 1917 that the most famous propaganda achievement of the war was launched with the story that the Germans were converting bodies of dead soldiers into lubricating oils, pig food and manure. This story originated from a mistranslation of a German newspaper article and the Department of Information cleverly used it to remind the population that, as it was fighting a "barbaric" nation, the struggle had to continue.[44] The first formal declaration of British war aims by Lloyd George in January 1918 was also intended to replenish depleted civilian fighting spirit.[45] The Prime Minister began his war aims speech by saying:

> When men by the million are being called upon to suffer and die, and vast populations are being subjected to the sufferings and privations of war on a scale unprecedented in the history of the world, they are entitled to know for what cause or causes they are making the sacrifice. It is only the clearest, greatest and justest of causes that can justify the continuance even for one day of this unspeakable agony of the Nations. And we ought to be able to state clearly and definitely not only the principles for which we are fighting but also their definite and concrete application to the war map of the World.[46]

This speech was certainly timely, for the first six months of 1918 saw morale on the home front severely tested. Not only did Britain stare defeat in the face as a result of the initial success of the German Spring Offensives, but also the government was forced to abolish all remaining exemptions to military service due to a manpower shortage caused by the massive loses of 1917. Yet, the nation continued to support the war, for, in the words of Brian Bond, "war-weariness is not synonymous with disillusionment".[47]

The nation was eventually rewarded for its patience and loyalty during the summer of 1918 when the Allied armies gained the initiative and forward momentum. By the autumn the population began at last to look forward to the realistic prospect of peace for the first time in the war. In early October *The Daily News* proclaimed:

> London is more crowded today than at any time in the memory of the present generation, and now that the war news is so magnificently encouraging it is a brighter London too...The hotels are full; there are queues at the best and most popular restaurants; the shops are reaping a rich harvest; and the theatres and music-halls are enjoying a boom.[48]

The war came to a sudden end on 11 November 1918. The celebrations that followed reflected the relief that was felt by a joyous nation, but the revelry did not last long. Soon Britain moved into a period of numb remembrance as the slow process of reconstruction began.

Between 1914 and 1918 the British home front supported the nation's participation in a war not because they were blissfully ignorant about the death and destruction that it caused, but because they thought that it was a war worth fighting. In 1918 Field Marshal Haig was seen not as a "butcher", but as a national hero who had led Britain to victory. Only in the late 1920s did a disillusioned Britain begin to lambaste the High Command and to question why the war was fought at all.[49] The result of this process was not only a flood of "anti-war" literature, but also the creation of a myth upon which the British perception of the First World War is still firmly based to this day.[50] Within this myth the massive oversimplification of complex issues relating to the war has meant that the whole issue of what motivated the British home front to support the war has been lost.

The reasons why British people supported the war can be found in three main factors: cultural conditioning, unintentional benefits, and just cause. Even before the war began, British people were being conditioned and mentally prepared for war by numerous non-governmental influences. Consequently, when war was declared, the nation was gripped by a surge of patriotic fervour and a feeling that war would be not only a great adventure, but also a miracle cure for Britain's ills. The unintentional benefits that the war brought to many sections of society, and most importantly to the working class, also helped to reinforce the morale of the nation between 1914 and 1918.

However, the single most important factor in the nation's support for the war was the righteousness of the cause. The British people believed that they were fighting not only to defend themselves against the aggression of others, but also to make the world "safe for democracy". Thus, rather than the war being an act of "senseless futility", it was fought and supported by a

British people who thought it necessary and just. Yet, despite this, the British national perception of the First World War has been dominated by a sense of revulsion since the 1930s. For historians wishing to add a sense of balance to the nation's attitude to the war, the task will be a long and difficult one – but the work has begun.[51]

* * *

I should like to thank Catriona Clark and my RMAS colleagues, G D Sheffield and Niall Barr, for their useful comments on this essay.

Notes

[1]   Due to the shortage of space, the author hopes that he will be forgiven for the many generalisations that he has to make during this essay. He is keenly aware that the use of the word "British" disguises the fact that the British population is no more predisposed to a unity of views than any other population in the world.

[2]   This perception of the First World War is still vigorous today. See G D Sheffield's essay in this volume, and "Editor's Introduction", in Brian Bond (ed), *The First World War and British Military History* (Oxford: Clarendon Press, 1991): 1-12.

[3]   The author of this essay is presently undertaking PhD research into the field of the creation and development of a British national perception of the First World War.

[4]   See Bernard Waites, *A Class Society at War: England 1914-1918* (Leamington Spa: Berg, 1987).

[5]   See Ian F W Beckett, "Total War", in Colin McInnes and G D Sheffield (eds), *Warfare in the Twentieth Century: Theory and Practice* (London: Unwin Hyman, 1988): 1-23.

[6]   Figure taken from Arthur Marwick, *The Deluge*, second edition (Basingstoke: Macmillan, 1991): 63.

[7]   See John Bourne, *Britain and the Great War, 1914-1918* (London: Edward Arnold, 1989): 201, and Tim Travers, *The Killing Ground: The British Army, the Western Front and the Emergence of Modern Warfare 1900-1918* (London: Allen & Unwin, 1987): 40.

[8]   A good example of such literature is William Le Queux's *The Invasion of 1910* (1906), which resulted in letters to the editors of various newspapers denouncing Germans who lived and worked in Britain. See I F Clarke, *Voices Prophesying War 1763-1984* (Oxford:

Oxford University Press, 1966).

9   See Travers: 39-40.

10   See John Springhall, *Youth, Empire and Society: British Youth Movements, 1883-1940* (London: Croom Helm, 1977).

11   Quoted in Brian Bond, *War and Society in Europe, 1870-1970* (London: Fontana, 1984): 75. Emphasis in original.

12   Ibid: 76-79.

13   See Peter Parker, *The Old Lie: the Great War and the Public-School Ethos* (London: Constable, 1987) and Michael C C Adams, *The Great Adventure: Male Desire and the Coming of World War I* (Bloomington and Indianapolis: Indiana University Press, 1990).

14   See Bourne: 229-230.

15   Caroline Playne, *The Neuroses of Nations* (1925), quoted in Bond: 96.

16   Anti-war groups were evident in Britain throughout the war, although some remained underground. Soon after war was declared in 1914, a group of Liberals and Socialists formed the Union of Democratic Control (UDC), which aimed at gaining a negotiated peace as soon as possible. The No Conscription Fellowship (NCF) was also established in 1914, and within twelve months had branches throughout the country. The NCF fought for the "rights" of conscientious objectors, of which there were 16 500 during the war. The vast majority of these objectors cooperated with the authorities, and 90% eventually accepted some form of alternative service. About 1300 "absolutists" refused all service and were imprisoned – 70 of these men died as a result of their imprisonment. See Bourne: 213-213, and Martin Ceadel, *Pacifism in Britain 1914-1945: The Defining of a Faith* (Oxford: Clarendon Press, 1980).

17   Quoted in Marwick: 73.

18   *The Daily News* 14 August 1914.

19   For recruitment, see Ian F W Beckett and Keith Simpson (eds), *A nation in arms: A social study of the British army in the First World War* (Manchester: Manchester University Press, 1985), and Peter Simkins, *Kitchener's Army: The raising of the New Armies, 1914-16* (Manchester: Manchester University Press, 1988).

20   For more on the role of British propaganda during the First World War, see the essay by Andrew Steed in this volume. See also M L Sanders and Philip M Taylor, *British Propaganda during the First World War, 1914-18* (London; Basingstoke: Macmillan, 1982), and

Cate Haste, *Keep the Home Fires Burning: Propaganda in the First World War* (London: Allen Lane, 1977).

[21] The phrase "Business as Usual" was coined by H E Morgan of W H Smith and Son in a letter to *The Daily Chronicle* suggesting such a policy on 11 August 1914. The slogan was then quickly adopted by a variety of businesses to show their intentions while Britain was at war. See Marwick: 79.

[22] It should be noted that many of the atrocity stories that appeared in British newspapers were derived from accounts first published in the French and Belgian press.

[23] Siegfried Sassoon, *Memoirs of a Fox-Hunting Man* (London: Faber, 1928): 221. See Peter Simkins, "Everyman at War: Recent Interpretations of the Front Line Experience", in Bond (ed): 289-313.

[24] Bourne: 208.

[25] Marwick: 92.

[26] See Kathleen Burk (ed), *War and the State: The Transformation of British Government, 1914-1919* (London: George Allen & Unwin, 1982), and David French, *British Economic and Strategic Planning 1905-1915* (London: George Allen & Unwin, 1982).

[27] Asquith had delayed the introduction of conscription by introducing the "Derby Scheme" in October 1915. The scheme was named after the Earl of Derby who was the Director of Recruiting and its aim was divide the adult male population into groups and invite them to show their willingness to serve, if called upon to do so. There was no compulsion in the scheme, but it created the foundations upon which conscription could be built.

[28] See Samuel J Hurwitz, *State Intervention in Great Britain: A Study of Economic Control and Social Response 1914-1919* (Columbia: Columbia University Press, 1949).

[29] F H Keeling, a middle-class Socialist writing on 27 February 1916 before the Battle of the Somme. Quoted in Marwick: 258.

[30] Between August 1914 and September 1916 prices rose by 65%. This inflation meant that those who did not benefit from large wage rises found it increasingly difficult to obtain even the barest essentials.

[31] This was aided by a tax system based upon direct taxation which affected the middle class more than the working class, and helped to keep down the cost of living.

[32] J M Winter, *The Great War and the British People* (Basingstoke:

Macmillan, 1986): 153.

[33] See Gail Braydon, *Women Workers in the First World War: The British Experience* (London: Croom Helm, 1981).

[34] Although these women were not paid at the same rate as men, they did benefit from higher wartime wages. The war allowed some women to gain economic independence for the first time in their lives.

[35] Quoted in Marwick: 137.

[36] See Martin Pugh, *Women's Suffrage in Britain 1867-1928* (London: Historical Association, 1980).

[37] See S D Badsey, "Battle of the Somme: British war-propaganda", *Historical Journal of Film, Radio and Television* 3: 2 (1983): 99-115, and Nicholas Reeves, *Official British Film Propaganda During The First World War* (Beckenham: Croom Helm, in association with the Imperial War Museum, 1986).

[38] Research is presently being conducted into this area by Eric F Schneider, a DPhil student at St Anne's College, Oxford.

[39] Nationally, *The Daily Telegraph* and *The Morning Post* published casualty lists until the 1916 losses meant that casualties were no longer news. *The Times* carried casualty lists of all ranks until the end of 1917, but from then onwards published only officer casualties.

[40] Quoted in Bourne: 206.

[41] Quoted in Marwick: 81.

[42] See L Margaret Barnett, *British Food Policy During The First World War* (London: George Allen & Unwin, 1985).

[43] Quoted in Marwick: 231-232.

[44] See Philip M Taylor, *Munitions of the Mind: War propaganda from the ancient world to the nuclear age* (London: Patrick Stephens, 1990): 166-167.

[45] Lloyd George was also under increasing pressure from the US President, Thomas Woodrow Wilson, to state British war aims.

[46] Quoted in Marwick: 256-257.

[47] Bond: 133.

[48] Quoted in Marwick: 298.

[49] See Paul Fussell, *The Great War and Modern Memory* (Oxford:

Oxford University Press, 1975); Samuel Hynes, *A War Imagined* (London: Bodley Head, 1990) and Modris Eksteins, *Rites of Spring: The Great War and the Birth of the Modern Age* (Boston: Houghton Mifflin, 1989).

[50] This flood of literature relates to the phenomenon between 1928 and 1933 which saw a massive number of novels and memoirs published about the war. See Edmund Blunden, *Undertones of War* (1928), Siegfried Sassoon, *Memoirs of a Fox-Hunting Man* (1928) and *Memoirs of an Infantry Officer* (1930), E M Remarque, *All Quiet on the Western Front* (1929), R C Sherriff, *Journey's End* (1928) and Robert Graves, *Goodbye to All That* (1929). The phrase "anti-war" is used only loosely here, as much of the literature has positive things to say about the First World War.

[51] See Bond (ed): 10.

"Oh! What a Futile War": representations of the Western Front in modern British media and popular culture
G D Sheffield

Captain Edmund Blackadder, Private S Baldrick and Lieutenant The Hon. George Colthurst St. Barleigh first marched onto British television screens in 1989, accompanied by a military band crashing out the *British Grenadiers*. Played by Rowan Atkinson, Tony Robinson and Hugh Laurie respectively, these three characters were first seen on the parade ground, passing a saluting base manned by General Sir Anthony Cecil Hogmanay Melchett (Stephen Fry) and, squinting around his general's elbow, his ADC, Captain Kevin Darling (Tim McInnerny). These were the five principal characters of *Blackadder Goes Forth*, a BBC television comedy set on the Western Front during 1917. The highly successful series was released on video and, six years after it was first screened, on audiocassette,[1] and has been repeated on television. A poster of Baldrick was issued in a magazine aimed at teenage girls. The ultimate accolade came in 1990, when British troops deployed to Saudi Arabia for the Gulf War named their large camp near Al Jubail "Baldrick Lines".

The success of *Blackadder Goes Forth* is largely attributable to the sheer quality of the scripts of Richard Curtis and Ben Elton, which blend perfectly with the sparkling performances of the actors to produce wonderful interplay between the scheming and cynical professional soldier, Blackadder, his gormless turnip-fixated soldier servant, Baldrick, and the naïve and enthusiastic wartime volunteer, Lieutenant George. The element of conflict, which lies at the heart of much great comedy, is provided by Blackadder's clashes with his real enemies, who are not the Germans but the brainless, braying Melchett and the cowardly, column-dodging Darling. But there is another reason for the success of *Blackadder Goes Forth*. It deals with a scar on the British national psyche which, although inflicted 80 years ago, has yet to heal.

All four series of *Blackadder* (the others were set in the Middle Ages, the Elizabethan era and in the 18th century) drew upon a half-remembered folk memory of the *1066 and all that* type. As the British national perception of the First World War is one of unmitigated disaster,[2] *Blackadder Goes Forth* has a dark side largely absent from the three previous series, in the last episodes of which the principal characters had met violent but comic deaths. When Blackadder, Baldrick, George and Darling finally go "over the top" into German machine-gun fire, the mood is deadly serious. Only a minimum of scene-setting was required to make *Blackadder Goes Forth* intelligible: nothing more than a shot of a trench was necessary to establish the context, and nor was any explanation required as to the conflict between Captain Darling living in a luxurious château, and Captain Blackadder in his rat-infested front line trench. The portrayal of British strategy and tactics – in one memorable scene, Field Marshal Sir Douglas Haig (played by Geoffrey Palmer) casually brushes model soldiers off a model of a battlefield and sweeps them up in a dustpan – is funny because everybody "knows" that British generals were incompetent and that their battles were invariably bloody failures. Even the modern British Army, which one might have thought had a vested interest putting forward a more positive view of the First World War, gave the series tacit endorsement by allowing the band of the Royal Anglian Regiment to appear onscreen. *Blackadder* builds not only on a shared knowledge of history, but also on a shared cultural heritage. The series contains echoes of works as diverse as those of the "War Poets" of 1914-18, R C Sherriff's 1928 play, *Journey's End*, and W E Johns's "Biggles" novels.

The slaughter on the Western Front is almost unanimously seen by modern Britons as a uniquely terrible episode in a conflict that achieved nothing. In classic Christian "just war" theory, conflicts have to be judged by two criteria: the reason for going to war (*jus ad bellum*) and the conduct of the fighting (*jus in bello*). According to the national perception, the First World War failed to measure up to the criteria for a just war on both counts, and thus offended the liberal principles of 20th century British decision-makers and opinion-formers.[3] It was a futile, pointless conflict that was fought about nothing and solved nothing. The British Army was led by bone-headed British generals who, faced with deadlock, could think of nothing more imaginative than to hurl long lines of troops against German trenches and barbed wire, where time after time they were cut down in swathes. The great battles of the First World War – "Gallipoli", "The Somme", "Passchendaele" – were colossal blood baths, utter disasters. The ordinary soldiers, who had enlisted almost in a holiday mood, became deeply disillusioned with the war and expressed their disenchantment by writing bitter poetry.

So deep has this image of the First World War been driven into the British psyche that "the Trenches" are constantly being invoked by modern Britons. A reference to the First World War is often used as a shorthand for stupidity, blind obedience, failures of leadership, and deadlock. In 1987 the political journalist, Ian Aitken, wrote that the turning point in his father's political development was witnessing "the botch-up made by the so-called officer class at the battle of Loos" when "the flower of Airdries's young men" were "killed or maimed...on a single day in September 1915".[4] Another use of Western Front imagery came in a newspaper article on "Britain's cola war". A marketing campaign launched by a leading brand of fizzy drink was described as "unlikely to deliver an ultimate victor" in the long-running competition with its major rival. As befitted such a situation of near-stalemate, the article included the almost obligatory reference to "trenches".[5] The First World War is occasionally also used as a more positive metaphor. In 1995 a Cabinet Minister enduring criticism was described by a supporter as coming from a tradition of "great-uncles who, when the whistle blew, walked towards the guns and got shot dead"; as one commentator pointed out, it was perhaps an "unfortunate metaphor" in the circumstances.[6]

It was not necessary to place any of these references into context: no one had to explain what happened on the Western Front. As the popular success of *Blackadder Goes Forth* indicates, it is not only readers of the quality press who can be relied upon to recognise and understand references to the First World War. During the Falklands War of 1982, the populist tabloid newspaper *The Sun*, which ran an aggressively jingoistic campaign during the conflict, juxtaposed photographs of Royal Marines surrendering to the Argentine invaders with the headline of "LEST WE FORGET". This spread was intended to remind readers of the gravity of the issues at stake – the surrender being described as "a black moment in our history", with the Task Force being dispatched to "wipe out the memory and free our loyal friends".[7] In order to reinforce its ultra-patriotic message, *The Sun* dug deep into the British collective memory, for "Lest we forget" is a phrase soaked in associations with 1914-18. Taken from Rudyard Kipling's 1897 poem, "Recessional", after 1918 these words became an "emblematic text for remembrance"[8] synonymous with commemoration of the First World War. By linking the Falklands War with the 1914-18 war, *The Sun* risked reminding its readers not only of heroic, self-denying sacrifice, but also of the "futility" of war; this was precisely the opposite message to that which the newspaper wished to convey. Journalists and politicians across the political spectrum share similar views of the First World War. How accurate is this national perception of a conflict which is still familiarly known as the *Great* War?

In recent years, a generation of historians who lack the heavy emotional baggage of their predecessors have begun to assess the war, and their conclusions are often sharply at odds with received wisdom.[9] The war against Germany was formally ended by the Treaty of Versailles, signed in 1919. This treaty included Article 231, the so-called "War Guilt" clause, which blamed the war on the aggression of Germany and its allies. In the years that followed, Article 231 became discredited and was replaced in the mind of the British public with, among other ideas, the notion that the First World War was "accidental", that in 1914 the states of Europe slipped into the abyss of war. This view, popularised in the 1960s, particularly by the historian, A J P Taylor, is echoed in an episode of *Blackadder*, but it cannot be shared by anyone who has examined German foreign policy and strategy. While there is no single and simple "cause" of the First World War, and no power can entirely escape blame, the finger of suspicion must be pointed firmly at Germany and its ally, the Austro-Hungarian Empire. As early as December 1912, German leaders were willing, at the very least, to chance war to forestall an attack by France and Russia, or to achieve their aim of *Weltpolitik* (world hegemony).[10] One school of thought, associated with the German historian, Fritz Fischer, goes much further than this. Fischer has argued that in July 1914 German leaders urged on Austria-Hungary against Serbia, being prepared to risk a general war in order to achieve world power status. The German leadership was influenced in their actions by powerful social and economic forces, in particular plans for *Mitteleuropa*, an economic bloc demanded by some soldiers and industrialists which would be dominated by and organised for the advantage of Germany. These plans were, in part at least, implemented during the war itself. Fischer's work, with its implications for continuity of foreign policy and war aims between imperial Germany and the Third Reich, remains controversial but highly influential.[11]

The question rarely – if ever – asked by critics of Britain's role in the First World War is: what would have happened if Germany had won, or even if the war had ended with a compromise peace other than a return to the *status quo ante bellum* (and the evidence points away from Germany, let alone other powers, being prepared to accept such a peace)? The fate of occupied Belgium provides an answer to this question. Germany's so-called "September Programme" of 1914 had envisaged a series of annexations which would have crippled France as a great power and reduced Belgium to a German satellite. The second part of this programme was actually put into effect. The discrediting of the inflated atrocity stories current during the war has caused the sufferings of the Belgian population to be forgotten – at least in Britain. German policy was based on *Schrecklichkeit* ("dreadfulness" or "frightfulness"). During their advance through Belgium in 1914 the German Army massacred hundreds of civilians and burned down towns and villages in reprisal for acts of resistance, real or imagined, and to deter the population. Out of a population of 7.5 million, about one million Belgians became refugees. During the Occupation, the Germans effectively de-industrialised Belgium by destroying industrial plant or moving it back to Germany. About 120 000 Belgians were sent to

Germany to undertake forced labour, in addition to 100 000 men taken from Occupied France. Worst of all were the privations endured by the population of Occupied Belgium. Although a grave shortage of food was partially offset by a relief programme which allowed ships to pass through the Allied blockade, Belgian death and birth rates suffered a calamitous rise and decline respectively. German treatment of Occupied territories fell well short of the racially-inspired treatment meted out by the Nazis a generation later, but it was bad nevertheless. A British defeat or acceptance, however reluctant, of German victory over France would have condemned Occupied Europe to a grim future.[12]

Britain has traditionally fought to prevent one power from dominating the continent. It is very likely that Britain would have fought on after a French capitulation, mortgaging its future in return for arms and food from the United States. At best, peace with Germany would probably only have postponed a renewal of the war. Britain would have to have become a permanently armed camp, very likely declining to the status of a second-rate power, unless it willingly joined with Germany for share of the spoils. The latter is, given the willingness of the British people to fight a total war, psychologically very unlikely. This would have entailed acquiescence in the victory of an ideological foe, for liberal parliamentary democracy would surely have perished as a major force in a continental Europe dominated by the German military autocracy. In a very real sense, the First World War did make the world "safe for democracy".

It has been suggested that "war aims" – the objectives for which a state enters a conflict – should be considered separately from "peace aims" – the terms upon which a belligerent, scenting triumph, wishes to conclude a war, and it is true that Russia, France and Britain developed far-reaching war aims once the First World War was underway.[13] However, in early 1918 the Germans were in a position to impose their "peace aims" on defeated Russia. The terms of the Treaty of Brest-Litovsk were harsh in the extreme. Russia, in the grip of revolution and civil war, was deprived of strategically and economically valuable areas such as Ukraine, Poland, and the Baltic states. The Germans, who were also strengthening their grip on their Austrian ally, seemed well on the way to achieving *Mitteleuropa* early in 1918. Even if Germany had given up every scrap of land that it had occupied in the West, its power would have been much greater than it had been in 1914. The threat posed by Germany's newly-acquired Eastern empire caused much anxiety among the British military and political élite in 1918. The British people too, were shocked by the severity of Brest-Litovsk. It was seen as the latest in a long line of German "atrocities" such as the sinking of the *Lusitania* and the execution of Nurse Cavell. The decline in civilian morale, which had been evident in 1917, was reversed.[14]

Therefore, contrary to received wisdom, the First World War was a "good", justified war. The evidence strongly suggests that the British population, both military and civilian, capital and labour, understood the German threat and, as in the Second World War, was prepared to make enormous sacrifices to defeat it. Remarkably, in November 1918 British military and civilian morale and enthusiasm for the war were probably as high as they had ever been.[15] Trench warfare was a terrible experience, but the prospect of defeat at the hands of Germany was worse.

Within the last twenty years, prompted by the opening of archives, a revisionist school of chiefly English-speaking historians has re-examined the military history of the Western Front. The very idea that the British Army of the First World War was a skilful military instrument will appear ludicrous to many. However, recognition of the challenges imposed by the battlefield of 1914-18 has lead some historians to argue that the British Army experienced a steep "learning curve" in battle.[16] A combination of "high" technology (machine-guns and, especially, artillery), and "low" technology (trenches and barbed wire) had in 1914 led to a temporary dominance of the defensive over the offensive. The emergence of trench deadlock meant that, as there were no flanks to turn, every assault had to be made frontally, and an attempt to circumvent the problem by using naval power only resulted in a similar tactical stalemate occurring at Gallipoli, in Turkey. Finally, and crucially, the war was fought without battlefield commanders being able to exercise voice control and without a usable instrument of exploitation. Horsed cavalry was obsolescent, and the primitive, slow, and unreliable tank of the period was far from a war-winning weapon.

The British Expeditionary Force (BEF) had a hard apprenticeship during the initial phase of trench warfare in 1914-15. It was first committed to battle on a large scale on 1 July 1916 (the notorious "First Day on the Somme") when it suffered very heavy casualties. However, during the 142 days of the Somme offensive, the BEF learned important tactical lessons and wore down the strength and morale of the German Army. The lessons were applied with some effect at the battle of Arras (April-May 1917) and at the Third Battle of Ypres (or Passchendaele, July-November 1917), battles which continued the process of wearing out the German Army. After a disappointing beginning, in late September and early October the Second Army under Plumer fought three model actions near Ypres which demonstrated the high level of tactical efficiency of the BEF and brought the Germans to the verge of defeat. Unfortunately, at that point the weather broke and Haig, the BEF commander, unwisely insisted on the battle being continued. In the spring of 1918, the Germans attacked and succeeded in reopening mobile warfare. The Allies fought the Germans to a standstill, and, beginning in late July launched a "Hundred Days" of offensives which inflicted a series of serious defeats on the Germans, steadily drove them back, took 385 400 prisoners (188 700 of whom were captured by the BEF) and in November forced them to sue for peace on whatever terms they could achieve. Modern warfare emerged from the crucible of the Western Front. The fighting of 1914 looked back to the era of Napoleon; the highly skilled BEF of 1918 used an embryonic version of the modern all-arms battle.

No one would claim that the learning curve was uniformly even, that all British generals were brilliant, or deny that the heavy loss of life was caused in part by mistakes. Yet, the losses must be balanced against the achievements of the British nation in arms. The professional army of 1914, trained and equipped for small-scale colonial warfare, was brought up to the size needed for a continental struggle by enlisting civilian volunteers and conscripts. The BEF of August 1914 had six infantry divisions; the BEF of November 1918 had 61 divisions. This improvised citizen army learned how to conduct modern industrialised warfare in the most difficult of situations, while actually fighting against an extremely tough and skilled enemy, the imperial German Army. The British state created a war machine which ultimately proved superior to that of Germany. In a democracy a total war can only be waged with the consent of the masses and in 1914-18 the conflict took on the nature of a "peoples' war". Only the willingness of the British people to work long hours in factories, to undergo privations, to fight in the armed forces (which consisted solely of volunteers until 1916), enabled the Allies to win. During the Hundred Days the BEF was the spearhead of the Allied offensive, and comprehensively outfought the Germans at every level. In terms of the size and power of the enemy army that was defeated and the high degree of military skill that was demonstrated, 1918 is the greatest victory in British military history. Furthermore it was a "vindication" of the least imperfect political system yet devised, liberal democracy.[17] A liberal parliamentary system had risen to the challenge posed by an expansionist military autocracy, and had defeated it.

Why, therefore, is the First World War regarded as a disaster? As long ago as 1940, George Orwell pointed out that the great battles of 1918 in which the German Army had been defeated had already been forgotten.[18] Clearly, the results of the struggle did not seem commensurate with the sacrifice involved. Using hindsight, we know that the threat of German militarism was not broken in 1918. It is arguable that the Allies should have continued to fight until Germany surrendered unconditionally, and then treat it much as the Third Reich was to be treated in 1945, although it is possible to make out a case that the Allies were not sufficiently powerful in 1918 to achieve this. The war having been won, the fruits of the peace were squandered. Defeated enemies, Machiavelli wisely observed, "must be either pampered or crushed".[19] The 1919 Treaty of Versailles did neither. It inflicted humiliations on Germany but did not cripple it. It was easy to reach the conclusion that it was "futile" to expend such effort only to see the defeated enemy re-emerge as a threat, hungry for vengeance, a mere twenty years later.

The defeat of imperial Germany cost the British Empire 947 023 military dead, of which 744 702 were from the British Isles. These enormous losses have in subsequent years overwhelmed any sense of achievement. They are higher than those sustained by Britain in any previous war, and certainly higher than the 264 000 suffered in the Second World War. Since 1945, Britons have tended to view the First World War through the lens of the Second – a "good" war, with a economical rate of casualties – and the earlier conflict has suffered by a simplistic comparison. In reality, the lower figures for 1939-45 reflected the fact that British forces were engaged for the most part on minor and subsidiary fronts, and fought nothing approaching the scale of the 1915-18 battles on the Western Front. It should be stressed, however, that on occasions – such as in the 1944-45 campaign in North-West Europe – unit casualty rates in individual actions were similar to those of the Western Front.[20] Moreover, the common idea that conditions for the ordinary soldier on the Western Front were uniquely terrible is not one that can withstand an examination of conditions endured by British soldiers in, for example, the Italian campaign of 1943-45.[21]

In the BEF of 1914-18 the majority of officers, and a disproportionate number of the ordinary soldiers, were articulate members of the middle class. These temporary amateur soldiers of 1914-18 were better placed than their working-class comrades to articulate their feelings about the slaughter. Had the war been fought without the active military participation of the middle class, it is doubtful whether it would have gained quite such an appalling reputation. The 1.8 million German fatalities of 1914-18, and the 27 million deaths, military and civilian, sustained by the USSR between 1941 and 1945 put the British figure for 1914-18 into sobering context. Yet, no matter how dispassionately one views British casualty statistics, no matter how carefully one places them into context, one cannot escape the fact that the "million dead" of 1914-18 represents one million human tragedies and a psychic shock unparalleled in modern British history. A study of the media in the last decade of the 20th century, 80 years on from the killing, reveals that Britain has not yet come to terms with the experience.

Popular interest in the First World War began to reawaken in the late 1950s. J B Priestley, himself a veteran of the Western

61

Front, suggested that reading about shelling was a form of escapism for a generation threatened with nuclear destruction.[22] A series of popular histories, including Leon Wolff's *In Flanders Fields*, Alan Clark's *The Donkeys* and, above all, A J P Taylor's *The First World War*, powerfully reinforced the British national perception of the war and helped to redefine it in the wake of the 1939-45 conflict.[23] These books are still influential, and many later additions to the genre have continued their basic theme. The opening of the British official archives for 1914-18 in the late 1960s revolutionised academic study of the war, but the popular impact of such archival-based works has been severely limited. The short print runs, exorbitant price and forbidding appearance of many "academic" history books conspire to ensure that they are read only by other scholars, while operational and tactical military history has until very recently been a deeply unfashionable subject with "serious" historians. In sharp contrast, popular works of military history sell well, are widely read, and are reviewed in the general press. It is instructive to compare two reviews of a book by a popular writer about the First World War, Lyn Macdonald. The first, a generally favourable piece written by a novelist and published in *The Sunday Times*, included a reference (apparently serious) to *Blackadder* in a discussion of the failures of British generalship. The second, written by an historian and published in a specialist journal, was highly critical.[24]

There are now two distinct perceptions of the First World War. The majority of people view it as a unique cultural event, essentially "outside" history. In contrast, an élite of historians sees the war in the context of political and military history. This is not to deny that important work has been produced by authors based outside academic institutions – Martin Middlebrook's seminal *The First Day on the Somme* being an outstanding and obvious example. Since the start of the 1970s, there has been an upsurge in publication of good popular and "amateur" history of the First World War, due in no small measure to the activities of the Western Front Association.[25]

Welcome as this trend is, it appears to have made little impact on the public perceptions of the First World War. Even those books which do not blindly follow traditional views tend, however unconsciously, to reinforce the stereotype by concentrating on British disasters, rather than British successes.[26] It is significant that no one has produced an oral history of the Hundred Days campaign of 1918. Moreover, by concentrating – as so many do – on the experiences of the ordinary soldier, popular histories can create a distorted picture. The published diary of Captain Edwin Campion Vaughan describes an attack made at Ypres in 1917. This is an exceptionally powerful piece of descriptive writing, which brings out the horrors of war – death, mud, fear, mutilation – in a stark and unforgettable manner. Yet, in military terms, this attack resulted in the capture of a tactically important position and was far from "futile".[27] Moreover, it is often forgotten that the majority of the infantryman's time was not spent holding trenches, and still less in battle. Indeed, by contrasting the care that the army took of their soldiers with the everyday life of working-class civilians, one historian has even argued that some privates had a better standard of living on the Western Front than they did at home.[28]

While there is often a delay in academic ideas becoming accepted or even noticed by the general public, the difference between academic and popular perceptions of the First World War is especially marked.[29] Key Stage 3 of the National Curriculum that currently operates in British schools dictates that the First World War is one of the historical subjects that has to be studied in outline by every fourteen-year-old pupil, and the Western Front is an option which can be studied in depth. The National Curriculum gives a certain amount of flexibility to teachers, and allows them to introduce elements of revisionism into their teaching.[30] However, a strong case can be made that it is teachers of English, not history, that have had the greatest impact on the shaping of views on the First World War through the teaching of war poetry. It is not generals and politicians, but the War Poets, a small group of junior officers, who are the most quoted British figures of 1914-18. Their popularity can be gauged by the fact that at least one company runs tours to the battlefields for schoolchildren studying the War Poets, and an annual GCSE War Poets Day is held at the Imperial War Museum. While the latter does include an input by an historian, it is relatively rare for material on the War Poets to contain much objective material on their historical background or to reflect a revisionist viewpoint.[31]

The single most influential recent book on the First World War is Paul Fussell's *The Great War and Modern Memory*. Fussell, an American Professor of English, uses literature to explore the British experience of the conflict, treating the First World War as a unique cultural event. Unlike most academic historical writing on the First World War, Fussell's influence extends to the classroom and, crucially, the general press; in 1994, nineteen years after its publication, *The Great War and Modern Memory* was described as "brilliant" and a "classic" respectively in two quality newspapers.[32] Fussell does indeed bring important insights to our understanding of the First World War, but his approach, which is "emphatically not historical",[33] has led two historians, Robin Prior and Trevor Wilson, to argue that, as history, *The Great War and Modern Memory* has numerous defects. Prior and Wilson take a conventional approach to the writing of history. They point out that Fussell's book contains a number of factual errors, but that, far more importantly, it ignores the war at sea and the mobilisation of British society and economy for total war. These immensely important facets of the war were "not tragic, ironic, or self-evidently futile", and yet Fussell is solely interested in the "futile" aspects of the Western Front. Moreover, in keeping his view of the "senseless" nature of the 1914-18 conflict, Fussell does not include a worthwhile discussion of the causes of the war, or the issues at stake, and the Allied victories of 1918 are all but ignored.[34]

Fussell, and Prior and Wilson, thus represent two very different schools of thought about the First World War, which might be called the "cultural" and "politico-military" schools. It is the former rather than the latter that dominates so much of the British media and popular culture. It is also reflected in teaching of the War Poets in schools, which has contributed powerfully to the dominant position that has been assumed in British culture by figures such as Robert Graves, Wilfred Owen, Siegfried Sassoon and – the one ranker among this collection of officers – Isaac Rosenberg. It is virtually impossible, for example, to read the phrase "Dulce et Decorum Est Pro Patria Mori" without reading into it the bitter irony of Owen's poem, for the original sentiments are now buried beyond retrieval. It would be foolish to deny that poetry represents a valid expression of a particular individual's experience. What is not seen as valid by the revisionist school is to rely primarily or even solely upon these poems as a means of understanding the First World War – still less to see the War Poets as representing "typical" British soldiers. At best, these poems provide a very limited and skewed view of both the war as a whole and the experience of the front line infantryman.[35]

Closely associated with the "poets' view of the war" is the notion of widespread disillusionment among soldiers, as they realised that their initial ardour for combat had been woefully misplaced, and that the war was in fact futile.[36] There is actually little evidence that large numbers of soldiers became disillusioned during the war itself, and such wartime disenchantment that occurred was usually with the army and military life, not the cause for which they fought.[37] Although the subject is in dire need of a proper study, it is likely that most disillusionment occurred after the end of the war, and was prompted by the less than perfect world to which the soldiers returned. However, one should be very cautious about assuming that the majority of British soldiers became disenchanted even after 1918. The war book boom of 1928-33 saw the publication of a large number of books whose authors displayed ambivalent or even positive attitudes to the war.[38] When Siegfried Sassoon issued his statement of opposition to the war in 1917, he most assuredly did not speak for the majority of British soldiers.

If used with care, literary sources can be valuable aids to understanding the past, yet they are highly misleading if they are not placed within an historical context.[39] Literature has a disproportionate influence on the way in which the First World War is depicted in the media. Unlike most academic military history, "serious" novels and literature about the First World War tend to receive attention in the general press (and are often reviewed by novelists or journalists, and not by historians). The perspective of the War Poets appeals to the liberal tradition. It is the general press, not specialist historical journals, which by definition reach the widest audience, which includes teachers and other opinion-formers. At bottom, the media obsession with a handful of unrepresentative soldiers reflects the fact that British perceptions of the First World War too often stem from literary rather than historical sources. At least some of the original audience at R C Sherriff's *Journey's End*, which appears to end on a note of defeat, would have known that the German offensive failed, and that the subsequent Allied counter-offensive won the war. In contrast, viewers of the film, *Oh! What a Lovely War* – in which the fighting simply stops, with the trench systems apparently intact – generally lack the knowledge to recognise that an important section of the war has, quite literally, been written out of the script.

Even when writing about the Second World War, journalists automatically reach for the poets of 1914-18 to provide headlines. In the space of a fortnight in 1995, at a time when VE Day fever gripped the media, if not the country, an article about the end of the war in 1945 was headed "Goodbye to all that" (the title of Robert Graves's semi-fictional memoir of the Western Front), while a review of two anthologies of poetry from that war had the Owenesque headline, "ANTHEMS FOR DOOMED YOUTH".[40] It is almost as if a media item about either world war is regarded as incomplete without a reference to the War Poets. A particularly ludicrous example occurred on a television programme in 1986 when a discussion about Haig's generalship between two historians – neither of them of the "lions led by donkeys" school – was concluded with a wholly inappropriate clip of an aged Robert Graves singing "Hanging on the Old Barbed Wire". It was as if the BBC had decided that their viewers could only take so much serious historical debate before they were given something comfortable and familiar to hold onto.[41]

Twenty years after the publication of *The Great War and Modern Memory*, the First World War continues to be "an engaging source of myth and imagery for living writers and their readers".[42] While a new generation of historians is shedding the emotional baggage of the last 80 years and beginning to assess the First World War in a detached fashion, their role as custodians of the British national perception has been assumed by novelists. In many ways this is an obvious development, for it is natural that a people that has gained an understanding of an event largely through the medium of fiction should express their reaction to it through the same medium. In writing his 1993 novel, *Birdsong*, which is partly set on the Western Front, Sebastian Faulks employed some of the methods of an historian, researching in soldiers' letters and diaries, but using them as "food for the imagination", rather than as a conventional historical source. The result is both a restatement of the traditional view of the war and a brilliantly imaginative recreation of an appalling human experience. The "traditionalist" position is even more clearly stated in *The Missing of the Somme*, a meditation on the war by the novelist, Geoff Dyer. For Dyer, the battles on the Western Front were futile blood baths. He does not confront and refute the revisionist case (of which, to judge by his bibliography, he is aware); he simply ignores it. That, rather than the various literary sins for which his reviewers took him to task, is the reason why *The Missing of the Somme* is far from being "the great Great War book of our time".[43]

The decade of the 1960s was a time of questioning of traditional values and mores, and this was reflected in treatments of the First World War on stage and screen. Major films include the story of a private shot for desertion, *King and Country* (1964), which was in turn based on a stage play, *Hamp*; and *Oh! What a Lovely War* (1969), directed by Richard Attenborough and based on Joan Littlewood's 1963 "anti-authority" play of the same name.[44] It was through the medium of television, however, that images of the First World War were to have the greatest impact on a mass audience. In 1964 the BBC showed the 26-part television series, *The Great War*. Produced by Tony Essex, with the historian Basil Liddell Hart as historical consultant, each episode attracted an average of eight million viewers. One of the principal scriptwriters (his work included the all-important programmes covering the Somme and Third Ypres) was John Terraine. Terraine's views, expressed in ten books published from 1960 to 1982, were sharply at odds with the popular perception of the war and, indeed, the views of Liddell Hart. According to Terraine, Haig pursued a strategy of attrition – the only possible strategy, given the circumstances – which wore down the German Army and prepared it for the *coup de grâce* delivered by the Allies in 1918. Even though many of the new wave of revisionist historians do not agree with Terraine's assessment of Haig as a Great Captain, his fundamental thesis – although frequently assailed over the last 30 years – has yet to be demolished.[45]

The BBC television series apparently matched the man with the hour; here at last was a golden opportunity to present an alternative viewpoint to a mass audience. Yet, as Alex Danchev has argued, this viewpoint was ignored or at least not understood by the audience; instead, the series reinforced the existing perception of the war as a futile waste of life.[46] In the case of the Passchendaele episode, entitled "Surely We Have Perished", it seems that revisionism was overwhelmed by extracts from the poetry of Owen and Sassoon.[47] The public reaction to *The Great War* suggests that programmes do not have to carry an explicitly anti-war message in order to build up negative images in viewers' minds: all they need to do is to show scenes of carnage. It may be the case that the viewers' responses simply reflected their existing impression of the war. The showing of documentaries on the Second World War, which often feature gory footage, does not seem to have changed the public perception of this conflict as a "good" war, in which men died to achieve a discernible and laudable end.

The First World War continues to be a favourite subject for television documentaries and dramas. Probably the most important documentary made since *The Great War* is Malcolm Brown's *The Battle of the Somme* (first shown by the BBC on the 60th anniversary of the battle in 1976, and reshown in 1986). Inspired by Middlebrook's book, the programme made a powerful impact by juxtaposing archive footage with a duffle-coated Leo McKern wandering across the present-day battlefield. Although the programme does not carry an explicitly anti-war message, the concentration on the human disaster of 1 July 1916 serves to reinforce traditional perceptions of the war. 1986 also brought a sharp reminder of how emotive an issue the First World War remains. The anti-war, anti-establishment themes of the "docudrama", *The Monocled Mutineer*, which was viewed by about ten million people, caused considerable controversy and raised important questions about the relationship between historical fact and dramatic imperatives.[48]

A new genre is that of the video documentary, which, cheaply priced and on sale in High Street shops, is a means of entertaining and informing the public about a variety of subjects, including the First World War. Most videos on 1914-18 reflect received wisdom, including – perhaps surprisingly – *The Official History of the British Army*. This takes a fairly traditional view of the war, with the section on Third Ypres saying nothing about the improved tactical performance of the British Army or about the near success of Plumer's three offensives.[49] The video has the immediacy of the television programme without its perishability, but, to judge from offerings currently available, video-makers seem unwilling to deal with complex issues onscreen. A partial exception is the commercially successful video, *The Story of the Great War*, which uses an academic revisionist historian as script consultant and attempts to place the Western Front into context by discussing the technology of war.[50]

Possibly the most viewed television programme dealing with a First World War topic was neither a documentary nor even a conventional drama, but a commercial for beer shown in the 1970s. This featured a Great War Tommy, returning from leave, quietly singing "Goodbyee", a sentimental song of the period. The poignancy of the commercial, and hence its power, lies in the fact that the audience knew that the soldier was going to France to face death. That pint was probably the last taste of bitter – that emblematic English drink – which the soldier would ever have. The context of the commercial was the rise of lager, a continental drink, as a serious challenge to the traditional British brew. A captive audience of television-viewers who may not have had the slightest interest in history saw this image, which sought to enlist the sympathy of the audience for a doomed youth by appealing to values of courage and tradition. This was a version of the 1914-18 myth that reached a truly mass audience. It is perhaps not entirely coincidental that the last episode of *Blackadder Goes Forth* was entitled "Goodbyeee".

A theme of this essay has been the failure of revisionist military historians to put across their message to a wider audience. There are some signs, however small, that this is changing. On 11 November 1993, the 75th anniversary of the Armistice of 1918, *The Times* carried a leader headed "History's Trenches: Orthodox views of the first world war should be questioned", which cited the work of John Terraine. On the same day, *The Guardian* carried an article by Professor Norman Stone which argued the case for the First World War as "a just war fought to counter German aggression". This article was balanced by the front page of *The Guardian* tabloid which featured a poppy and Owen's "Anthem for Doomed Youth". Nearly two years later, on the 50th anniversary of VE Day, *The Independent*'s leader contrasted Britain's "unambiguously good" role in the 1939-45 war with that in the First World War, which "could be seen with hindsight as a pointless slaughter". The love affair between the media and the British national perception of the First World War is far from over.[51]

Does the constant reinforcement of the national perception of the First World War matter to anyone except revisionist historians? The answer is an emphatic Yes. The First World War is not a dead antiquarian subject, but a live and emotive issue. The belief that Britain's role was a disaster reaches to the highest levels of decision-making. The author of *The Donkeys* became Minister of State for Defence in Margaret Thatcher's Conservative government.[52] Furthermore, the British national perception has implications for popular support of the use of British forces in a campaign that threatens to be bloody and protracted. At best, distorted views of history are unhelpful; at worst, they can be disastrous. Although the British myth of the war may seem to be relatively benign, the product of a liberal state's horror at mass carnage, the denial of the fact that the British Army inflicted a crushing military victory on the German Army aided Hitler's rise to power. Finally, it is surely right and fitting that the Million Dead should be remembered not as a useless sacrifice, but as the terrible price that had to be paid for victory in a just and necessary war.

*   *   *

I would like to thank Lloyd Clark, Nigel de Lee, Martine de Lee, Tony Heathcote and, especially, Stephen Badsey for their help and advice.

Notes

[1]   BBC videocassettes, BBCV 4349 and 4350; BBC *Radio Collection* audiocassette.

[2]   I have assumed, perhaps rashly, that there is such a thing as a British national perception of the First World War. This assumption is based on observation of the media, and discussions with a large number of people over a period of some fifteen years. We lack a properly conducted study of public opinion on the matter, but the preliminary findings of my Sandhurst colleague, Lloyd Clark, suggest that there is a general awareness of the First World War as a uniquely terrible experience, and that perceptions of this war tend to colour perceptions of conflict in general.

[3]   For attitudes to war, see Martin Ceadal, *Thinking about Peace and War* (Oxford: Oxford University Press, 1987); Michael Howard, *War and the Liberal Conscience* (Oxford: Oxford University Press, 1981).

[4]   *The Guardian* 12 January 1987: 21.

[5]   *The Guardian*: 24 April 1995: 16.

[6]   *The Observer* 9 April 1995: 22.

[7]   *The Sun* 8 April 1982, quoted in Robert Harris, *Gotcha! The Media, the Government and the Falklands Crisis* (London: Faber and Faber, 1983): 45.

[8]   Bob Bushaway, "Name Upon Name: The Great War and Remembrance", in Roy Porter (ed), *Myths of the English* (Cambridge: Polity Press, 1992): 145. For the evolution of the process of commemoration and attitudes towards the war, see this source and Adrian Gregory, *The Silence of Memory: Armistice Day 1919-1946*

(Oxford: Berg, 1994). Jane Leonard, Fiona Douglas and Angela Gaffney are currently working on the Irish, Scottish and Welsh experiences respectively.

[9]   Brian Bond, "Editor's Introduction", in Brian Bond (ed), *The First World War and British Military History* (Oxford: Clarendon Press, 1991): 1.

[10]   James Joll, *The Origins of the First World War*, second edition (London: Longman, 1992): 104-105, 234-235.

[11]   For a convenient short summary of Fischer's ideas, see his "German War Aims 1914-1918 and German Policy before the War", in Barry Hunt and Adrian Preston (eds), *War Aims and Strategic Policy in the Great War 1914-1918* (London: Croom Helm, 1977): 105-123.

[12]   Matthew Bennett, "The German Experience", in Ian F W Beckett (ed), *The Roots of Counter-Insurgency: Armies and guerrilla warfare, 1900-1945* (London: Blandford Press, 1988): 60-82; Bernard Thorold, "Invasion", in Peter Young (ed), *Purnell's History of the First World War* 1: 5 (London: Purnell's, 1969): 128-130; Jacques Willequet, "Belgium: Life under German Occupation", *Purnell's History* 5: 3 (1971): 1877-1879.

[13]   Joll: 169.

[14]   Benjamin Schwarz, "Divided Attention: Britain's Perception of a German Threat to Her Eastern Position in 1918", *Journal of Contemporary History* 28 (1993): 103-121; John Bourne, *Britain and the Great War, 1914-18* (London: Edward Arnold, 1989): 210; Nicholas Reeves, "The Power of Film Propaganda – myth or reality?", *Historical Journal of Film, Radio and Television* 13: 2 (1993): 186.

[15]   For British military morale, see G D Sheffield, "Morale in British Army on the Western Front, 1914-18", Occasional Paper for the Institute for the Study of War and Society, De Montfort University, (forthcoming); for civilian morale, see Reeves.

[16]   The following books espouse, to varying degrees, the revisionist case: Trevor Wilson, *The Myriad Faces of War: Britain and the Great War, 1914-1918* (Cambridge: Polity Press, 1986); Paddy Griffith, *Battle Tactics of the Western Front: The British Army's Art of Attack, 1916-18* (New Haven; London: Yale University Press, 1994); Bourne; Correlli Barnett, *The Collapse of British Power* (Gloucester: Alan Sutton, 1984); Peter Simkins, *World War I 1914-1918: The Western Front* (Godalming: Colour Library Books, 1991); Bill Rawling, *Surviving Trench Warfare: Technology and the Canadian Corps 1914-1918* (Toronto: University of Toronto Press, 1992); Robin Prior and Trevor Wilson, *Command on the Western Front: The Military Career of Sir Henry Rawlinson 1914-18* (Oxford: Blackwell Publishers, 1992).

Two important books by Tim Travers are more sceptical about the British Army's "learning curve": *The Killing Ground: The British Army, the Western Front and the Emergence of Modern Warfare 1900-1918* (London: Allen & Unwin, 1987) and *How the War Was Won: Command and Technology in the British Army on the Western Front, 1917-1918* (London; New York: Routledge, 1992). Peter Simkins, G D Sheffield, and John Lee are working on *Haig's Army: An Operational, Social and Organisational Study of the British Army on the Western Front, 1916-18*. For John Terraine, see note 45.

[17] Robin Prior and Trevor Wilson, "What Manner of Victory? Reflections on the Termination of the First World War", *Revue Internationale d'Histoire Militaire* 27 (1990): 96.

[18] George Orwell, "The Lion and the Unicorn", in Sonia Orwell and Ian Angus (eds), *The Collected Essays, Journalism and Letters of George Orwell, volume 2: My Country Right or Left* (Harmondsworth: Penguin Books, 1970): 80.

[19] Niccolò Machiavelli, *The Prince*, translated with an introduction by George Bull (Harmondsworth: Penguin Books, 1975): 37. See also Barnett.

[20] John Terraine, *The First World War 1914-1918* (London: Papermac, 1984): 183-184; Jeffery Williams, *The Long Left Flank: The Hard Fought Way to the Reich, 1944-1945* (London: Leo Cooper, 1988): 318-319. The Second World War is now subject to some revisionism, but there is little evidence that this has affected popular views of this conflict – witness the public controversy surrounding a biography critical of Churchill's wartime premiership: John Charmley, *Churchill: The End of Glory* (London: Hodder and Stoughton, 1993); *The Times* 2 January 1993: 12 (review by Alan Clark); *The Sunday Times* 10 January 1993: Sec. 3, 6 (review by Anthony Howard).

[21] Here it is instructive to compare John Ellis's book on the Western Front, *Eye-Deep In Hell* (London: Croom Helm, 1976), with his study of the fighting man in the Second World War, *The Sharp End of War* (London: Corgi, 1982).

[22] J B Priestley, *Literature and Western Man* (London: Heinemann, 1960): 370.

[23] Leon Wolff, *In Flanders Fields: The 1917 Campaign* (London: Longmans, Green and Co, 1959); Alan Clark, *The Donkeys* (London: Hutchinson, 1961); A J P Taylor, *The First World War: An Illustrated History* (London: Hamish Hamilton, 1963).

[24] Reviews of Lyn Macdonald, *1915: The Death of Innocence* (London: Headline, 1993) by Kate Saunders, *The Sunday Times* 19 December 1993, and by A J Peacock, *Gun Fire* 29: 63-66.

[25]   Peter Simkins, "Everyman at War: Recent Interpretations of the Front Line Experience", in Bond (ed): 289-313. Martin Middlebrook, *The First Day on the Somme: 1 July 1916* (London: Allen Lane, 1971). For a more recent example, see Leonard Sellers, *The Hood Battalion. Royal Naval Division: Antwerp, Gallipoli, France 1914-1918* (London: Leo Cooper, 1995). Compare this, however, with J H Johnson, *Stalemate! The Great Trench Warfare Battles of 1915-1917* (London: Arms and Armour Press, 1995). This is a throwback to the 1960s, based on published sources, and containing little in the way of originality.

[26]   For example, an otherwise excellent history of 36th (Ulster) Division concentrates heavily on 1 July 1916. Philip Orr, *The Road to the Somme: Men of the Ulster Division Tell Their Story* (Belfast; Wolfeboro, NH: The Blackstaff Press, 1987).

[27]   Edwin Campion Vaughan, *Some Desperate Glory: The diary of a young officer, 1917* (London: Papermac, 1985): 220-231; James E Edmonds, *Military Operations, France and Belgium, 1917* II (London: Imperial War Museum; Nashville: Battery Press, 1991): 208.

[28]   C Barnett, "A Military Historian's View of the Great War", *Essays by Divers Hands, Being the Transactions of the Royal Society of Literature* 36 (1970): 1-18.

[29]   A school textbook in current use, for example, does not reflect revisionist thinking on the fighting on the Western Front; Colin Shephard, Andy Reid, Keith Shephard, *The Schools History Project: Discovering the Past Y9 Peace & War* (London: John Murray, 1993).

[30]   I am indebted to Roger Coombes and his Year 9 history set at Collingwood College, Camberley, and to Keith Grieves for their guidance on history in the National Curriculum. Similar thanks are due to Gerda Bennett for her advice on the teaching of poetry.

[31]   For examples, see Christopher Martin, *War Poems* (London: Collins Educational, 1991) which pursues a "traditionalist" agenda, and Michael Marland, *The Times Authors No. 5: The War Poets* (London: Times Newspapers, n.d.). The latter is an information pack aimed at schoolchildren and edited by a teacher. Bernard Bergonzi, *Heroes' Twilight: a Study of the Literature of the Great War* (London: Macmillan, 1980), and especially Andrew Rutherford, *The Literature of War: Five Studies in Heroic Virtue* (London: Macmillan, 1978), chapter 4, place the War Poets in historical context.

[32]   These comments are taken from reviews of a book influenced by Fussell, Geoff Dyer's *The Missing of the Somme* (London: Hamish Hamilton, 1994); *The Sunday Times* 23 October 1994: Sec 7, 11 (Kate Saunders); *The Independent*, undated clipping, 1994 (Mick Imlah).

[33]   Bond (ed): 1.

[34]   Paul Fussell, *The Great War and Modern Memory* (London: Oxford University Press, 1975); Robin Prior and Trevor Wilson, "Paul Fussell at War", *War in History* 1: 1 (1994), especially 66-72. Fussell's attempt in *Wartime: Understanding and Behavior in the Second World War* (Oxford: Oxford University Press, 1989) to depict the 1939-45 war as "futile" has received much less sympathy.

[35]   Barnett (1984): 428-435.

[36]   Robert Wohl, in Tim Cross (ed), *The Lost Voices of World War I: An international anthology of writers, poets and playwrights* (London: Bloomsbury, 1988): 382; Anne Powell (ed), *A Deep Cry: Literary Pilgrimage to the Battlefields and Cemeteries of First World War British Soldier-poets Killed in Northern France and Flanders* (Aberporth: Palladour Books, 1993): xiv.

[37]   See C E Montague, *Disenchantment* (London: Chatto & Windus, 1922); S F Hatton, *The Yarn of a Yeoman* (London: Hutchinson, n.d.).

[38]   A selection would include Charles Edmonds, *A Subaltern's War* (London: Peter Davies, 1929); R C Sherriff's play, *Journey's End;* and H E Harvey, *Battle Line Narratives 1915-1918* (London: Brentano's, 1928).

[39]   A textual analysis of media images underpins French philosopher Jean Baudrillard's articles, "The Reality Gulf" (*The Guardian* 11 January 1991) and "La Guerre du Golfe n'a pas eu lieu" (*Libération* 29 March 1991). Christopher Norris's *Uncritical Theory: Postmodernism, Intellectuals and the Gulf War* (London: Lawrence and Wishart, 1992) seeks to counter what he regards as the dangers of an approach seemingly disconnected from the specific historical and political context of that conflict.

[40]   *The Times* magazine 6 May 1995: 8; *Independent on Sunday* magazine 23 April 1995: 31.

[41]   *Newsnight* BBC Television, 1 July 1986. The two historians were John Terraine and Keith Simpson.

[42]   Bergonzi: unpaginated preface.

[43]   Sebastian Faulks, *Birdsong* (London: Hutchinson, 1993) and Sebastian Faulks, "Back to the Front with Tommy", *The Guardian* 15 September 1993: 1-2; Geoff Dyer, *The Missing of the Somme, The Observer* 30 October 1994: 24 (review by Valentine Cunningham).

[44]   Bond (ed): 9, and Alex Danchev, "'Bunking' and Debunking: The Controversies of the 1960s", in Bond (ed): 281-288.

[45] For concise statements of Terraine's thesis, see his "Haig", in Field Marshal Sir Michael Carver (ed), *The War Lords* (London: Weidenfeld and Nicolson, 1976) and his *The First World War 1914-1918*. For a critical assessment of Terraine's thesis, and a listing of Terraine's works, see Danchev: 273-280, and Keith Simpson, "The Reputation of Sir Douglas Haig", in Bond (ed): 151-155, 161-162.

[46] Danchev: 279-281.

[47] This episode is shown to schoolchildren at the annual Imperial War Museum War Poets Day. I am grateful to Anita Ballin and Rebecca Strike for their advice on this matter.

[48] See Julian Putkowski, "Toplis, Etaples and the 'Monocled Mutineer'", *Stand To!* 18 (1986); Julian Petley, "Over the Top", *Sight and Sound* 56: 2 (spring 1987): 126-131.

[49] *The Official History of the British Army* (Castle Vision, CVI 1852).

[50] *The Story of the Great War 1914-1918* (Castle Vision, CVI 1842). Despite its ghastly title, *Blood and Mud: Trench Warfare in the West 1914-1918* (PolyGram Video, 632 932-3) also deserves an honourable mention.

[51] *The Times* 11 November 1993: 19, and *The Guardian* 11 November 1993: Sec. 2, 2-3; *The Independent* 8 May 1995: 14.

[52] Bond (ed): 11. For the use of history as a guide for British defence policy-makers, see David French, *The British Way in Warfare 1688-2000* (London: Unwin Hyman, 1990).

Presenting arms: portrayals of war and the military in British cinema
Ian Stewart

It has been claimed that there have been more films made about war than about any other subject-matter,[1] and – although by no means the only source of information and impression – cinema has undoubtedly played an important role in colouring the perceptions of war and the military in British culture in the 20th century. Part of the reason for this surely lies in the apparent credibility of the film-watching experience: this "easy" medium invites the viewer to look on as recorded "reality" unfolds.

How accurate are cinema's representations of war and conflict? Are war films, as common sense would seem to suggest, the nearest simulation of the reality of battle which the cinematic apparatus can achieve?[2] Or are portrayals of war and the military, as this essay will argue, as much the combined product of cinematic conventions, generic formats and the commercial aspirations of a film industry, rather than any pretence to actuality?

To examine this view further, one needs to look at the development of the cinematic conventions that have come to characterise commercial cinema and at some of the ways in which these have influenced the representation of war and the military on film.

Popular film utilises certain formal devices in its depiction of reality – the "classical Hollywood style"[3] – thereby creating in viewers an expectation of the narrative and stylistic features to be found in any given film. An obvious example is the conventional narrative form. This decrees an opening, where the scene is set and the characters are introduced; a middle section, in which the narrative develops; and a dénouement, where the various narrative themes are brought together and a sense of completion is engendered. The reality of international relations and armed conflicts means that real wars, however, invariably lack clearly defined narrative openings, developments or closures. Represented in mainstream cinema, however, war will as a matter of course exhibit conventional narrative features, and naturally this is the form in which war is commonly conceptualised. Our culture, steeped in a narrative tradition, tends to impose this reading upon the phenomenon of war, whether appropriate or not.[4] When one writer described the 1991 Gulf War as having "a movie script happy ending",[5] was she describing the conflict itself, or an interpretation of this conflict rooted – like film portrayals of war in general – in narrative traditions?

In addition to these elements in the "grammar" of popular cinema, there are generic[6] codes and conventions. The cinema-goer is well aware of the formal differences over and above the manifest differences in content between, for example, a detective film and a musical. Similarly, the war film has its own generic codes and conventions. For example, it focuses on the exploits of a few soldiers or sailors, even though the film itself may revolve around battle scenes that depict thousands. This concentration on the few means that the human-interest aspect of the narrative is foregrounded, rather than any wider political questions which the war might raise. A common feature of the "classic war film"[7] is the absence of discussion about the war in question – war films tend to centre on action rather than analysis. This is not to say, however, that the representation of the military, thus removed from politics, is rendered apolitical. In fact, the removal from contemporary politics allows the representations of the military to function more freely as a metaphor for the nation.

The stylistic conventions and generic forms found in popular film are, of course, intrinsically linked to the commercial aspirations of the film industry which supports them. In the case of the portrayal of war and the military in British cinema, one should be aware of the economic, social and political forces that have shaped the British film industry during the 20th century.

To examine film representations of war and the military while referring to the touchstones of cinematic style, generic form and commercial enterprise, it seems appropriate to begin by looking at some of the earliest images of war recorded and their relationship both to the ways of representing reality that were developing within the cinematic mode of address, and to the commercial aspirations of the nascent film industry.

Early cinema and war

> Absolutely astounding, and if I had seen it on a cinematograph film I should have sworn that it was faked![8]

Since its invention at the end of the 19th century, cinema has enjoyed a particularly close relationship with war, and especially modern warfare. This relationship is apparent in their respective technologies: the simultaneous development of the repeating rifle and Marey's camera should be noted, as should the many military uses of cinematic and video-based sighting and reconnaissance devices.[9]

Why war and conflict should provide such popular subject-matter for filmmakers seems obvious. Apart from the centrality of war in political and social terms, war is also an ideal cinematic subject, promising many of the ingredients that have driven commercial cinema: a high level of physical action; the interplay of powerful people; extraordinary acts of selfless bravery and heroism; the photogenic qualities of military technology; and so on.

However, it is important to note that these ingredients are not used in their raw form, but are worked into a commercial cinematic product. This is especially true in the case of battle scenes. Real battles are very different from their cinematic counterparts. When he visited Europe during the First World War, D W Griffith – whose *The Birth of a Nation* (1915) features perhaps the first truly cinematic battle – said "viewed as a dogma, the war is in some ways disappointing".[10] The cinematic conventions developed in films such as *The Birth of a Nation* are the templates on which later representations of conflict are based. In this sense, the largest influence on the way in which a battle in a film is portrayed is how battles have been portrayed in other films.

The practice of filming reconstructions of war, so common in the early days of the cinema, helps to underline this point. Given the logistical problems of filming actual wars and conflicts (they were usually far away and the time difference between filming, developing, editing and finally exhibiting was great), the attraction of simply faking battle scenes was enormous. These reconstructions, however, were very popular with audiences, as the war correspondent Fredrick De Villiers found to his cost. De Villiers had actually filmed the battle of Volo in April 1897, the first battle ever to have been captured on film. However, by the time he had returned to England, Star Films of Paris had cornered the market with reconstructions of the fighting. Demand thus fulfilled, his product was worthless in commercial terms. The question is: why should an audience, already served by a fictional version that conformed better to their expectations of what a battle looked like, show any interest in the real thing? Authenticity alone was not sufficient – audiences wanted close-ups, identifiable characters, and a continuous and resolved narrative. In fact, audiences demanded the cinematic conventions that the burgeoning entertainment cinema delivered so well. Moreover, of course, this commercial cinema was growing fast: *Bioscope* reports that by 1910 London had over 300 cinemas, Manchester 111 and Liverpool 33. Significantly, most of these outlets were affiliated to cinema chains. Films that were good at the box office were exhibited all over the country and people demanded more of the same.

Cinema, therefore, soon became truly a mass medium: cinema-goers throughout the British Isles could see the same films, be exposed to the same cinematic conventions that were developing, and have the same reference points. This growing demand for similar commercial products helped further to crystallise the developing generic codes and conventions of what constituted a film and, in turn, how film portrayed reality.

It may appear that this discussion of the developing cinematic conventions has little relation to newsreels, the prime source of moving images of the First World War for the home audience – these films purported simply to record the realities of war. However, two points should be borne in mind. Firstly, the cinema industry was also part of the total war effort. Films such as *Britain Prepared* (1915), *The Battle of the Somme* (1916) and *The Battle of the Ancre and the Advance of the Tanks* (1917) not only provided information, but also were part of a wider propaganda campaign.[11] Secondly, even "objective" newsreels were not free from the influence of cinematic conventions. Where the most popular documentary of this period, *The Battle of the Somme*, lacked "real" footage, scenes such as the famous over-the-top sequence were reconstructed. Clearly, the staged character of this important sequence allowed the filmmakers to impose their version of "reality". Significantly, this faked sequence was often incorporated into later fictional films, no doubt to inject a sense of the "real".

The reconstruction of a key sequence can be justified on practical grounds. However, the fact remains that the newsreels were bound by the same stylistic and narrative demands – the makers of *The Battle of the Somme* just could not leave out such an important sequence. The cinematic conventions within which they were working demanded that it be included.

Filmmakers keen to record the conflict also presented problems for the military authorities charged with prosecuting the war in question. Keen to maintain control over both the battle area and information, the military were loath to allow free access.[12] Removed to a distance, the filmmakers were often left with poor shots of the action. This meant, however, that many images which could be useful from the combatant's point of view – to promote the aims of the war effort and to bolster public support – could not be generated. It would seem that contemporary Western military doctrine has recognised the dilemma and sought to accommodate the production of such images.[13]

When US forces landed in Somalia on 9 December 1992, the first sight the Navy Seals met on the beach was a CNN camera crew. The US government had arranged the landing to coincide with prime-time American news bulletins. This seemed to have hailed a new development in the relationship between the military and the media. However, there had been a number of military leaders who recognised the power of images somewhat earlier. For example, on 3 January 1914 Pancho Villa, the Mexican bandit, signed a contract with Mutual Film Corporation, which gave them exclusive rights to cover all his battles. Under this agreement, Villa would ensure the cameramen access to the battlefields and generally accommodate their wishes. Indeed, he went as far as to ensure that all battles would be fought in daylight, appreciating the difficulties of night-time filming. He even postponed his attack on the city of Ojinaga until a camera operator could be present![14]

The role of British cinema during the Second World War

> one of the most valuable tasks which the cinema could perform in wartime was to project an image of the national character and the national identity that would promote support for the war effort and attract the sympathy and support of overseas allies.[15]

In the 40 or so years between the first picture shows and the outbreak of the Second World War, the British cinema industry had evolved into a significant economic and social institution. There were almost 4500 cinemas, selling between them 963 million entrance tickets a year. It is estimated that there was a solid cinema audience of some twenty million, and, for a considerable proportion of that audience, two or three cinema outings in a single week was not an unusual occurrence.

By definition, it is the film industry, which produces, distributes and exhibits motion pictures, that determines the type of films that the public sees and, by implication, those it does not see. A film not only requires a great deal of artistic input, but also needs to be supported by an industry which coordinates the necessary materials, sets, actors, processing, administration, distribution and exhibition.

By the middle of the 1920s, this industry was well established in Britain and a number of production companies and cinema chains were in existence. Of course, these cinemas were not showing only British films. In fact, home-produced films accounted for less than a fifth of their total programming. The biggest single source of these foreign films was the United States of America. The Hollywood machine was already functioning well by this point, and some 80% of the films screened in Britain's growing number of picture palaces were produced there.

There were many problems with this heavy reliance on American product. The British circuits' need for American films – and it was a common practice for a single cinema to change its programme two or three times per week – put the Americans producers in a strong bargaining position. They were able to dictate, to some extent, the terms under which British exhibitors screened their films. Many of them, for example, demanded that the exhibitors bought whole packages of films from them. They could also ensure that the films of their choosing were given priority when it came to release dates and billing.

The fact that British cinemas were contractually obliged to give special treatment to American films often meant that the release of British films had to be fitted around their programming of the big American features. Consequently, many of them received only very short runs or their release was delayed, sometimes for months. Significantly, these developments also meant that British exhibitors were educating their own public to appreciate a certain type of product – the Hollywood movie – and, in doing so, they stimulated an appetite that would never be wholly satisfied.

The economic consequences for the young film industry in Britain were obvious and detrimental. When a film received only a limited or postponed release, the revenue the film producers finally received was often too little and too late to recoup the initial investment required to make the film. Furthermore, depending on the financial health of the studio and the nerve of their shareholders, it could naturally dissuade or delay the studio from investing in their next project.

As the very idea of what constituted a film – in terms of generic form, narrative structure and production values – unsurprisingly came to be based on the Hollywood model, British films consequently suffered in comparison. The British film industry was increasingly viewed as little more than a supporting feature to the grand show of Hollywood. This did not go unnoticed: Prime Minister Baldwin warned of "[t]he enormous power which film is developing for propaganda purposes and the danger to which we in the country and our Empire subject ourselves if we allow that method of propaganda to be entirely in the hands of foreign countries".[16]

It was this kind of fear that inspired the Cinematograph Films Act of 1927, which bound the film industry to screen a certain number of British films. Although there were difficulties with the implementation and interpretation of the Act, it did mean that more British films were produced and shown during the decade it was in place than in the previous one. Thus, the "quota quickie" came into being: cheap, quickly made "British" films that satisfied the conditions laid out in the Act. George Pearson, for example, made eight films in one year for MGM at the Twickenham Studios. The films churned out during this time were often – and sometimes accurately – castigated as simply programme-fillers devoid of any artistic or commercial qualities. However, this tells only part of the story, as the quickie system also allowed studios to blood young directors – both Michael Powell and Alexander Korda acquired valuable experience making quota quickies – which would set the industry in good stead to meet the challenges of the war economy. Money, materials, technical equipment and time would all be limited, and the need to reflect and promote the British way of life would never be more pressing. The lessons learnt under the quota system – of producing straightforward, direct films cheaply and quickly – would prove invaluable.

The film industry in Britain had already lived through one world war and, indeed, had been praised for its role in "inspiring the nation to victory". *The Times* encapsulated this feeling in an article in 1919: "good propaganda probably saved a year of the war, and this meant the saving...of at least a million lives". However, the lessons learnt during that period only partly prepared it for the conditions in which it would be forced to operate during the Second World War. Whereas the First World War was a long and bloody campaign involving up to four million British soldiers, it was nevertheless a war fought exclusively overseas. In this sense, it was removed from the everyday lives of people in this country. The Second World War, however, was very much "the people's war", fought in the butcher's shop as well as on the battlefield. The war impinged on every facet of life in this country, and the cinema was no exception.

The war's effects on the film industry were felt almost immediately. Mindful of the possible consequences of so many people in a confined space (such as in a cinema) during an air raid, the government closed down all the cinemas. However, the predicted air raids did not immediately materialise, and by 11 September cinemas outside London were able to reopen. Gradually, picture houses in London were allowed to follow, and by the end of the year it was business as usual for exhibitors. It was not long, however, before exhibitors experienced problems, especially when it came to maintaining the stringent air raid precautions which the government demanded with a workforce undergoing radical change. Although chief projectionist was regarded as a reserved occupation, it was not long before conscription deprived the exhibitors of a large proportion of their young, male employees. Consequently, increasing numbers of women came to work in the business, replacing the men lost to the Armed Forces. The exhibitors, however, were not short of films to show, since Hollywood maintained its enormous production levels throughout the war.

The period of the Second World War is seen as something of a "golden age" of British filmmaking, when the industry produced films that were truly popular, whilst also reflecting and promoting traditional British values and culture. A number of factors were responsible for this. Primarily, there was the newly defined sense of purpose of the film industry: this was a world war where the future of the nation was perceived to be at stake. Therefore, it is not surprising that filmmakers, producers and writers saw themselves as having a significant role to play in the war effort. For example, Alexander Korda's *The Lion Has Wings* (1939) was

81

the producer's personal contribution, while the patriotic overtones of Laurence Olivier's *Henry V* (1944) – which is prefaced by a message to the soldiers serving overseas – are quite obvious.

There can be no doubt that many filmmakers relished the role of commentators in providing a focus for the nation in difficult times, not only presenting and supporting the national case, but also suggesting the collective way forward. One popular film was entitled *The Way Ahead* (1944), which charts the experiences of a group of recruits undergoing basic training. In these films the Army functions as a "microcosm of the nation", in which the soldiers put aside their class and other differences for the greater good. The usual cast of characters tends to comprise an Englishman, a Scotsman, an Irishman and a Welshman. "Recruit" films lent themselves particularly well to comedy: for example, *King Arthur Was a Gentleman* (1942), starring Arthur Askey, follows the exploits of comedians answering the call to arms. Such a film effectively combines the roles of showing a nation pulling together in a difficult time and of providing some much-needed comic relief.

The formalisation of the film industry's role of "projecting Britain" took place with the re-establishment of the Ministry of Information (MoI). The remit of the MoI was to present the national case both to the public at home and to those abroad – in other words, to be responsible for the preparation and issue of national propaganda. Although the thrust of its efforts was concerned with the preparation of its own films, the MoI did finance some feature films, perhaps most notably Powell's *49th Parallel* (1941). However, the Ministry had certain other important powers. As celluloid was deemed an essential material, it was able to control its supply. Given their hold on this vital resource, they were able to demand that they "vetted" any potential film. Celluloid was only released to the producers after the MoI had studied a synopsis of the shooting script and had been granted access to information about the production company and the personnel they intended employing on the project.

It would be fair and correct to conclude that this all seems like an infringement of the film industry's freedom of working conditions. Cinema was a powerful and influential medium and the government through its agencies was determined to exploit it to its fullest potential. The blatant use of film for such purposes in Nazi Germany had not gone unnoticed in Britain or elsewhere.

The MoI's powers amounted virtually to a state-controlled industry, where only officially sanctioned films were made and shown. However, every film passed by the British Board of Film Censors, established in 1912, had in effect been an officially sanctioned film; the MoI merely extended that privilege a little. Indeed, the MoI did not have to extend the existing arrangements very far. Since the early 1930s it had become an accepted practice for production companies to submit scripts to the board for pre-censorship. It was easier and cheaper to make any required cuts or modification before shooting, rather than after.

In essence, therefore, the censorship rules regarding the making of feature films were hardly changed by the war, and the existing procedures efficiently ruled out "undesirable" films. If anything, this process worked too well and some of the guidelines had to be relaxed during the war. To take an example especially relevant to this discussion, they were loosened regarding the cinematic portrayal of the military, in order to accommodate the more "realistic" approach used in the feature, *Waterloo Road* (1944). *The Life and Death of Colonel Blimp* (1943) is also interesting in this respect. Although the film was advertised on its release as a "banned film" and Prime Minister Churchill publicly criticised it, the fact remains that had the MoI seriously sought to prevent this film from being made or released, it could easily have done so.

Cinema attendances grew significantly during the war. By 1945, over 30 million people were regular cinema-goers, and some 30% of adults went at least once a week. However, it must be remembered that there were far fewer social activities competing with a night at the pictures in those days than there are now. For example, the hours of public houses (barely acceptable social venues for women in any case) had been trammelled due to rationing. In addition and very importantly, the newsreels were as they had been in the First World War – invaluable sources of information about the war. However late or edited these films were, "seeing" was still believing.

Post-1945 British cinema

> Why is it in those war films the Scotsman and the Welshman are digging the tunnels and the Englishman is the officer giving the orders? (Max Boyce, comedian)

The period after the end of the Second World War saw the British film industry experience something of a renaissance. What has become known as the "Indian summer"[17] of the British film industry saw high levels of production, much of it on the subject of war, and especially the most recent wars.

Until now I have discussed film's ability to present a convincing version of reality without mentioning its ability to represent history. Between the wars there were many films reflecting on the role of the British military in the Great War. Films such as *Tell England* (1931), *The Dawn Patrol* (1930), *The Lost Patrol* (1934) and, perhaps most importantly, the film version of R C Sherriff's *Journey's End* (1930) were important in that period during which British society was reflecting from the distance of a decade or so on its involvement in the Great War.[18] In world cinematic terms, *All Quiet on the Western Front* (1930) and *La Grande Illusion* (*Grand Illusion*, 1937) are key films in this regard.

In respect of the Second World War and Britain's appraisal of its involvement, *Dunkirk* (1958) seems especially important. Made eighteen years after the historical events which it seeks to portray, sufficient time had elapsed for the events of Dunkirk to be placed within the wider context of a war that had been won – as a narrative voice proclaims towards the end of the film, "a great defeat and a great miracle". Rather than having been a humbling and dispiriting defeat, it was now read as the experience that above all others hardened British resolve to prosecute the war successfully. To see how the film constructs this portrayal, one should look at the incorporation of archive and newsreel footage which, allied to a pseudo-documentary style, helps give the film a powerful sense of authenticity, which allows it to deal credibly with the issue of truth vs. misinformation during wartime.

The film opens with newsreel footage from the period. This anchors the film in the "real world", in a specific time and place. The documentary film has a reputation for recording reality in a way that a fiction film does not. And realism, however acquired, allows documentary films "to be mobilized in the public service to give image and perspective to the national and international scene".[19]

Dunkirk borrows that reputation and so helps construct an authority it would otherwise lack. It also uses some of the conventions of the documentary style – for example, the scant use of close-up. Although this device is a convention of the feature film (particularly war films, where such shots can greatly emphasise the anger or pain on a face and so motivate identification with a character), *Dunkirk* only rarely employs the device. By adopting such stylistic procedures, it triggers a set of audience expectations rooted in documentary and newsreel consumption. The reception of the documentary is predicated on the assumption that the camera is merely recording, not interpreting, reality for the audience.

That the experienced cinema spectator is sufficiently sophisticated to be able to see the difference in film stock that is apparent when documentary footage is inserted into a fiction film is not a weakness. Although the technique is visible, rather than serving to emphasise the fictional nature of the film drama, it merely underlines the authority of the account. Such is the strength of realist convention engendered in the documentary and newsreel.

An example from *Dunkirk* might help better to explain this point. In the section where the soldiers are in a field under attack from Stukka aircraft, the difference between Leslie Norman's footage of the actors playing soldiers and the library shots of the aeroplane is obvious. The apparent wear on the documentary shots is only one aspect of this, as is the juxtaposition of perspective (perspective and frame composition of the documentary differ from those used in the feature film) and soundtrack – again a difference, since in fiction films the sound is "better", in that the acoustics can be artificially manipulated, whereas in documentary the sound is less worked upon and consequently has a harsher tone. However, this disparity demeans neither the newsreel nor the fiction film, but supports both. It does this by drawing attention to the film's blurred fictional status: the spectator knows that this is a drama, but equally that "Dunkirk" really happened. The viewer is bound to accept the documentary evidence because its appeal for validity goes beyond the parameters of the filmic experience and invokes his/her knowledge of the real world, which in this case supports the newsreel. Consequently, the status of the drama is raised. More than simple play-acting, it is the retelling of history. The film's review in *Variety* is telling in this respect:

> 'Dunkirk' is a splendid near-documentary which just fails to reach magnificence...The film throughout is deliberately underplayed, with no false heroics and with dialog which has an almost clinical authenticity.[20]

This new status accorded to the fiction is also useful in giving validity to events which happen within the fictive world. For example, when the soldiers witness the brutal shooting down of French refugees, this event is presented as one which did (or at least could have) happened. The fact that that may not have happened (or, if it did, certainly not as presented in the film) is overridden.

By the end of *Dunkirk*, the tensions with which the film opened – the frustration of the civilians unable to do their bit for the war effort, their difficulty in assimilating the varied information with which the public is inundated, the (ultimately trivial) rivalries that exist within the Army structure – rank, nationality and so on – are cleanly resolved. As the narrative voice describes, it is now a nation no longer made up of "civilians and fighting men, only people", and the "nation has been made whole".

Such messages of national unity of course go much further than specific historical events, however traumatic. They are essential for the health of the nation state. The medium of cinema and, in particular, treatment of the Armed Forces are especially effective in the constructions of such messages. The Army, as an apparent microcosm of British society, provides an excellent metaphorical vehicle for exploring issues of class, privilege, gender and social structure. Any film about the British Army is also a film about British society.

The postwar period saw films such as the Boulting brothers' *Private's Progress* (1956) which, although similar to the recruit films of the Second World War, is different in one significant aspect. With no total war to wage, the conscript's service is no longer essential. This frees the film to question many of the class-based assumptions of British society and to trace the changing values of the contemporary society without presenting the nation at risk. In a similar way, *Tunes of Glory* (1960) uses the Army as a vehicle to question accepted forms of organisation and power. The film focuses on the competition between the up-through-the-ranks Alec Guinness character and the born-to-lead John Mills character. Significantly, neither succeeds; the Mills character commits suicide and the Guinness character is unable to hold himself together and turns to drink.

The friction that can exist between individuals and institutionalised power relations are also dealt with in *The Hill* (1965). Set in a prison camp in North Africa during the Second World War, the scene is a familiar one – films such as *The Wooden Horse* (1950), *The Colditz Story* (1954), *The Great Escape* (1963) have ensured this. However, in *The Hill* it is a prison camp run by the British Army itself, and the convicts are all British Army soldiers.

As in any film dealing with the Army, the power relations in *The Hill* are aligned in the first instance by the Army rank mechanism. However, the convicts, guilty of breaking King's Regulations, are without rank, a fact which is played upon by the King character (note the pun). He places himself in a position effectively outside the control and authority of the Army. Consequently, the rules and regulations represented by the NCOs and the Commanding Officer are terminally undermined.

King is also treated as an outsider in terms of his skin colour. In fact, not only is attention drawn to his skin colour by a number of racist remarks, but also his very right to be in the British Army is frequently challenged. King's presence involves not only the issue of race, but also, by extension, that of imperialism. Many members of the British Commonwealth served during the Second World War, a fact that often goes unrepresented in films of and about the period. "You are black", he is told by the Regimental Sergeant-Major. His reply, "I know that already", is important. The humour of the remark unsettles and momentarily repositions the guard. This is a major issue of King's relationship with the guards: it is constantly renegotiated. This negotiation process opens with the question of his right to be there, and closes with a dispute over their right to control him.

King is ultimately unmanageable. It is difficult not to see the

King character as analogous to the contemporary state of British imperialism. Audiences of the mid-1960s were familiar with the difficulties which successive British governments were having in the former colonies. One should also note the "Zulu" films of this period: *Zulu* (1964) and *Zulu Dawn* (1979), in addition to *The Long and the Short and the Tall* (1960) and *A Hill in Korea* (1956), set in Malaysia and Korea respectively and dealing with British military experience in other theatres of war; all these films question Britain's role in the world.

In *The Hill*, apart from King's specific position, all the soldier-convict characters cause difficulties to the system. The smooth running of the organisation is endangered in one way or another by their behaviour. It is the role of the prison guards not only to punish them, but also to send them back as rehabilitated and effective soldiers. In this respect, the "hill" of the title, a large mound in the centre of the camp yard that the convicts are made to run up and down, stands for the Army's – and by extension, society's – attempts to bring the unruly dissenters back into line. Importantly, unlike many other films dealing with the Army, there is no neat resolution of these differences to be found in the dénouement of *The Hill*. Compare, for example, the mixture of differences, rooted chiefly in class differences, that are resolved in *In Which We Serve* (1942). But, of course, *The Hill* is not a war film in the same sense: it was not made or shown during the war that provides it with its subject-matter.

The League of Gentlemen (1960) also uses the Army to question social values, in this case what the nation owes its soldiery: all the would-be robbers are victims of the Army redundancies of the 1950s. The representations of the Army found in the cinema and later on television are not fixed, but – like the values of the contemporary society – are subject to change and modification.

Films can of course present an opportunity for the institution of the Army to be seemingly criticised or commented upon. This is often done by contrasting the values and behaviour of the Army with the society around it. These comparisons can exist within the film text, as in *The Breaking of Bumbo* (1970), where the traditions and way of life of the footguards are set against the backdrop of revolutionary 1960s politics, or in *The Bofors Gun* (1968), where the soldier's power struggles are played out in the Cold War era. But, given that the "army" in each of these films also a metaphorical dimension of "nation", these films viewed today can be seen to be as much, if not more, about their contemporary social and political milieu as about the Army.

The First World War was also undergoing something of a reappraisal. *King and Country* (1964) and *Oh! What a Lovely War* (1969) are particularly interesting in this respect. In 1989 the BBC television comedy, *Blackadder Goes Forth*, continued this process.

In *The Charge of The Light Brigade* (1968) or *Conduct Unbecoming* (1975), the values of an earlier era can be contrasted with those values of the film's contemporary audience. The assumptions of audiences can also be challenged. In the independently funded Irish film, *Hush a Bye Baby* (1989), made and set in Derry, the scene in which a British Army soldier who answers a Republican youth in Irish Gaelic does exactly that. It also suggests that the filmmakers know that their audiences are not used to seeing soldiers presented in this way in this context.

Conclusion

The example drawn from *Hush a Bye Baby* is also evidence that the British (and Irish) publics hold a set of assumptions about how soldiers are represented, and that these assumptions are triggered whenever an image of a soldier appears on a cinema or television screen. Of course, the form of these representations varies. We have examined only a handful of films and tried to detect a few central themes. In this way, the form of film representations of war and the military can provide a valuable insight into the changing face of British society and politics in the 20th century. War threatens a nation's well-being, and perhaps its existence. But in addition to this potential destruction, war can bring a disparate nation together and forge a unified national identity. Nowhere is this sense of national identity more pronounced than in the Armed Forces who "represent" the nation.

Films about war and the military often seem more concerned with simple adventure or action. At one level, they are simply entertainment. But these films are also documents of British society's attitudes to questions such as class, gender, race and nationhood, and the role of Britain in world affairs. It is by regarding war films as such that they are most useful as cultural artefacts. It could be argued that they are far richer in result than the unreasonable demand that cinema should provide, by vicarious experience, an insight into the realities of battle or military life. The key to unlocking these other aspects of the meaning of a war film is to look beyond the content of these films. We should also examine the cinematic and generic conventions in which the particular representation is framed, bearing in mind at all times the commercial industry which supports the production, distribution and exhibition of the resulting product.

Notes

[1]   Jay Hyams, *War Movies* (New York: Gallery Books, 1984): 9.

[2]   For a discussion of the way in which specific battles have been represented on film, see the essays by Edmund Yorke and G D Sheffield in this volume.

[3]   For a detailed explanation of this term, see David Bordwell, Janet Staiger and Kristin Thompson, *The Classical Hollywood Cinema: Film Style & Mode of Production to 1960* (New York: Columbia University Press, 1985).

[4]   Nigel de Lee's essay in this volume remarks upon the tendency of military history also to do this.

[5]   Ann McFeatters, quoted in Bruce Cumings, *War and Television* (London: Verso, 1992): 118.

[6]   Much of my thinking on genre is drawn from Stephen Neale, *Genre* (London: British Film Institute, 1980). Although an invaluable text on genre, this book, as with much published work on genre, makes little reference to the war film as such.

[7]   By this term, I mean particularly war films dealing with the Second World War, although there are many others dealing with earlier and later wars which are similarly focused on action. British-made examples of this genre, or films dealing with British military experiences, are *The Desert Rats* (1953), *The Battle of the River Plate* (1956), *I Was Monty's Double* (1958), *Ice Cold in Alex* (1958), *The Longest Day* (1962), *The Battle of Britain* (1969) and *A Bridge Too Far* (1977). One could argue that the genre of the anti-war film is at least partly defined by the *inclusion* of comment, explicit or otherwise, about the specific war in hand, or war in general.

[8]   Captain Sir Edward H W Hulse in a letter from the French Front. Quoted in Modris Eksteins, "The Cultural Impact of the Great War", in Karel Dibbets and Bert Hogenkamp (eds), *Film and The First World War* (Amsterdam: Amsterdam University Press, 1995): 209.

[9]   For a fuller discussion of this relationship, see Paul Virilio, *War and Cinema: The Logistics of Perception*, translated by Patrick Camiller (London: Verso, 1989).

[10]   Quoted in Kevin Brownlow, *The War, the West and the Wilderness* (London: Secker & Warburg, 1979): 148.

[11]   See, for example, Philip M Taylor, *Munitions of the Mind: War propaganda from the ancient world to the nuclear age* (London: Patrick Stephens, 1990), especially 159-232, Nicholas Reeves, *Official British Film Propaganda During The First World War* (Beckenham: Croom Helm, in association with the Imperial War Museum, 1986), and S D Badsey, "Battle of the Somme: British war-propaganda", *Historical Journal of Film, Radio and Television* 3: 2 (1983): 99-115.

[12]   See John Allen's essay in this volume.

[13]   See Stephen Badsey's essay in this volume.

[14]   Brownlow: 91-92.

[15]   Jeffrey Richards, "National Identity in British Wartime Films", in Philip M Taylor (ed), *Britain and the Cinema in the Second World War* (London: Macmillan Press, 1988): 43.

[16]   Parliamentary Debates (Commons) 29 June 1925, volume 185, Col. 2084.

[17]   James Park, *British Cinema: The Lights That Failed* (London: B T Batsford, 1990): 88-105.

[18]   Naturally, this is an ongoing process. See the essays by Lloyd Clark and G D Sheffield in this volume.

[19]   John Grierson, "Documentary: The Bright Example", in Forsyth Hardy (ed), *Grierson on Documentary* (London: Faber and Faber, 1966): 187.

[20]   *Variety* 26 March 1958.

Cultural myths and realities: the British Army, war and Empire as portrayed on film, 1900-90
Edmund J Yorke

The popular perception of the British military prior to the arrival of moving film images in the early 20th century was by no means wholly positive. During the 18th, 19th and indeed for the early part of the 20th centuries, the British Army in particular had enjoyed a nefarious reputation amongst significant sectors of the British population. This was due largely to its unenviable role in suppressing civil disorders before the establishment of a regular, nationwide police force.[1] The Army's anarchic role in the containment of the 1780 anti-Catholic Gordon Riots, for example, prompted the often quoted remark by the politician, Charles James Fox, that he would "much rather be governed by a mob than a standing army".[2]

Despite victories such as Waterloo, the reputation of the British military at home was further tarnished by the heavy-handed policing actions conducted by both local militia and regular forces during the post-Napoleonic war disturbances and the Chartist disorders of the 1840s.[3] Of these, the 1819 "Peterloo massacre", when a dozen men and women were cut down by the sabres of an ill-disciplined local militia and contingents of regular Hussars, left a legacy of hatred in working-class areas of Lancashire which lingered on for decades.[4] The image of the army as an "instrument of class war" in many working-class areas was further enhanced by its role in the suppression of the post-1880 industrial disturbances, culminating in the 1910 "Tonypandy incident", when two miners were allegedly killed by troops. (This event apparently played a significant role in delaying the deployment of troops as rescuers during the Aber-fan disaster of 1966, when elements of local mining communities were perceived by local authorities as being inimical to a military presence in the area.) Indeed, as late as 1919, two striking dockers were shot dead by troops as the government reacted sternly to postwar "Bolshevik" activities.[5]

Despite these latter incidents, from the mid-19th century the British Army was beginning to restore its reputation to the level of its Royal Navy counterpart, whose enduring heroic image had been irrevocably established in the popular mind by Nelson's stunning exploits during the Napoleonic Wars. A variety of institutional, social and political factors was responsible for this. The dispatches of William Russell from the Crimea, dramatically exposing the shortcomings of the Victorian military establishment, and the resultant sufferings of the troops excited much popular sympathy, as did the reports of the stirring medical work of Florence Nightingale. Similarly, wide-ranging reforms from the 1870s created a more professional army, with both the abolition of purchase of commission and more brutal army punishments, and the promotion of closer community ties clearly through the "linked battalion" system at town and county levels. Popular writers, such as Rudyard Kipling and G A Henty, extolled the "virtues" of war and the military, while the Church gave a new moral respectability to military ethos through, for example, the foundation of the Salvation Army.

But, as Professor John MacKenzie has succinctly observed, it was "*colonial* war" which played a vital part in transforming the reputation of the military and placing it on a standing equal to that of the navy.[6] The proselytizing mission of Empire and its overall moral integrity was promoted in the popular imagination by, for example, news of "barbarisms" at Kābul, where a British army was annihilated in 1842 by "treacherous" Afghans, and the massacre of British women and children at Cawnpore (Kanpur) during the 1857 Indian Mutiny by "blood-thirsty" renegade sepoys. Similarly, heroic deeds such as the defence of Rorke's Drift and General Gordon's defence of Khartoum were magnified and perpetuated by a plethora of popular newspapers (e.g. Penny Dreadfuls), books, music-hall songs, and the writings of war correspondents such as Archibald Forbes.[7] The military could be safely portrayed as both civiliser *and* avenger, a vital instrument of imperial order and an important distraction from its hitherto more questionable role as guardian of domestic peace.

It was a role ripe for exploitation by the embryonic film industry which tentatively emerged in the late 1890s. Crude extracts of moving Biograph Company film depicting scenes from the Anglo-Boer War (1899-02) excited popular imagination as never before, and reinforced earlier Victorian perceptions of the heroic role of the military abroad. Silent, moving film images of trench warfare during the First World War carried the jingoistic traditions of "King and Empire" to even greater heights, even though some film excerpts have been recently exposed as overt reconstructions of battles for propaganda purposes.[8] Even costly imperial defeats such as Gallipoli (1915) and Kut (1915-16), both at the hands of the "uncivilised" Turks and largely due to the incompetence of senior commanders, failed to diminish popular enthusiasm for the British military abroad.

Ironically, it was only in the late 1920s, with the advent of sound in filmmaking and the Empire showing definite signs of decline, that the cinema itself reached its full status as an art form. Nevertheless, with a mass audience largely reared on school textbooks and fictional novels depicting the glorious and romantic imagery of Empire, the stage was set for a series of imperial epics which, with few exceptions, hid the realities of life for subject peoples. It was indeed a "heroic age" for imperial filmmaking, which reached its zenith just before the Second World War.[9] There were a number of reasons for this phenomenon. Firstly, these films catered for a largely uneducated audience reared before the postwar Butler reforms and physically cut off from the realities of Empire by limitations of transport and travel. Secondly, the subject-matter itself was highly saleable, visually attractive and largely based on legends and myths perpetuated by writers such as Kipling, Yeats-Brown, A E W Mason and H Rider Haggard. Finally, realism was *costly*. Film companies could not afford exterior locations in India and Africa, for example, and most were studio-based.

Key films of this ultra-jingoistic period with a wholly or partial imperial/military theme include *The Charge of the Light Brigade* (1936), *Clive of India* (1934), *The Drum* (1938), *The Four Feathers* (1939), *Gunga Din* (1939), *Lives of a Bengal Lancer* (1934), *The Lost Patrol* (1934), *Mutiny on the Bounty* (1935), *Rhodes of Africa* (1936), *Sanders of the River* (1935) and *Stanley and Livingstone* (1939). Of these, *Sanders of the River*, *Gunga Din*, *The Charge of the Light Brigade* and *The Four Feathers* were perhaps the most influential and representative of the heroic imperial/military tradition. *Sanders of the River*, described by one writer as a "[m]uch-caricatured African adventure of the very old school",[10] epitomises the classic, romanticised portrayal of Empire. It set the political overtone for most other British and American films focusing on the Empire theme, depicting an isolated district commissioner (Leslie Banks) ruling firmly and wisely over "treacherous natives", solidly supported by Paul Robeson playing a friendly but highly deferential African chieftain. Robeson was later much criticised for his "degrading" role, and the film gave no indication of the harsher aspects of British rule in Africa, such as forced labour policies on white mines and farms.

Gunga Din, set in imperial India and starring Cary Grant, Victor McLaglen and Douglas Fairbanks Jnr as three British sergeants, is a classic Hollywood portrayal of an outnumbered British force gallantly confronting treacherous "Thugs". Loosely based upon Rudyard Kipling's famous poem, this rousing period action film with comedy asides emphasised loyalty in an otherwise peaceful Raj, as, for example, an Indian servant sacrifices his own life to "save the regiment".[11] This again provided a stark contrast to the realities of 1930s British India where Mahatma Gandhi's Indian National Congress Party was already actively challenging British rule. The "treacherous native" image appeared in another popular 1930s epic, *The Charge of the Light Brigade*, a glamorous but wildly inaccurate historical epic which starts in India in the 1857 Mutiny period (three years after and thousands of miles away from the 1854 Crimean battle of the same name!).

The British imperial military epic, *The Four Feathers*, set in imperial Sudan, directed by Zoltán Korda and based upon A E W Mason's famous novel, again stresses the courage of British officers and men in maintaining order throughout the Empire. Ralph Richardson plays Harry Faversham who, after initially being branded a coward, redeems both his own and regimental honour by a series of heroic feats, including the rescue of three fellow British officers from the clutches of the "Mahdi". Again, the "savagery" of the Mahdi's forces is starkly contrasted with the "decency" of the British, while, for example, the devastating impact of British rifle and artillery fire upon Mahdi soldiers (in what was a grossly one-sided final battle at Omdurman) is glossed over.[12] Indeed, in only a few 1930s films, notably *Rhodes of Africa* and *Stanley and Livingstone*, was there any attempt to achieve a balance between the romantic legend of the story-books and the realities of war and Empire.

A major watershed in the context of imperial filmmaking was reached with the advent of the Second World War, as imperial myths began to give way to imperial reality. For a number of reasons, the war provided a catalyst for a revisionist approach to the military and Empire on film. Firstly, "combat" documentaries made by British Service Film Units, notably *Desert Victory* (1943), based upon Montgomery's victory at El 'Alamein, and *Burma Victory* (1945), based on Field Marshal Slim's victories in Burma, inevitably revealed the horrors and sacrifices of modern warfare. Vivid pictures of dead and dying on the battlefield provided a salutary lesson to a British public hitherto largely immunised from live-action coverage, while Richard Dimbleby's film exposé of Nazi war crimes at Belsen revealed the grossly inhuman side of warfare closer to home.

Secondly, with its mass call-up and new, wider opportunities, the war encouraged a leftwards shift in British public attitudes and politics, which was epitomised by Labour's stunning victory in the 1945 General Election. The ravages of the Blitz, for example, encouraged a war-weary population, reinforced by demobilised soldiers, to consider more pressing domestic issues, such as housing and social security, rather than those of a far-flung and already disintegrating Empire. Educational reforms and the growth of communications made the public much more aware of the inequalities and, indeed, the dark side of Empire.

Finally, the Second World War, unlike the First World War, provided vivid evidence of Britain's strategic vulnerabilities both at home and abroad.[13] The desperate isolation of 1940-41 following Dunkirk, the initial sense of impotence against Nazi expansion in Europe, and the emergence of two giant superpowers, the Soviet Union and the United States, all contributed to the loss of confidence in the Empire. The twin defeat by Japan at Hong Kong and Singapore were particularly devastating to British morale. At Singapore the surrender of over 100 000 imperial and British troops in February 1942 shattered forever the myth of British military invincibility and provided a major stimulus to nationalist agitation across the Empire. In 1942 the British were even forced to concede postwar independence to Indian nationalist leaders in order to forestall a Japanese invasion of India. Even Britain's closest imperial allies, Canada, Australia and New Zealand, experienced disillusionment as British tactical errors led to defeats, not only in the Far East, but also in Europe, and notably at Dieppe. Indeed, while in 1914 all three white Dominions had unconditionally declared war in support of Britain, in 1939 the decision was put to the vote.

This change of attitude to war and Empire, both at home and abroad, permeated filmmaking throughout the 1950s and 1960s and was reinforced by Britain's steady retreat from its colonial possessions. By 1948 India, Pakistan and Ceylon (Sri Lanka) had been granted independence, and between 1957 and 1964 most of the African colonies were freed from British rule. One of the first postwar films investigating the darker side of Empire was *Cry, the Beloved Country* (1951). Although not strictly concerned with military issues, the film, by examining racial inequalities in South Africa at ground level, was an important omen. *Simba* (1955) deals with white settler intransigence *and* Mau Mau extremism in colonial Kenya, thereby injecting both balance and realism into this imperial conflict. This is not to say that the old-style pre-war imperial epic was dead. Heroic myths were still perpetuated in films such as *Bengal Rifles* (1954), featuring Rock Hudson as a British (!) officer bravely suppressing a "native" rebellion, *Storm over the Nile* (1955), a remake of *The Four Feathers*, and *Northwest Frontier* (1959), featuring Kenneth More as a British officer escaping from yet another Indian rebellion. David Niven maintained the British stiff upper lip in *55 Days at Peking* (1962), which tackles the 1900 Chinese Boxer rebellion.[14] However, none of these films attracted the mass audience appeal of the 1930s epics.

In the aftermath of the 1956 Suez Crisis – a humiliating landmark in the retreat from Empire – a new, critical light emerged more fully in a spate of films focusing wholly or partly on the imperial military experience. These new-style epics questioning root attitudes to Empire included Otto Preminger's controversial film, *Exodus* (1960), David Lean's *Lawrence of Arabia* (1962) and Basil Dearden's *Khartoum* (1966). *Exodus* was one of the first postwar films to take a rabidly anti-British perspective. Focused upon the postwar crisis in Palestine, the film highlights the ruthless methods employed by the British to stem the mass Jewish immigration into this area while, at the same time, romanticising the role of Jewish "terrorist" groups such as Irgun and the "Stern Gang".

Lawrence of Arabia also highlights the "Arab perspective" through Peter O'Toole's sensitive portrayal of T E Lawrence, as well as revealing, in an uncompromising way, the brutalities of an imperial war. For example, the scene depicting the merciless massacre of a Turkish column by Lawrence's Arab irregulars suggests how both Arabs and Turks were perhaps the ultimate victims of British imperial machinations in the region. Similarly, in the epic *Khartoum* we see a General Gordon sensitively played by Charlton Heston, troubled by his Christian conscience and overall moral obligation to rescue the local Sudanese, as he wrestles with British government orders callously to abandon Khartoum and its inhabitants to the tender mercies of the Mahdi's forces.

The new postwar critical style emerged most clearly, however, through the extremely popular imperial military epic, *Zulu*, released in 1964. The brutality and futility of war were exposed to an unprecedented extent, as the film depicts barely 150 British soldiers successfully defending the Rorke's Drift Mission Station against approximately 4000 Zulus. Filmed largely on location not far from the actual battle site, Cy Endfield's directorial masterpiece was, in the words of one reviewer, "[a] film with dignity on both sides but no self-importance, it manages to extoll (sic) heroism without glorifying war. It is also one of the few films to actually show the sheer physical arduousness of battle – it ends not with triumph and jubilation but with sheer exhaustion".[15] In the film there is a conscious effort to demonstrate Zulu culture, heroism and sacrifice, a far cry from the noble or more often "insidious savage" imagery so copiously projected in pre-war films. Military ethos is directly challenged in memorable action sequences. A strong, anti-war tone emerges in some scenes with a drunken missionary (skilfully played by Jack Hawkins) berating the British defenders over the wickedness of their cause, while the hard-pressed surgeon, Major Reynolds (Patrick Magee), questions the futility and wastage of war as he struggles to save a dying young private in the bloodstained makeshift field hospital. In the final scene, the two exhausted officers, Chard and Bromhead (Stanley Baker and Michael Caine, respectively) are sickened by the surrounding carnage and Baker is left to collect scores of shields from piles of Zulu corpses in a final atmospheric scene, fraught with tragedy and pathos.

Nevertheless, elements of jingoism are by no means completely absent in *Zulu*, with British coolness and discipline exemplified by Nigel Green as a hard-pressed Colour Sergeant Bourne, steadying panicky young soldiers and later struggling to maintain his composure as he takes the final roll-call. Again, in the words of Trevor Willsmer the film was "*our* epic, a celebration of national courage (but not nationalism) with its eyes wide open".[16] This probably explains the mass appeal of a film which reflected the postwar mood of residual pride, but which also carried a new awareness of the harsher realities and consequences of empire-building for both conquerors and conquered.

A second – this time British – film version of *The Charge of the Light Brigade*, directed by Tony Richardson and released in 1968, reflected the enhanced cynical mood of the late "revolutionary 60s", when the anti-Vietnam War protests were reaching their height both at home and abroad.[17] The horror and senselessness of war are again graphically demonstrated with overt criticism of corrupt, incompetent leaders such as Lord Cardigan (played by Trevor Howard). The film focuses heavily upon the plight of the neglected Victorian soldier living in disease-ridden squalor and fighting a thankless – indeed, meaningless – war thousands of miles from home.[18] There can be no starker contrast with the 1936 Hollywood "hokum" version starring David Niven and Errol Flynn at their swashbuckling best!

During the past two decades, filmmaking with regard to the imperial military genre appears to have taken an even more cynical twist. For example, the 1979 sequel to *Zulu*, *Zulu Dawn* (based on the earlier catastrophic British defeat at Isandhlwana), presented a much more acerbic, questioning view of the same imperial war. In this dark, foreboding film, imperial motives are even more deeply and persistently challenged. The cynicism behind British moves in 1879 both to provoke a Zulu war and to annex Zululand is stressed, while doomed British soldiers and their victorious Zulu protagonists are ultimately projected as innocent victims of an imperial war. Graphic scenes of brutality towards the Zulu captives, of the merciless hunting-down of fleeing Zulu warriors after the initial invasion, are complemented by vignettes depicting the war correspondent, Charles Norris-Newman (played by Ronald Lacey at his acidic best) repeatedly challenging the British column commander, Lord Chelmsford (Peter O'Toole) regarding the justice of his cause.

The "anti-heroic" period of the 1980s and 1990s was again underlined by several films initially examining the "imperial role" of the British Army. Two Australian-produced and directed films, *Gallipoli* (1981) and *Breaker Morant* (1980) – the former based on a disastrous 1915 defeat by the Turks with heavy ANZAC casualties, and the latter depicting the fortunes of several Australians executed for "war crimes" during the 1899-1902 Anglo-Boer War – proved virulently anti-imperial and, indeed, anti-British in tone. The blunders of Gallipoli were almost solely attributed to British incompetence, with young Australian soldiers depicted as innocent victims of yet another senseless war. *Breaker Morant* again portrays Australian volunteers as victims of British injustice and betrayal. Both must be seen as representative of the new wave of nationalism sweeping an Australia which was slowly shaking off the shackles of its imperial past. A similar, even more cynical view of the Empire at war can be discerned in the recent Canadian drama-documentary television series, *The Valour and the Horror*, based on the controversial wartime role of Air Chief Marshal "Bomber" Harris, and the disasters at Dieppe and Hong Kong.

The iniquities of the British Army's record in empire-building were also by no means spared in, for example, Richard Attenborough's film version of the life of Gandhi (1982). The scene depicting the massacre of over 300 unarmed Indian protestors by a British colonial force can be seen as an accurate re-enactment of General Dyer's infamous action at Amritsar in 1919, and the film as a whole reveals – more powerfully than before – the racial tensions which lay beneath the panoply of Empire.

Thus, for the past three quarters of a century, the medium of moving film has provided a graphic illustration of changing political attitudes to the military as an instrument of Empire. In the 1920s and 1930s film provided a welcome, uncritical justification of Empire and a diversion from the past, less glorious *domestic* role of the British Army as a protector of social order at home. A less informed and rarely travelled British public, largely denied visual images of "real" war and anxious to escape from the ravages of the Depression, still hungered for Victorian romanticised stereotypes of the imperial military at war.[19] The impact of the Second World War, with, for example, feature-length combat documentaries encompassing all the sounds, sights and unpleasant realities of war, led to a decisive switch, both in public mood and style of filmmaking. Postwar decolonisation further brought home the starker realities underpinning British imperial rule; the increasing independence of these areas, notably Australia and India, led to a corresponding ambition by *local* film producers and directors to record their own, if sometimes heavily biased, images of the British political military role in its imperial context. The shock of the Suez Crisis of 1956 and the new liberalism of the 1960s (encompassing a strong anti-war movement) had already encouraged *British* filmmakers similarly to question the ethos of the Empire and, with it, the British Army's role as an instrument of imperial power. In recent times, this more critical approach may have swung the pendulum too far. The 1988 US/British film, *For Queen and Country*, for example, depicting a black soldier returning to squalid civilian life in Britain, plumbed new depths of cynicism and vitriol.

More worrying is the apparent obsession with Britain's

political-military role during the imperial period. It is hoped that future filmmakers will redress the balance with a greater focus upon cultural interaction or the socio-economic legacies of Empire, as epitomised in films such as Michael Radford's *White Mischief* (1987), which examines the sybaritic lifestyle of white settlerdom in colonial Kenya, and David Lean's *A Passage to India* (1984), in which an English girl accuses an Indian doctor of rape. Such films have attracted large audiences – as did traditional "action epics" such as *Zulu* and *Gallipoli*. Moreover, they will provide a broader, more valid base for a balanced interpretation – and, indeed, judgment – of Britain's imperial past.[20]

Notes

[1]   For a comprehensive treatment of the military and social order in Britain, see especially Charles Townshend, *Making the Peace: Public Order and Public Security in Modern Britain* (Oxford: Oxford University Press, 1993) and Anthony Babington, *Military Intervention in Britain: From the Gordon riots to the Gibraltar incident* (London; New York: Routledge, 1990).

[2]   See, for example, Babington: 21-31.

[3]   See E J Hobsbawm, *Primitive Rebels: Studies in Archaic Forms of Social Movement in the 19th and 20th Centuries* (Manchester: Manchester University Press, 1959), E J Hobsbawm and George Rudé, *Captain Swing* (London: Lawrence and Wishart, 1969), E P Thompson, *The Making of the English Working Class* (London: Victor Gollancz, 1980), for the origins of these disturbances, and Babington: 59-114, for the military response.

[4]   See Robert Walmsley, *Peterloo: The Case Reopened* (Manchester: Manchester University Press, 1969), Joyce Marlow, *The Peterloo Massacre* (London: Rapp and Whiting, 1969) and Babington: 46-58, for the social and political implications of this event for the public perception of the military.

[5]   See Babington: 115-152, and Townshend: 36-55, 80-81.

[6]   John M MacKenzie (ed), *Popular imperialism and the military 1850-1950* (Manchester: Manchester University Press, 1992): 3. Emphasis added.

[7]   See, for example, Dave Russell, "'We carved our way to glory': the British soldier in music hall song and sketch, c. 1880-1914"; Jeffrey Richards, "Popular imperialism and the image of the army in juvenile literature"; and Roger T Stearn, "War correspondents and colonial war, c. 1870-1900", all in ibid: 50-79, 80-108, 139-161 respectively.

[8]   See, for example, R Brooks and R Davies, "Immortal images of Somme battlefield were faked for newsreels", *The Observer* 23 June 1991.

[9]   Among the millions of avid film-goers in 1930s Britain was one Margaret Thatcher who recalled the stirring impact of films such as Korda's *The Four Feathers* on her emerging political philosophy (*Sunday Times Thatcher Memoirs*, 28 May 1995: 2).

[10]   Leslie Halliwell, *Halliwell's Film Guide*, eighth edition (London: HarperCollins, 1992): 477.

[11]   A film described by Pauline Kael in 1968 as "one of the most enjoyable nonsense adventure movies of all time". Quoted in ibid.

[12]   Nevertheless, even Graham Greene felt compelled to testify to its enormous popularity: "It cannot fail to be one of the best films of the year...even the richest of the ham goes smoothly down, savoured with humour and satire". Quoted in ibid: 406.

[13]   For the "decisive" impact of the Second World War in terms of imperial decline, see, for example, John Darwin, *Britain and Decolonisation: The retreat from empire in the post-war world* (London: Macmillan, 1988): 34-68.

[14]   For a similar "patriotic" and uncritical approach, see the early scenes depicting Churchill's military career in *Young Winston* (1972).

[15]   Trevor Willsmer, "*Zulu*", *Movie Collector* 1: 8 (1994): 31.

[16]   Ibid. Emphasis in original.

[17]   Perhaps not surprisingly, Tony Richardson figured prominently in the anti-Establishment "Angry Young Men" movement that blossomed briefly among British intellectuals such as John Osborne in the late 1950s and early 1960s. See Ephraim Katz, *The International Film Enyclopaedia* (London: Macmillan, 1979): 972.

[18]   See also Sergej Bondarčuk's *Waterloo* (Italy/USSR, 1970) for graphic battle scenes depicting the carnage and wastage of war.

[19]   It was a "denial" greatly assisted by the British Board of Film Censors (no doubt tacitly approved of by the mainly Conservative government) which ensured that more socially challenging and "less patriotic" films – for example, *Love on the Dole* (1941) – were restricted viewing.

[20]   As MacKenzie has observed, "colonial warfare has been ill-served by historians" and "individual colonial campaigns need to be placed not only in the cultural frameworks of the *European* combatants but also in those of the indigenous peoples of empires" (221). Emphasis added. The film industry provides one medium through which this can be achieved.

Reporting terrorism: the British state and the media, 1919-94
Susan L Carruthers

In the 75 years between 1919 and 1994, a revolution occurred in mass communication. The nature of terrorism was arguably also unrecognisably transformed between these dates, with many commentators positing a direct correlation between changes in communications technology and alterations in terrorist technique.[1] Some have even claimed that "terrorism proper" only emerged in the satellite television era: 1968 marked not only satellite's transformation of Western broadcasting, but also the birth of international terrorism, at which new communications technology was the midwife.[2]

However, terrorism has had much greater longevity, if one takes terrorism to be "whoever is classified and prosecuted as such"; given the fluidity of the word's meaning, this seems the most appropriate way to proceed.[3] Certainly, British governments have *perceived* their opponents to be "terrorists" from at least the later years of the 19th century – mainly then in the guises of the shadowy, nihilistic Russian revolutionary or the bungling Fenian bomber. London in the 1880s feared the destruction of symbolically significant buildings at the hand of Irish "terrorists" as much as it did in the 1980s.[4] This is not to deny that those deemed "terrorist" have employed very different tactics according to the time and place of their actions. There is little similarity between, for example, Mau Mau's panga attacks on its victims and the Semtex bombings of the modern Irish Republican Army (IRA), other than a desire to inspire terror and to raise the costs (physical and/or material) of a continued presence by British forces in a disputed territory. Those who resort to violence make what use they can of the available technology – whether a sharpened knife or the latest lightweight explosive. However, this essay argues that the ways in which governments have responded to "terrorism" demonstrate remarkable consistency over this period, especially when we consider how the state has sought to constrain and define media reportage of terrorism. This thesis has not (to the author's knowledge) been comprehensively illustrated before, although similar general points have been mooted hitherto. For example, Jennifer Hocking and Philip Schlesinger have both argued that Britain's counter-terrorist theory and practice derive from the experience of colonial counter-insurgency, and that a significant component of both has been "information control".[5]

To illustrate my contention that there is considerable consistency in how British governments have dealt with media reportage of terrorism, examples are drawn from a number of spatially and temporally disparate insurgencies, which saw the British (or colonial) state in opposition to "terrorists" struggling to free themselves of the imperial yoke. This is also how Irish Republicans have understood their "armed struggle" – although their reading of history is widely disputed. It is their activities which frame this discussion: from the Anglo-Irish "War of Independence" of 1919-21 to 1994, the year of the paramilitaries' cease-fire and (significantly, for our purposes) the lifting of the 1988 Broadcasting Ban, the most far-reaching governmental attempt to circumscribe media coverage of terrorism of this entire period. In the intervening years, the discussion will alight on Palestine, where Arabs violently opposed the British Mandatory authorities' policy on Jewish immigration in the 1930s, and Zionists took up arms against Britain's presence in the 1940s; Malaya, where a state of emergency existed between 1948 and 1960, as British and indigenous security forces fought against armed members of the Malayan Communist Party; Kenya, where a movement known as "Mau Mau" opposed the colonial presence, although in the process killing many more Kikuyu than white settlers; and Cyprus, where in the late 1950s Ethniki Organossis Kyprion Agoniston (National Organisation of Cypriot Fighters - EOKA) embarked on a campaign of violence aimed at removing Britain from the island, in order that it could be united with Greece. The focus is thus upon instances of terrorism in which the British state has been *directly* involved, on the grounds that British governments have had both a greater perceived need and a greater ability to intervene in the process of media representation of these insurgencies than of terrorism generally.

Why the media matter: publicity as "the oxygen" of terrorism

Before examining the ways in which British governments have sought to influence media reportage of terrorism, we need to understand why the state has consistently believed such interference necessary. When Margaret Thatcher made her often repeated observation that publicity constitutes "the oxygen" of terrorism (a phrase which her memoirs acknowledge was, in fact, borrowed from the former Chief Rabbi, Lord Jakobovits),[6] her words chimed with the prevailing orthodoxy on both sides of the Atlantic amongst politicians and "terrorologists" alike.[7] Her remark was made in the context of the US media's reportage of the 1985 TWA hostage crisis, not of Irish terrorism. It has often been assumed that IRA activity prompted Thatcher's words because they seemed more than just a theoretical proposition, but rather a policy prescription, leading almost inexorably to the Broadcasting Ban of October 1988.

The Broadcasting Ban, which prohibited members of certain Northern Irish organisations (and those whose words could be construed as support for them) from speaking in an official capacity on television and radio, was a departure from traditional, more covert forms of governmental pressure on the media.[8] In many respects, the Ban was the product of other factors than simply a belief that new ways had to be found to prevent the media from (generally unwittingly) playing the terrorists' game by affording them the publicity they so craved. The Thatcher government was increasingly exasperated with the IRA, and wanted to hang tough without taking steps even more contentious than the reporting restrictions, such as the reintroduction of internment. The government was also rattled by the growing electoral success of Sinn Féin in Northern Ireland since the hunger strikes of 1981, and, according to Ed Moloney, was seeking ways of delegitimising the party in order to bolster the government's refusal to talk to its representatives.[9]

Thatcher's exasperation with television programme-makers and managers was also mounting after a series of highly publicised disputes between government and broadcasters over programmes relating to Northern Ireland: the BBC's interview, after Airey Neave's assassination, with a representative of the body responsible, the Irish National Liberation Army (INLA);[10] *Panorama*'s filming of an IRA roadblock at Carrickmore (which allegedly drove Thatcher "scatty with rage");[11] the documentary, *At the Edge of the Union*, in BBC's *Real Lives* series, which depicted the lives of Martin McGuinness and a Loyalist counterpart;[12] and, most famously, Thames Television's *Death on the Rock*, which questioned the government's version of events surrounding the killing of three unarmed IRA members on Gibraltar by the SAS, and in the process reanimated a longer-running controversy over the operation (or not) of a "shoot to kill" policy by British Security Forces.[13] These programmes reinforced Thatcher's animus against the broadcast media in general, doubtless serving to reaffirm her commitment to shaking up British broadcasting by subjecting it to the rigours of the free market.[14]

The Ban's broad context is worth explaining in some detail in order to strengthen the specific point that there was nothing inherently new about Thatcher's understanding of the relationship between terrorism and the media, and that the Ban was not an inevitable product of her "oxygen of publicity" remark. Indeed, wherever British governments have perceived terrorism to be at work, they have generally also believed those terrorists to be seeking publicity and the media to be furnishing it.

These twin sentiments have been expressed with varying

degrees of bluntness by politicians or colonial officials during each insurgency. Even between 1919 and 1921, Cabinet Ministers believed Sinn Féin to be intent, above all else, on bringing the Home Rule question to the British public's attention: "nothing", opined the Secretary of State for War in August 1919, "would annoy the Irish so much as the conviction that they were not absorbing the minds of the people of Great Britain".[15] Yet, the Irish appeared to possess many advantages in this respect. Lloyd George maintained that "almost every Irishman is a natural propagandist for his country".[16] More particularly, the Irish rebels had a sophisticated propaganda organisation, employing the talents of gifted columnists and novelists, including Erskine Childers, author of *The Riddle of the Sands* (1903). The persuasiveness of Sinn Féin propaganda, rather than weaknesses in the British case against Irish Independence or the excesses of the specially drafted paramilitary police known as the "Black and Tans", was credited with swaying international and British opinion against the government:

> so successful [were Sinn Féin] in their methods of carrying on this propaganda that they not only induced persons all over the world who were evilly affected towards the British Empire to receive and even to credit the charges which they made, but they actually induced large numbers of English people to take the view...that the balance of censure inclined in the direction of the forces of the Crown.[17]

Similarly, in Palestine, when Zionists launched a campaign of violence against the British Mandatory authorities in 1944, the High Commissioner (Sir Harold MacMichael) reported a growing belief that "extremism is an effective method of drawing attention to Zionist demands".[18] Even "responsible" Jewish leaders could not "resist the idea that publicity for these [terrorist] crimes tends also to bring into the limelight the claims of Jewry, and the urgency of solving the problem of Palestine in a way favourable to themselves".[19] It is not surprising, therefore, that the terrorists should be intent on securing as much publicity as possible. Having served in Palestine, a number of British officials then presided over the Malayan Emergency, and derived from their experience of Zionist terrorism a belief that the Malayan Communists were similarly publicity-driven. One such, the High Commissioner, Sir Henry Gurney, ruefully wrote to the Colonial Office in April 1950:

> An unfortunate feature of terrorist campaigns (as distinct from war) is that we do the terrorists' publicity work for them. The BBC is the worst offender in creating the impression that life in Malaya (as in Palestine) consists of a

series of incidents. The aim of the grenade thrower is to hit the headlines, and our press and broadcasting do the job for him to his complete satisfaction.[20]

While Mau Mau were not considered publicity-seekers in quite the same way, largely because colonial officials generally refused to understand the movement as rational or employing coherently thought-out tactics, EOKA were perceived in like fashion to the Zionist insurgents and Malayan Communists. A British Intelligence report from November 1955 (a few months after the start of the Cypriot Emergency), written as if by the terrorist leader himself, stated that the aim of uniting Cyprus with Greece would by realised by "the effect which my activities in Cyprus will have on public opinion here, in the UK and in the US. My main object of attack is public opinion, *not* any particular physical target."[21]

The assertion that terrorists want publicity as a primary goal has generally been accompanied by a governmental contention that, in this respect, the incumbents of power are at a distinct disadvantage to their terrorist challengers. There are a number of components to this belief: that terrorists receive over-abundant media attention because their acts are so newsworthy, and this makes it hard to prevent the media from playing into their hands; that, whereas terrorists can indulge in any manner of lie or distortion that suits their purposes, government propagandists (or publicists, as governments prefer to term them) are obliged to tell the truth; moreover, because officials or the Security Forces are obliged to check their facts before distributing a story to the media, the terrorists' version of events has a head start, and consequently is much harder to refute. More particularly, the governmental sense of disadvantage stems from a conviction that for terrorists *any* publicity is good publicity. It does not matter if the media accept or reject the gloss the terrorists put on their own activities, for the latter's overwhelming objective is simply to snatch the headlines.[22]

Furthermore, the longer the terrorists sustain their campaign, the more likely that their protracted existence alone will appear to represent a serious challenge to the state. As a senior mandarin in the Colonial Office wrote at the start of what was to be a 12-year state of emergency in Malaya: "The danger we fear is that, by the very fact of their continuing resistance against authority, men who were at the start no more than a band of thugs preying on the law-abiding members of the community may attract to themselves some of the glamour of national heroes".[23]

A certainty that terrorists both desire and receive publicity holds clear (albeit non-specific) policy implications. As Jennifer Hocking has argued, from this belief "follows a prescription of counterterrorism measures by the state that includes at its heart a controlling of the alleged media/terrorism symbiosis".[24] The belief that such a nexus exists is, however, just that: an article of faith rather than an empirically verified standpoint. Arguably the terrorism/media symbiosis is not verifiable. Any social-scientifically acceptable method of testing the hypothesis is open to question, or not "scientific" at all.[25] One could ask the "terrorists" whether and why they desire publicity, but they could lie – they are, after all, unlikely to concur that bad publicity suits their purposes – or be victims of a "false consciousness".[26] One could read their memoirs, but they too are party to the same pitfalls (with the addition of memory's inherent vagaries).[27]

If, in the absence of solid evidence, one were to accept that terrorists *do* want publicity, one should nevertheless be wary of assuming that the terrorist strategy is flawless. Bad publicity may harm, rather than favour, their ends. The manner in which the media present terrorism may, in fact, favour the state, building a consensus around counter-terrorism measures of often questionable legality.[28] Nor is it always clear how the gaining of publicity will serve the terrorists' ends. Presumably, if terrorists do want media attention, they desire it in order that various audiences will change their behaviour as a result of what they read, view or hear, placing pressure on their government to act in a way consistent with the terrorists' goals.

However, this has not always been held as the central reason why terrorists seek publicity. British governments have generally been rather sketchy on how public opinion figures in the terrorist strategy, partly because their concern about media portrayals of terrorism is grounded in a "contagion theory" of media effects, not simply in concern over public attitudes. In other words, they believe that media attention to terrorism encourages more of the same. Again, one can see this attitude at work in various historical settings. For example, in Malaya the High Commissioner asked the local press to refrain from publishing news of rubber tree slashings in Perak state, "so as to avoid putting similar ideas into the heads of bandits in other areas".[29] In Palestine during the Arab Rebellion of the late 1930s (sparked by the large influx of Jewish immigrants fleeing Nazi Germany), the British Mandatory authorities imposed a ban on any mention of the Mufti of Jerusalem – believed to be the chief inspirer of Arab "terrorism" – which extended to all his activities, his whereabouts and his very name.[30]

To sum up, the contention is that British governments (and they are certainly not alone in this) have traditionally perceived the media to be doing the terrorists' work for them, and consequently have tried to limit the amount and type of publicity terrorists receive, using various methods which will be considered below. In his study of Britain's "civil wars", Charles Townshend argues that: "Since the development of a full-scale 'psychological warfare executive' and apparatus in the Second World War, propaganda has become an obsession of media-saturated western societies. The belief that terrorism is fuelled by publicity has become an *idée fixe*, although it has no historical basis."[31] Perhaps it would be truer to state that it has no empirical basis: the belief, however questionable it may be, certainly has a long historical pedigree, and doubtless has gained force precisely because terrorists have been perceived as publicity-seekers for so long.

Why visual images matter

Governments have historically been particularly sensitive to certain forms of publicity which the media may afford terrorists. One broad generalisation is that visual media, even before the television age, have been the subject of more intense governmental anxiety than the written word. Visual images have at times been assumed to possess certain talismanic qualities. During the Irish campaign of 1919-21, the government came to regard pictures of "terrorist leaders" as seditious in their own right. For example, in 1918 the British government considered banning the sale of photographs of rebel leaders, and discussed the effect on the level of violence of censoring the appearance of De Valera's portrait in newspapers.[32]

In the newsreel age, the recurrent anxiety was that visual news stories from troubled colonies showed images of the aftermath of terrorist atrocities, which highlighted the terrorists' "success". Terrorism by its nature was (and remains) clandestine – perpetrated away from the human eye or camera. If newsreel cameramen were looking for action stories, as they generally were, the only action which they could film – because they knew exactly where and when it would occur – was that of the Security Forces. This was not always something that pleased the authorities: the newsreels' concentration on troops rounding up suspects or fanning out through jungle or woodland in search of elusive terrorists tended to highlight in one case the Security Forces' repressiveness, and in the other, the hopelessness of their task.[33] At the height of the Mau Mau insurgency, for example, MI5 (in an area not normally within its sphere of interest) expressed concern that the "general impression" left by the commercial newsreels was of "Africans being manhandled and oppressed by white imperialists".[34] As a result, the Colonial Office urged Governor Baring to influence "those responsible for the newsreel material" so that they would "treat matters more objectively and comprehensively, and perhaps even be given facilities to do so".[35] In Malaya the government tried to ensure that newsreel images and commentaries ran along favourable lines by providing the commercial companies with both raw film footage and suggested textual accompaniments.

With television came a new headache: the televised interview with a terrorist leader. British politicians have shown profound unease about the leaders (or presumed leaders) of terrorist organisations appearing on British television for rather longer than one might have imagined. In 1957 Archbishop Makarios was released from the Seychelles, where the British authorities had held him in detention for a year, after certain evidence came to light which, it was alleged, demonstrated his complicity in EOKA terrorism. News that Makarios had been invited to a conference of religious leaders in London the following June, and that the BBC planned to use the occasion to interview him, prompted panic in Westminster. Charles Hill, Chancellor of the Duchy of Lancaster, was prevailed upon by the Cabinet to raise the matter with the assistant to the BBC's Director-General, Harman Grisewood, during one of their regular "informal chats". Although the BBC held firm, Hill was reassured that any interview would be made "the occasion for severe hostile questioning of the gentleman".[36] The BBC had adopted a similar position in 1955, when Sir Ian Jacob (the then-Director-General) rebuffed a request to refrain from broadcasting an interview with Makarios – believing that the exchange between Makarios and Woodrow Wyatt had been "a fair and interesting exposure of a shifty rascal".[37]

During the most recent phase of the "Troubles" in Northern Ireland, televised interviews with terrorists have generally been the sorest point in government-media relations, despite their infrequency and the fact that broadcasters have continued to treat terrorists as "hostile witnesses". Long before the Broadcasting Ban, broadcasters were extremely wary about interviewing terrorists and, indeed, in the nine years prior to the Ban they had not done so.[38] Much of the complicated system within the BBC of "referring upwards" matters pertaining to Irish terrorism was evolved specifically to deal with occasions when terrorist interviews were under consideration.[39] In 1971 the BBC decided that "such interviews should only be filmed and transmitted after the most serious consideration, and that the BBC *should be seen to be clearly opposed to the indiscriminate methods of the extremists*".[40] Following this decision, which effectively meant that the Director-General himself had to authorise such interviews, the BBC transmitted one in 1972, another in 1974, and none between 1974 and 1977.

The Prevention of Terrorism (Temporary Provisions) Act (PTA), first introduced in 1974, was widely interpreted by broadcasters as outlawing interviews with terrorists, as it created a criminal offence of the failure to pass on information relating to terrorist whereabouts or activities.[41] This reading of the PTA was not challenged until the BBC's interview with the INLA, after their assassination of Airey Neave in 1979. In the ensuing furore over the interview (which had been "approved" by the Director-General), the Attorney General made it clear to the BBC that he had *considered* taking action under the PTA. No proceedings were brought, but the Corporation seems to have taken the intended message, abstaining from further interviews within the context of news and current affairs programming.[42]

The most far-reaching governmental attempt to curtail television interviews with terrorists was the 1988 Broadcasting Ban. Given broadcasters' extreme caution in this matter, one might wonder why such a move was necessary. In introducing the measure to the House of Commons, the then-Home Secretary, Douglas Hurd, offered the government's public rationalisation:

> For some time, broadcast coverage of events in Northern Ireland has included the occasional appearance of representatives of paramilitary organisations and their political wings, who have used these opportunities as an attempt to justify their criminal activities. Such appearances have caused widespread offence to viewers and listeners throughout the United Kingdom, particularly just after a terrorist outrage. The terrorists themselves draw support and sustenance from access to radio and television – from addressing their views more directly to the population at large than is possible through the press.[43]

The Ban was an anomalous measure, open to numerous interpretations and perhaps wilfully vague, precisely in order to encourage even greater circumspection amongst broadcasters. One of its peculiarities was its inattention to press interviews with terrorists, the Ban's strictures being aimed primarily at television (radio being, one suspects, an incidental target). The reason proffered for the singling out of broadcasters was that their interviews, received by mass audiences, caused "widespread offence" – although both the BBC and the IBA (now the ITC) claimed that their listeners/viewers never did complain in large numbers on the rare occasions when terrorists were interviewed.[44] The Ban certainly did not direct itself at the feature of television which is generally held to make it such a powerful medium: its visual quality. Rather the Ban fetishized the *voices* of terrorists (or those whose words could be construed as supporting terrorism). It did not ban interviews, nor the reported speech of such people. Their *words* could still be transmitted to viewers – via subtitles or actors – but not their voices. Hurd's remark, shortly after the Ban, that "broadly, we are putting broadcasters on the same basis as representatives of the written press", and thus that broadcasters should not feel unfairly singled out, was unconvincing in the extreme. As the freedom of expression group, Article 19, pointed out, Hurd's utterance was "true only in the obvious sense that in the written press the words cannot be heard; there is, however, nothing to stop the papers from allowing anyone full access to their columns".[45]

Managing the media

Governments have therefore encouraged the visual media to show or give voice to terrorists as infrequently as possible, by various means ranging from pressure on newsreel or television companies (whether a discreet word in the appropriate ear, or a threat to pull a specific programme, as in the case of *Real Lives*) to legislation (such as the PTA).[46] They also have at their disposal a panoply of other news-management techniques. Many of these do not relate solely to the reporting of terrorism, but rather form part of any government's repertoire of devices for encouraging media dependence on official sources, and, more broadly, a news reportage which meets with governmental approval.

That the media do indeed often rely heavily on official sources when reporting political or military stories is only partly the result of governmental public relations techniques. News-gathering routines and the institutionalised practices of journalists often make them turn initially to state sources, to which reporters accord greater credibility than to alternative sources. Such reliance can be reinforced in various ways, of which the most blatant (although probably not the least effective) is to ply journalists with "hospitality". David Miller cites one Northern Ireland information officer recalling the early days of the "Troubles": "In those days I don't think any of us realised that there was a great deal more to dealing with journalists than just pouring them gallons of drink and being a hail-fellow-well-met".[47]

The slowness with which information officers in Northern Ireland polished their professional skills is somewhat surprising, given that their job, in essence, was not so very far removed from that done by information officers in Ireland between 1919 and 1921, and in a whole series of colonial campaigns thereafter. (In each case, special information staffs were appointed *within* the troubled territories; these dealt with the local media and correspondents from UK-based and international media organisations, while the Westminster Lobby and various Whitehall information officers continued their work of briefing and "spinning" at the London end.) As Philip Schlesinger has remarked, modern-day tactics for encouraging media dependence are essentially the same as those employed in 1919-21.[48]

During that war, a journalist was appointed to head the British government's Public Information Department at Dublin Castle in 1920. Basil Clarke termed his approach "propaganda by news", the crux of which was that Dublin Castle should make itself indispensable to journalists by providing a steady stream of news:

> About 20 Pressmen, Irish, British and foreign, visit the Castle twice daily, take our version of the facts – which I take care are presented as favourably to us as may be, in accordance with truth and verisimilitude – and they believe what I tell them. And they can't afford to stay away. That is an advantage which no system of Press propaganda other than the news propaganda system, could win...Our Press reports as a result spread all over the world and influence public opinion in every country in which they appear.[49]

Clarke was undoubtedly over-optimistic about how far journalists *believed* what they were told, for, as already noted, many in Whitehall believed that Sinn Féin's word was more widely accepted than that of the government.[50] Given the need to refute Sinn Féin propaganda, Clarke was also adamant that the government needed to be quicker off the mark in distributing their version of events, otherwise Sinn Féin's speedier account would gain an unshakeable toe-hold. The rapid dissemination of news was also regarded as a priority (although often an unrealisable one) in every subsequent "emergency".[51]

Encouraging journalistic dependency may be easier where correspondents are reliant on officials not only for news, but also for physical access to the scene of operations. This was arguably far more the case in the colonial insurgencies of the 1940s and 1950s than in Northern Ireland since 1968. In Malaya, for example, journalists who wanted to see the Security Forces in action could only do so with their express acquiescence, as operations were largely conducted in Malaya's dense jungle interior, which was inhospitable to soldiers, let alone journalists. While David Charters is right that in Malaya "thousands of miles from home, operations beyond the jungle fringe could be conducted in almost complete secrecy", the Malayan authorities did not always welcome this secrecy, and on occasion encouraged journalists to observe the difficulty of the Security Forces' task.[52] Indeed, in the early phase of the Emergency, Gurney was exasperated by the press's inattention to it, complaining that the British press was "not doing enough to present to the people at home a true picture of the work being done in Malaya by the Government and security forces".[53]

Where journalists have sought access to certain physical locations, inaccessible without military permission, the Security Forces' role in news-management has often consequently been elevated. Frequently, the Army has not particularly relished finding itself at the sharp end of state-media relations. Relations between correspondents and the military in Palestine during the

Zionist insurgency were often tense, with the former resenting being shepherded by Army "minders" who supervised press interviews with both the military and civilians.[54] In Malaya and Cyprus, the military "supremos", Templer and Harding, were both inept in their handling of the press, with even Templer's sympathetic biographer noting that the General's personal relations with the press were "singularly unsuccessful".[55]

The Army also assumed in some emergencies a news-releasing role, which rarely worked to the state's unambiguous advantage. In Kenya the Colonial Office viewed with alarm the decision to let the Army release news, because their "sitreps" (situation reports) had too gung-ho a flavour – making operations against the Mau Mau resemble a hunt for big game.[56] The broader problem with having the Army assume too high-profile a public relations role was that this appeared to contradict the central tenet of British counter-insurgency practice: namely that the civil power remains in overall charge, with the military acting in its support.[57] As this "law and order" approach to terrorism was emphasised in Northern Ireland during the 1970s, so the Army assumed a subordinate position, both in public relations and more generally, while the Royal Ulster Constabulary (RUC) became more prominent. Whereas in 1976 the Army had more than 40 press officers, by 1981 there were 21, and by 1989 Army HQ at Lisburn had only three.[58]

Even where journalists were not reliant, physically, on the state, the latter's control over access to information gave it a further "weapon". In effect, official news sources could operate a "carrot and stick" approach where journalists needed the raw material of news: "good behaviour" (copy which did not contradict the official version or, even better, broadly concurred with the state's counter-terrorist objectives) could be rewarded by allowing a handful of chosen journalists privileged access to certain particularly "juicy" morsels of information. For example, during the campaign against Mau Mau, details of the latter's oath ceremonies (which were believed to be too depraved for the government to publish openly, even in the form of a White Paper) were circulated to a number of "responsible" Fleet Street editors.[59] Clearly the intention was that editors would come to regard (if they did not already) Mau Mau as an atavistic movement which sought to return the Kikuyu to a pre-colonial state of savagery, rather than as a progressive force for self-rule. On the other hand, journalists whose reports the authorities considered unhelpful could be punished by being "frozen out" of the official briefing system.[60]

The differential treatment of journalists by government officials operated at a number of levels, not simply that of who was privy to confidential material and who was not. As David Miller points out with reference to the recent "Troubles", the

Northern Ireland Office (NIO) has operated a "hierarchy of access". Broadcast journalists have received preferential treatment to their print colleagues; international journalists and London or Belfast-based representatives of the UK media have been accorded higher status than their counterparts representing local or Dublin media outlets.[61] Much the same pattern is discernible in various colonial counter-insurgencies. During the Malayan Emergency, the government was particularly eager to encourage US journalists to visit the territory, and was prepared to offer incentives such as free transport courtesy of the RAF: the reason being that, when the Korean War broke out in 1950, Attlee's government was keen to prove to Truman's administration that Britain was doing its bit to contain Communism in South-East Asia.[62] Those who suffered most, in all the colonial cases, were representatives of the local, indigenous press, who were generally regarded as purveyors of tendentious reports, at best. In Ireland between 1919 and 1921, printing presses were frequently seized.[63] During the 1930s Arab Rebellion, the local press was regarded as so unreliable that the Mandatory authorities compelled local papers to restrict their coverage of the rebellion to official communiqués, which had to be carried verbatim.[64] General Templer sought similar powers over the local press during his period as "Supremo" in Malaya, only to find that the Colonial Office in London was most reluctant to concur, while in Cyprus in the 1950s the local press became the object of Governor Harding's vitriol.[65] His assumption of powers to ban any publication deemed prejudicial to the anti-terrorist campaign was branded by the *New Statesman* as "the most punitive press law ever enacted in a British territory".[66]

During each insurgency, colonial officials routinely were of the opinion that the local newspapers were the *worst* they had ever encountered.[67] The resulting harshness with which the press was dealt in Palestine, Malaya, Kenya and Cyprus outstripped any general "maltreatment" which the local press in Northern Ireland may have faced – although the latter too was seen as troublesome, and the *Republican News/An Phoblacht* has certainly not always been tolerated willingly.[68] However, one feature of the post-1968 "Troubles" has been a profusion, rather than a prohibition, of local community-based journalism.[69] In this sense, Miller and Charters are doubtless right that Northern Ireland's proximity to the UK "mainland" – its very accessibility to journalists – meant that the Province was not susceptible to being treated in *entirely* the same way as colonial territories.[70]

Delegitimising the enemy

The way in which the state's behaviour shapes media reportage of terrorism, and public perceptions more generally, is not confined to these news-management techniques. Any campaign of terrorism involves the state and insurgents in a competition for legitimacy. The terrorists challenge the state's right to govern a particular territory (and often the fashion in which it is governed), justifying their resort to violence as a legitimate response to injustice. For its part, the state denies the validity of any grievances and the terrorists' violent pursuit of their rectification, asserting its own sole right to employ force. Speeches by politicians, statements in the Houses of Parliament (the inspired Parliamentary Question being a favoured mechanism by which the government can promote its own case), the publicity materials produced by various government departments, and so on, all make clear the government's view of where legitimacy lies in any insurgency, just as the terrorists' own public declarations, pamphlets, newspapers or interviews present their opposing case.

One key level at which legitimacy is contested is that of language itself. As Conor Cruise O'Brien has stated:

> in political and ideological struggles, words are weapons, not analytical tools...The use of the designation 'terrorism' constitutes a declaration of illegality of the political violence referred to. So whether we use the term, refrain from using it, or hesitate to use it, has a bearing on how long the political violence is likely to continue and how many lives it will cost.[71]

Language has been recurrently fought over. David Miller writes, with reference to the "Troubles", that "[i]t is the active concern of both [British government and the IRA] to label the other side as the *real* 'terrorists'".[72] However, throughout the period under consideration, state and insurgents have battled to call their opponent "terrorist" – and have that pejorative designation stick.

Government officials have thus been self-conscious in their choice of vocabulary when describing their opponents, with "terrorist" generally being seen as the most damning label, although not always the sole one. In Ireland between 1919 and 1921, the IRA were referred to variously as "terrorists", a "murder gang" and "cowardly murderers". For their part, Sinn Féin propaganda presented British aggression in Ireland as the source of all trouble: a pamphlet by Erskine Childers, entitled *Military Rule in Ireland*, detailed the British administration's 35 636 acts of aggression, 45 murders and seven prisoners' deaths due to maltreatment – "the most notorious acts of organised terrorism".[73]

As for the "Stern Gang" and Irgun Zvai Leumi in Palestine, the Mandatory authorities decided in 1944 that these should not be called "gangsters" – with its apolitical overtones; rather the government should "bring out the fact that terrorists openly avow they are acting for political aims".[74] They remained "terrorists" until Irgun bombed the Tel Aviv Goldsmith Officers' Club in March 1947, at which point the Middle East Land Forces rejected that term: "It is no longer possible to differentiate between passive onlookers and active armed members of the Jewish population, and the word 'terrorist' is no longer being applied to differentiate one from the other".[75] The Army had other reasons for wanting to avoid the word. When the Brigadier commanding the 6th Airborne Division in Palestine issued an order prohibiting use of the word "terrorist", he did so on the grounds that it "invests the individuals concerned with a certain amount of glamour, and raises them on a pedestal all by themselves, thus drawing publicity to them". The preferred alternatives were "armed Jews, Jews, thugs, murderers".[76]

In Malaya, the Palestine model was rather reversed. Members of the self-styled Malayan Races Liberation Army (MRLA) were designated initially as "bandits", becoming "Communist Terrorists" officially in 1952. The rationale behind the terminology was complex. "Bandits" was initially chosen in part because any governmental suggestion that a civil war was under way in Malaya would render the British government, rather than private insurance companies, liable for reimbursements to tin-mining companies and rubber-plantation owners, whose businesses had been targeted by the MRLA.[77] The word was also thought to constitute a declaration of illegitimacy, as was the word "terrorist", which was also frequently employed. The formal order, announcing that the MRLA were henceforth to be "Communist Terrorists", reflected the government's determination to link the "bandits" more closely with international Communism.[78] This had the advantage of demonstrating to onlooking audiences that events in Malaya were not just an isolated phenomenon or the result of colonial misrule, but part of the Kremlin's South-East Asian scheme. For their part, Mau Mau and EOKA were throughout their respective campaigns more straightforwardly "terrorist" in official parlance.

But have the state's linguistic strategies for stigmatising its opponents carried force? In other words, has the official discourse been reproduced by the mass media? While the answer would generally appear to have been in the affirmative, one should beware assuming that the media *automatically* served merely to mirror dominant meanings and interpretations produced by the state. Indeed, at times the media proved highly critical of the government's preferred terminology: the labelling of the Malayan Communists as "bandits" came in for a good deal of Fleet Street ridicule. The reason that the media have occasionally wished to renegotiate terminology with the state has stemmed, however, from a shared belief that language was a crucial weapon against terrorists, and that the media itself should actively participate in the battle. In the Malayan case, the press criticised "bandit" as signalling insufficient governmental harshness towards the terrorists.

It should come as no surprise, therefore, that some news organisations have established guidelines governing the appropriate usage of contested terms such as "terrorist" and "guerrilla".[79] Different sections of the British media, however, have conceptualised how they can best serve the counter-terrorist end in divergent ways. Many British tabloids during the 1980s became increasingly immoderate in their condemnation of the IRA as "bastards" and "scum" – delegitimising language which, while it may have been in keeping with at least some of their readers' preferences, was certainly not to the taste of the BBC. The latter, for its part, has tended to regard its duty in the fight against terrorism as maintaining its objectivity: providing a service trusted by both communities in Northern Ireland, as around the world (via the World Service) for its detachment and impartiality. This means avoiding inflammatory language. The Corporation has had guidelines on the use of language since the 1970s, and these caution that it is often preferable to avoid the emotive "terrorist" in favour of "gunman" or "IRA member", although news reporters should never employ "terms by which terrorist groups try to portray themselves as legitimate".[80]

The battle to delegitimise the enemy has never, of course, been simply a matter of semantics. What underlies the linguistic battle is a substantive contest over political power and who has the right to exercise it. In all these case studies, the state has challenged the terrorists' self-representation as a nationalist force and/or as a representative expression of widespread popular feeling. In other words, the state has not simply attacked terrorism *per se*, but the terrorists' very grounds for resorting to such methods. Thus, British governments laboured to show that a Zionist state would encroach on Arab rights, unsettling the whole Middle East, while Cyprus – if enjoined to Greece – would similarly oppress the Turkish minority, while destabilising NATO. The terrorists' "unrepresentativeness" has also been played on heavily: official propaganda stressed that the Malayan Communists represented only the sectional interests of a fraction of Malaya's Chinese population (itself a minority), just as Mau Mau could only claim to speak on behalf of some of Kenya's Kikuyu.[81]

While the state has denigrated the methods of terrorism and the recourse to it, the "terrorists" have attacked the state's counter-terrorist practices. To substantiate their claim that the state and its agents are the *real* terrorists, insurgent organisations have customarily pointed to the extra-legality of many anti-terrorist measures, and to atrocities committed by the Security Forces. Moreover, as Thomas Mockaitis has pointed out, "in counterinsurgency an atrocity is not necessarily what one actually does but what one is successfully blamed for".[82]

Such atrocity allegations have recurred in all Britain's counter-insurgencies, although British governments have frequently been keener to denounce the allegations than to refute them via independent and public investigations of the charges. During the Anglo-Irish war of 1919-21 the Black and Tans' "reprisals" were so widespread that Basil Clarke considered resigning because they made his task hopeless.[83] The "Stern Gang" and Irgun's campaign in Palestine was, according to Mockaitis, "more conspicuous for allegations of abuse than for documented cases of actual wrongdoing".[84] It is debatable whether this suggests that the allegations were ill-founded or that attempts to verify them were half-hearted. Certainly the allegations were legion, as they were during the Kenyan Emergency of the 1950s, where horrific charges were laid (and on occasion proved) against the Security Forces.[85] Meanwhile, EOKA's campaign in Cyprus saw the honing of what the British government branded the "smear technique", with the Greek government assisting EOKA's dissemination of charges against the Security Forces. As for Northern Ireland in more recent years, such charges have again become common currency. The introduction of internment without trial in August 1971, coupled with the use of "in-depth" interrogation techniques, unsurprisingly fuelled an outcry not only from the internees, their relatives and the Republican movement, but also from civil liberties organisations. Indeed, in 1976 the European Commission on Human Rights condemned in-depth interrogation as torture.[86]

While the allegations have frequently centred on the treatment meted out to those interned or detained on suspicion of (or having been found guilty of) terrorist offences, many other charges have been recurringly made: house-to-house searches made with scant respect for property; unfair trials for terrorist suspects; summary justice practised by the Security Forces (allegations of "trigger-happiness" were rife during the campaign to quash Mau Mau – a precursor to more recent claims that a "shoot-to-kill" policy has been operated with regard to Irish Republican terrorists). Frequently, charges have also been made that measures which were supposedly anti-terrorist have slid into harassment of the particular community or ethnic group from which the terrorists sprang: Jews in Palestine made this charge, as did Malaya's Chinese population, Kenya's Kikuyu, and Northern Ireland's Catholics.

Allegations against the state have frequently been reported by the British media, even if the latter have not been essentially predisposed towards those making the claims. This has made it hard for governments simply to ignore reported "atrocities". Each counter-insurgency has therefore seen the British government attempt to discredit the charges, in some cases by alleging in turn that the manufacture of atrocities is a routine part of *any* terrorist campaign. This line was employed during the Cypriot Emergency, with a government pamphlet stating: "Wherever terrorism has been employed in the pursuit of political ends, part of the technique has been to try to discredit the forces of law and order by accusing them of scandalously abusing their powers and of indulging in terrorism on their own account".[87]

The state may of course counter with atrocity stories of its own: sometimes this has involved stressing particular methods of the opponent, often with gruesome photographic evidence. Thus, photographs of Mau Mau's victims – both human and animal – slashed and in some cases almost severed limb from limb – were given a widespread distribution.[88] Similarly, journalists invited to visit the residence of the Governor of Cyprus were treated to private photographic displays of EOKA's victims. Damaging details about the opponent have also been, if not always invented, certainly exaggerated: thus, official propaganda's stress on the bestial sexual practices supposedly involved in Mau Mau's oath ceremonies (although government publications had to hint at much that was left to the imagination to supply). Terrorist oaths resurfaced in Northern Ireland during the early 1970s. One of the pieces of misinformation originating with the Army's controversial press officer, Colin Wallace, was a "Sinn Féin oath". According to the briefing document for Army officers in which the oath appeared, the latter pledged members to "fight until we die wading in the fields of Red Gore of the Saxon Tyrants and murderers of the glorious Cause of Nationality".[89] Wallace also fabricated "evidence" that Republican paramilitaries were engaged in black magic rituals – a piece of misinformation which, he suggests, was so successful that the RUC (unaware of who had supplied the black candles and chicken's blood found in IRA "covens") began to warn parents not to let their children walk home alone from school.[90]

Conclusion: the tensions in the strategy

Having enumerated some of the recurrent concerns of British governments in dealing with terrorism and the media's reportage of it, this conclusion will outline some of the enduring tensions in the state's counter-terrorist practice, especially as it concerns media relations. The predominant tension is a confusion over whether or not a campaign of terrorism and the state's response constitute a state of war. British counter-insurgency theory suggests clearly that an insurgency should not be handled as a war: hence the insistence that the military acts in support of the civil power. In practice, however, where a state of emergency has been declared (or even where one has not), a shadowy area of legal confusion has been entered, and the state's seeming uncertainty as to how far it can act as though at war has extended its dealings with the media. Sometimes the "war against terrorism" is given a literal expression in measures which transgress the normal peacetime rule of law. Thus, Margaret Thatcher defended the Broadcasting Ban on the grounds that "[t]o beat off your enemy in a war you have to suspend some of your civil liberties for a time".[91] This equation of terrorism with war begs the question, as Paul Gilbert has pointed out, as to "what restrictions on freedom of opinion and expression a war against terrorists might justify".[92]

The degree to which any war necessitates information being withheld from journalists, or their reports being censored, is always a matter of negotiation. There are no standard "rules of war" with regard to military-media relations. Where terrorism has been treated as war, government-media relations have not thereby been clarified, although the result has been that governments have expected considerable deference from the media – and arguably far more than they have a right to expect in what is formally peacetime.

We should, however, note that while British journalists challenged the legality of the Broadcasting Ban, in general broadcasters have often themselves likened the situation in Northern Ireland to a war. They have done this in particular when attempting to convince sceptical governments that their reporting has not treated the British Army and the IRA as equally legitimate. Lord Hill (at that time Chairman of the BBC) famously wrote in 1971 to the Home Secretary that "as between the British army and the gunmen, the BBC is not and cannot be impartial".[93] His sentiments were echoed more crudely by Lord Aylestone (Chairman of the ITA): "As far as I'm concerned, Britain is at war with the IRA in Ulster and the IRA will get no more coverage than the Nazis would have done in the last war".[94] Broadcasters have made such points in the past precisely to stave off governmental regulation of their reporting of terrorism – claiming that they could censor themselves quite happily without government assistance. The Ban of October 1988 signalled that the broadcasters had failed to convince the government that in this "war" they were taking self-censorship sufficiently far.

It has often been assumed that in these quasi-wars British governments have encouraged the media to concentrate on terrorism. Contrary to the assumption that the state has regarded a decontextualized emphasis on terrorism as wholly serving its interests, British governments have, in fact, frequently tried to stress "good news", while stigmatising the methods of their opponents. Accordingly, there have been further tensions in the state's media strategy: good news vs. bad, and more news vs.

119

less. On occasion it *has* appeared strategically appropriate to stress terrorism – in other words, to ensure the prominence of more "bad news". During the Zionist insurgency in Palestine in the 1940s, British officials urged a relaxation of wartime censorship in the Middle East, in order that more news of the Irgun and "Stern Gang"'s activities could be released. News of terrorist incidents would, it was hoped, help turn moderate Zionists (in the United States especially) against the militant organisations.[95] There have certainly also been times when British governments have sought greater publicity for IRA activities – quite often with a similar view to dissuading American audiences from funding Republican militancy. But giving too much prominence to news of terrorism could have unfortunate and often unforeseen consequences. For example, Irgun's hanging of two British sergeants in July 1947 – an atrocity which was widely reported in Britain (in some cases in an inflammatory manner)[96] – sparked anti-Semitic riots in a number of British towns and cities.

Governmental attempts to draw media attention to terrorism have often occurred in tension with a desire to illustrate that disorder was under the state's control: that the terrorists represented only a small minority of troublemakers, and that life for the law-abiding majority was, on the whole, peaceful and "normal". Bernard Ingham stressed that his and Thatcher's aim had been "to underline the positive achievements in Northern Ireland, to highlight the peaceful normality of life over most of the province".[97] Again, what was attempted during the "Troubles" was nothing new. In the colonial insurgencies considered above, government officials frequently attempted to encourage journalists to write "good news" pieces, pointing out how colonial rule had benefited the indigenous peoples.[98]

Photographic material and story-lines were made available to the world's press by the British Information Service, or COI, although finding suitable subjects could prove problematic. During the Emergency in Cyprus the Governor's specially appointed publicity adviser in London, John Fletcher-Cooke, wrote of the "difficulty of finding photographic subjects which are likely to increase appreciation of the British policy in Cyprus at present".[99] Amongst the edifying activities chosen for photography were Governor Harding's visits to mixed villages in the wake of clashes between Greek and Turkish Cypriots, bumper crop harvests, and Lady Harding's charitable activities. But, although the government's publicists seemed quite pleased with their efforts, a more jaundiced eye might question whether these images were sufficiently powerful to achieve the intended effect.

More broadly, of course, the good news strategy was – and remains – problematic. Miller's observations on its current employment in and on Northern Ireland are resonant with regard to past colonial experience: "The 'good news' part of British strategy meets with relatively little success in the news media, foundering on a contradiction within the strategy of official sources and on the rock of news values".[100] "Good news" for the media is often no news at all. This was recognised during the Malayan Emergency, when a Colonial Office official wryly pointed out:

> not only the BBC but also the UK Press tend to direct nearly all their attention to terrorist activities in Malaya. As you will know from your experience in Palestine, this is simply because exciting incidents in the terrorist campaign are 'news', whereas ordinary peaceful development which is going on all the time is not news.[101]

In short, while the British media have often been willing foot soldiers in the "war against terrorism", their imperatives and those of the state have not always coincided. The media have not, therefore, always simply fallen in behind the state.

To sum up, British governments' responses to terrorism have shown considerable continuity since 1919. This is not to say that terrorists – or the media in their reporting of it – have met exactly the same response from one insurgency to the next. The continuity consists less of a set of practices than a set of paradoxes. While governments have been certain that terrorists are essentially publicity-seekers, they have been less sure of how to deprive terrorists of their "oxygen", and even whether such suffocation is to be desired. It may even aid the state to *have* terrorists accorded media attention. As one official remarked of Makarios during the Cyprus insurgency: "it would almost *pay* us to put him on TV – black beard, shifty glances, prevaricating replies and all".[102] One might speculate that some Cabinet Ministers argued much the same about the desirability of Gerry Adams's being seen and heard on television when the Ban was under discussion. While giving terrorists less publicity has certain advantages, governments have also frequently preferred to invoke Voltaire's prayer: "Oh Lord, let my enemies make themselves ridiculous".[103]

Notes

[1]   The most thorough treatment of this theme is Alex P Schmid and Janny de Graaf, *Violence as Communication: Insurgent Terrorism and the Western News Media* (London: Sage, 1982).

[2]   This point is made by the French social scientist Gerard Chaliand in *Terrorism: From Popular Struggle to Media Spectacle* (London: Saqi Books, 1987): 7.

[3]   G Soulier, "European integration and the suppression of terrorism", *Review of Contemporary Law* 2 (1978): 30, cited by Jennifer Jane Hocking, "Governments' Perspectives", in David L Paletz and Alex P Schmid (eds), *Terrorism and the Media* (Newbury Park; London; New Delhi: Sage, 1992): 88.

[4]   For an account of the Irish-American bombing campaigns of the 1880s, see K R M Short, *The Dynamite War: Irish-American Bombers in Victorian Britain* (Dublin: Gill & Macmillan, 1979).

[5]   Hocking, in Paletz and Schmid: 99-100. She also acknowledges a debt to Philip Schlesinger, whose article, "On the shape and scope of counter-insurgency thought", in Schlesinger's collection, *Media, State and Nation: Political Violence and Collective Identities* (Newbury Park; London; New Delhi: Sage, 1991), was a precursor to her own. In that piece, Schlesinger also makes the point that many current news-management techniques are, in fact, derivative of Britain's experience in Ireland between 1919 and 1921.

[6]   Margaret Thatcher, *The Downing Street Years* (London: HarperCollins, 1993): 408.

[7]   The "orthodoxy"is well represented in Abraham Miller, *Terrorism, the Media and the Law* (New York: Transnational, 1982) and in Yonah Alexander and Richard Latter (eds), *Terrorism & the Media: Dilemmas for Government, Journalism & the Public* (Washington: Brassey's, 1990), while the orthodoxy's critics are better served in Yonah Alexander and Robert·G Picard (eds), *In the Camera's Eye: News Coverage of Terrorist Events* (Washington: Brassey's, 1991) and A Odasuo Alali and Kenoye Kelvin Eke, *Media Coverage of Terrorism: Methods of Diffusion* (Newbury Park, CA: Sage, 1991).

[8]   The Ban and its background are analysed in Article 19, *No Comment: Censorship, Secrecy and the Irish Troubles* (London: Article 19, 1989); Liz Curtis and Mike Jempson, *Interference on the Airwaves: Ireland, the Media and the Broadcasting Ban* (London: Campaign for Press and Broadcasting Freedom, 1993); Lesley Henderson, David Miller, Jaqueline Reilly, *Speak No Evil: The British Broadcasting Ban, The Media and the Conflict in Ireland* (Glasgow: Glasgow University Media Group, 1990); and Ed Moloney, "Closing Down the Airwaves: the Story of the Broadcasting Ban", in Bill Rolston (ed), *The Media and Northern Ireland: Covering the Troubles* (Basingstoke: Macmillan, 1991): 8-50.

[9]   Moloney: 18-21.

[10]   Liz Curtis, *Ireland: the propaganda war. The British media and the 'battle for hearts and minds'* (London: Pluto Press, 1984): 164-165; Philip Schlesinger, *Putting 'reality' together: BBC news*, second edition (London: Methuen, 1987): xviii.

[11]   See Curtis: 165-167; and Roger Bolton (then *Panorama*'s Editor),

Death On the Rock And Other Stories (London: W H Allen, 1990): 64-83.

[12]   An account by the BBC's Director-General at that time is contained in Alasdair Milne's *DG: The Memoirs of a British Broadcaster* (London: Coronet, 1988): 186-199.

[13]   See Bolton; and David Miller, "The Media on the Rock: the Media and the Gibraltar Killings", in Rolston: 69-98. The inquiry into the programme has also been published: *The Windlesham/Rampton Report on* Death on the Rock (London: Faber and Faber, 1989).

[14]   Moloney: 15-17.

[15]   WC(606A), Cabinet Minutes, 5 August 1919; CAB 23/15. [All official papers cited are held in the Public Record Office, Kew.]

[16]   Cited by D G Boyce, *Englishmen and Irish Troubles. British Public Opinion and the Making of Irish Policy 1918-22* (London: Jonathan Cape, 1972): 83.

[17]   Ibid: 84.

[18]   Telegram from MacMichael to Stanley (Secretary of State for the Colonies), 19 February 1944, #238; CO 733/456/6.

[19]   Telegram from MacMichael to Stanley, 24 March 1944, #363; CO 733/456/6.

[20]   Letter from Gurney to J D Higham, 25 April 1950; CO 537/6579.

[21]   Cyprus Intelligence Committee, "Appreciation by Dighenis on 18 November 1955", CIC(55)28, 19 November 1955; CO 926/454. Emphasis in original.

[22]   This was also the belief of a number of orthodox theorists of terrorism, whose views held sway with the Thatcher-Reagan administrations of the early/mid-1980s; Abraham Miller, for example, contended that "for terrorists, it is not really important if the self-portrayal is publicly approved or disapproved" (4).

[23]   Letter from Sir Thomas Lloyd to Sir Franklin Gimson (High Commissioner for Singapore), 23 August 1948; CO 537/3758.

[24]   Hocking, in Paletz and Schmid: 87.

[25]   On the inadequacy of attempts to prove the connection, see R Picard, "News Coverage as the Contagion of Terrorism: Dangerous Charges Backed by Dubious Science", in Alali and Eke, *Media Coverage of Terrorism*; David Miller, *Don't Mention the War: Northern Ireland, Propaganda and the Media* (London: Pluto Press, 1994): 247-250; and David L Paletz and John Boiney, "Researchers'

Perspectives", in Paletz and Schmid: 6-28.

26   See Cynthia L Irvine, "Terrorists' Perspectives: Interviews", in Paletz and Schmid: 62-85.

27   See Robin P J M Gerrits, "Terrorists' Perspectives: Memoirs", in ibid: 29-61.

28   These points have been argued elsewhere; see Philip Schlesinger, "'Terrorism', the Media and the Liberal-Democratic State: A Critique of the Orthodoxy", in Schlesinger (1991): 17-28; and Philip Schlesinger, Graham Murdock and Philip Elliott, *Televising 'Terrorism': political violence in popular culture* (London: Comedia, 1983).

29   Telegram from Gurney to Creech Jones (Colonial Secretary), 26 November 1948, #1515; CO 537/3758.

30   Cab 36(37), Cabinet Minutes, 6 October 1937; CAB23/89.

31   Charles Townshend, *Britain's Civil Wars: Counterinsurgency in the twentieth century* (London; Boston: Faber and Faber, 1986): 36.

32   Correspondence on this matter can be found in CO 904/166.

33   An official in the Commonwealth Relations Office made this precise point with reference to EOKA's campaign in Cyprus: "The incidents are almost always shooting or bomb-throwing in the dark, or from behind walls, isolated individuals are set upon, and the only activities of the security authorities which can be properly photographed are the counter-measures. Since these generally consist of the arrests, search and interrogation of such suspects, in cordoning off districts, or in house-to-house searches, they are calculated to emphasize the repressive activities which the actions of the terrorists necessitate". Letter from Smedley to Millard (10 Downing Street), 18 June 1956, PG11926/16; FO 953/1693.

34   Minute by Mary Fisher to Harold Evans and Charles Carstairs (CO), 2 January 1953; CO 1027/7.

35   Draft letter from Carstairs to Baring, 8 January 1953; CO 1027/7.

36   See a note from Hill to the Prime Minister (Macmillan), 16 June 1958, and a letter from the Foreign Secretary (Selwyn Lloyd) to Ian Jacob (Director-General of the BBC), 13 June 1958; PREM 11/2226.

37   This anecdote is related by Harman Grisewood in *One thing at a time: An autobiography* (London: Hutchinson, 1968): 191.

38   Moloney: 10.

³⁹ On "reference upwards", see Schlesinger (1987): 207-222, and Curtis: 173-196.

⁴⁰ Curtis: 179, and Schlesinger (1987): 210. The IBA also had guidelines covering interviews with "people who within the British Isles use or advocate violence or other criminal measures for the achievement of political ends", which set out that a producer should not plan such an interview without previous discussion with his/her company's top management. Emphasis added.

⁴¹ Article 19: 14-15.

⁴² The controversial documentary, *At the Edge of the Union*, mentioned above, made use of interviews but in a very different context.

⁴³ Hansard, volume 138, 19 October 1988: Col. 885.

⁴⁴ Glasgow University Media Group: 43.

⁴⁵ Article 19: 26.

⁴⁶ The Broadcasting Ban took the form of a "notice" to the broadcasting authorities, and thus was not technically a piece of legislation.

⁴⁷ David Miller (1994): 76.

⁴⁸ Schlesinger (1991): 79. See also Steve Chibnall, *Law-and-Order News: An analysis of crime reporting in the British Press* (London: Tavistock Publications, 1977): 172-205.

⁴⁹ Memorandum on "Press Propaganda", 4 April 1921, Clarke; CO 904/168.

⁵⁰ Similarly, during the early period of the "Troubles", the Army's PR machine in Northern Ireland was so unreliable that it acquired the soubriquet "the Lisburn lie machine", with some journalists finding the IRA a more accurate source.

⁵¹ David Miller (1994) cites former Army press officer, Colin Wallace, to this effect: "The important thing is to get saturation coverage for your story as soon after the controversial event as possible. Once the papers have printed it the damage is done. Even when the facts come out, the original image is the one that sticks" (238).

⁵² David Charters, "Intelligence and Psychological Warfare Operations in Northern Ireland", *RUSI Journal* volume 122 (1977): 25-26.

⁵³ Minutes of the 15th Commissioner General's Conference at Bukit

Serene, 7 June 1950; CO 537/6011.

54   David A Charters, *The British Army and Jewish Insurgency in Palestine, 1945-47* (London: Macmillan Press, 1989): 125-126.

55   John Cloake, *Templer, Tiger of Malaya: The Life of Field Marshal Sir Gerald Templer* (London: Harrap, 1985): 292. During the EOKA insurgency, Colonial Office personnel became exasperated by Harding's belief that any hostile press comment should be dealt with by a senior mandarin briefing the offending editor. As Charles Carstairs, who headed the CO's Information Department, remarked, nothing seemed to make Harding "understand that there is no *sure* way of corking up the Press in this country or of preventing them from drawing their own conclusions and making their own comments on what are reported as *facts*". Minute by Carstairs to Sir John Martin, 28 May 1957; CO 926/880. Emphasis in original.

56   The Army was thought insensitive not only to the nuances of language, but also to the fact that counter-insurgency meant winning hearts and minds on the ground with new socio-political measures. As one member of the Colonial Office put it: "The presentation of emergency news, even if it is largely of an operational character, very often carries a political slant, and it is easy for this to be overlooked or not realised by an Army officer. We have had difficulties over this in Malaya." Minute by E B David to Charles Carstairs, 30 June 1953; CO 1027/40.

57   For a general treatment of British counter-insurgency theory and practice, see Thomas R Mockaitis, *British counterinsurgency in the post-imperial era* (Manchester; New York: Manchester University Press, 1995), and Townshend.

58   David Miller (1994): 81. On the RUC Press Office, see Curtis: 253-255.

59   Details of Mau Mau oath ceremonies were thought too obscene to be published with the 1954 White Paper, but the Cabinet decided that suitable newspaper proprietors could be circulated with the secret Appendix; CC(54) 10, Minutes of Cabinet meeting of 22 February 1954; CAB 128/27.

60   See Chibnall: 78-80. In the 1970s the correspondents Robert Fisk, Simon Winchester and Simon Hoggart were all on different occasions refused access to Army briefings on account of their "hostility"; see J Kirkaldy, "Northern Ireland and Fleet Street: Misreporting a Continuing Tragedy", in Yonah Alexander and Alan O'Day, *Terrorism in Ireland* (London: Croom Helm, 1984).

61   David Miller (1994): 106-107.

62   See a minute by P L Carter (FO Information Policy Dept.) 24 October 1950, PG 14545/6; FO 953/1031.

[63] The Cabinet heard in July 1917 that the Chief Secretary of Ireland had sufficient powers under the Defence of the Realm Act to authorise the military to take control of printing presses and stop the publication of any newspaper which published seditious speeches. War Cabinet 175, 4 July 1917; CAB 23/5.

[64] See the High Commissioner of Palestine's reports in CO 935/21.

[65] Templer's proposal that the press be made to carry reports on the counter-insurgency campaign verbatim was, the Colonial Office felt, "just the sort of thing which would be likely to annoy the Press". Minute by T C Jerrom to J D Higham, 16 June 1952; CO 1022/339.

[66] *New Statesman and Nation* 8 December 1956: 733.

[67] For example, the Colonial Secretary Oliver Lyttelton wrote of the Malayan press that there was "no Press which is more difficult to handle, more unpredictable in its comments, or more speculative in its guesses" (Lord Chandos, *The Memoirs of Lord Chandos* [London: The Bodley Head, 1962]: 364). Meanwhile, in Kenya, with the outbreak of Mau Mau disorder, the local vernacular press was deemed "full of anti-European propaganda and encouragement of race hatred", and restrictions on the press formed one prong of the repressive measures taken in September 1952 to deal with unrest. Note by W Gorrell Barnes on discussions with Kenya's Attorney General, 12 September 1952; CO 822/437.

[68] For example, Thatcher's press secretary, Bernard Ingham, complained that the Province's press, radio and television were "just about the most difficult to deal with in the whole of the United Kingdom". Cited in David Miller (1994): 116. On *Republican News*'s disruption by the Security Forces, see Curtis: 266.

[69] See Paul Arthur, "The media and politics in Northern Ireland", in Jean Seaton and Ben Pimlott (eds), *The Media in British Politics* (Aldershot: Gower, 1987): 205-206.

[70] David Miller (1994): 82 and 306n9, citing Charters (1977).

[71] Conor Cruise O'Brien, "Terrorism Under Democratic Conditions: the Case of the IRA", in M Crenshaw (ed), *Terrorism, Legitimacy and Power: the Consequences of Political Violence* (Middletown, CT: Wesleyan University Press, 1983): 93-94.

[72] David Miller (1994): 146. Emphasis in original.

[73] Erskine Childers, *Military Rule in Ireland* (Dublin: The Talbot Press, 1920): 34.

[74] Telegram from Lord Moyne (British Resident Minister in the Middle East) to Stanley (Colonial Secretary), 8 October 1944, #23; CO 733/457/9.

[75] CHQ MELF, Weekly Intelligence Review for week ending 7 March 1947, "Palestine Outrages"; WO 275/120.

[76] Memorandum by Brigadier J R Cochrane, General Staff of the Sixth Airborne Division; WO 275/86.

[77] Brief for the Cabinet Malaya Committee Meeting on 18 May 1950, FZ1017/11G; FO 371/84478. The CO was insistent that "on no account should the term 'insurgent', which might suggest a genuine popular uprising, be used". Minute from J D Higham to K Blackburne, November 1948; CO 537/4762.

[78] Memo from the Secretary for Defence, "Official Designation of Communist Forces", 20 May 1952; CO 1022/48.

[79] See Peter Taylor, "The Semantics of Political Violence", in Peter Golding, Graham Murdock and Philip Schlesinger (eds), *Communicating Politics: Mass communications and the political process* (Leicester: Leicester University Press, 1986): 211-221.

[80] David Miller (1994): 167. On the BBC's guidelines, see also Schlesinger (1987): 229-231.

[81] The actual propaganda themes pursued in each emergency are examined in detail in Susan L Carruthers, *Winning Hearts and Minds: British Governments, the Media and Colonial Counter-Insurgency 1944-60* (London: Leicester University Press, 1995): 170-177.

[82] Mockaitis: 37.

[83] Boyce: 89.

[84] Mockaitis: 41.

[85] Ibid: 47-48. See also Carruthers: 170-177.

[86] Charters (1977): 24.

[87] *Allegations of Brutality by British Forces in Cyprus Refuted*: 1; copy in FO 953/1825.

[88] At first this distribution was extremely discreet, as the pictures (like Mau Mau's oaths) were believed too shocking for the government to publicise openly and widely. However, the CO's Charles Carstairs reported in January 1953 that sets of photographs of "human atrocities in Kenya have been shown at great discretion to persons it is thought would benefit by seeing them". Carstairs to Mackintosh, 8 January 1953; CO 1027/7. In 1954 a government pamphlet full of "atrocity" photographs was produced "anonymously", but carrying a preface by Granville Roberts, the Kenya authorities' publicity officer in London.

89   Curtis: 231.

90   Wallace made these claims on a BBC2 *The Late Show* programme, "The Information War", broadcast on 16 August 1994.

91   Cited by Article 19: 25.

92   Paul Gilbert, "The oxygen of publicity: terrorism and reporting restrictions", in Andrew Belsey and Ruth Chadwick (eds), *Ethical Issues in Journalism and the Media* (London; New York: Routledge, 1992): 137.

93   Curtis: 10.

94   Ibid.

95   Correspondence on this matter can be found in FO 371/40133.

96   *The Daily Express*, which had printed a front-page photograph of the bodies (booby-trapped by Irgun), was censured in Parliament for its "descent from decent journalism and good taste". Hansard, volume 441, 12 August 1947: Col. 2354.

97   Bernard Ingham, *Kill the Messenger* (London: HarperCollins, 1991): 309, cited by Miller (1994): 151. As Miller points out, Ingham and Thatcher's claim, that only the media wished to dwell on the negative side of life in Northern Ireland, is somewhat disingenuous.

98   One reason why the CO was reluctant for the Army to assume control over the release of news in Kenya was that there had been "far too much purely military and security news", and "far too little about the good things and large areas of peace and progress, against which Mau Mau events should be seen". Letter from Lyttelton to Baring, 10 July 1953; CO 1027/40.

99   Letter from Fletcher-Cooke to Glass, 16 July 1956, PG11926/44; FO 953/1695.

100   David Miller (1994): 154.

101   Letter from J D Higham to Gurney, 7 May 1950; CO 537/6579.

102   "Note on Cyprus Publicity in the UK", 12 April 1957, by Charles Carstairs; CO 1027/155. Emphasis in original.

103   The prayer was invoked by two Colonial Office officials in a discussion on terrorism in Palestine in 1946. See a minute from Fitzgerald to Mathieson, 20 December 1946; CO 537/2289.

Media misperceptions of Saddam Hussein's army
Sean McKnight

The role of the (mostly) Western international media in the Gulf crisis and Gulf War has been the subject of lively debate. In the period leading up to the war, the media was seen as a powerful presence on the world scene, and the United States administration viewed winning the public relations war as an essential preliminary to taking military action against Iraq. Lieutenant-General Thomas W Kelly, Joint Chief of Staff Director of Operations, who regularly briefed the press at the Pentagon during the crisis, typified the concerns of the administration to retain public support in arguing that "[a]nybody who doesn't recognize that the support of the American people is a critical element of combat power is pretty dumb".[1]

The defeat of Iraq and the apparent ability of television to transmit news in "real time", coupled with the sheer power of the imagery of war appearing nightly on television screens throughout the world, seem to have convinced most people even more of the central importance of the media, and especially television.[2] Indeed, the "live" coverage of the Gulf War appeared to grant television a unique role[3] in furthering the popular understanding and appreciation of warfare. The purpose of this essay is to challenge this assumption by examining the misleading impression of Iraqi military strength that was given in the American and British media, and by exploring some of the reasons why an inaccurate picture received such wide currency.

At an academic conference on the Gulf War held at the University of Keele in September 1992, there was a disturbing silence on one topic. No one seemed particularly interested in why Iraq, after the end of its war with Iran, had been so poorly understood in the West in terms of its potential for using force to resolve international disputes, and in terms of the capabilities of its armed forces. These were matters on which many experts had been wrong, and even some of the participants at the conference had been spectacularly inaccurate in their predictions of events in the Gulf, something to which they seemed indifferent or oblivious. Nevertheless, the reasons why Iraq was so poorly understood are important, and exploring this ought to be a matter for scholarly questioning.

One group that, unlike the academic community, is extremely self-critical about its coverage of the war is the Western media.

Many journalists, particularly in the United States, have expressed their concern that coalition governments were allowed excessive freedom in managing the news. In this they have been joined by academics studying media matters. This feeling was not helped by the public pronouncements of some of President Bush's Cabinet after the war. Secretary of State, James Baker, told the press:

> The Gulf War was quite a victory. But who could not be moved by the sight of that poor demoralized rabble–outwitted, outflanked, outmaneuvered by the U.S. military. But I think, given time, the press will bounce back.[4]

Some writers have seen the media's role in the Gulf as reflecting Western, and particularly US, dominance of the international media. This interpretation paints the media as, at best, the dupes of the American administration, or, at worst, as knowing accomplices in furthering the violent birth of the US-dominated New World Order. This angst in part explains the extraordinary attitude of US journalists in refusing to cooperate with their government in covering Haiti prior to the recent "peaceful" US invasion, and the generally poor level of relations between the US government and its media since the war. A similar dispute has on the whole not taken place in Britain, because British journalists not only are more cynical in their expectations of government manipulation and secrecy, but also do not believe – in contrast to their American colleagues – that they have a special constitutional status.[5]

Understandably, the reasons why Iraq was underestimated as a potential aggressor and overestimated as a military threat are peripheral to subsequent examinations of the media coverage of the war. However – in contrast to other types of analysis of the Gulf War – they have not been completely ignored by these studies. It is in the writings of those most critical of the Western media that the clearest explanation for the failure to understand Iraq is outlined. According to many of these critics of Western policy, the United States either failed to warn Iraq against invading Kuwait, or tacitly (or even overtly) encouraged it to use force.[6] This analysis is supported by many in the Arab world who see the Iraqis as victims of a US plot designed to legitimise a Western destruction of an over-mighty Arab state. This view of American complicity in creating the crisis is joined by a belief that the media were deliberately misled over Iraqi military might by "Pentagon disinformation...about colossal fortifications, artillery powerful beyond our imagining, vast stocks of chemical and biological weapons at the ready, and so on".[7] In this view, the purpose of this elaborate deception of the media was "to help

131

justify the carpet and terror bombing of both the military and civilian 'assets' of this Third World country".[8] In the absence of any alternative explanation, this view of the reasons for exaggerating Iraqi military strength may become widely accepted, and has already done so in some circles.

The impression given of Iraqi military capabilities both in the Western press and on television before February 1991 can be divided into two broad categories. Firstly, there was what might be described as the "pessimistic" perspective, which suggested the Iraqi military were so capable that they would inflict major casualties upon the coalition and, even if they were ultimately defeated, would succeed in prolonging the ground war for some months. This "pessimistic" perspective was important in the media, but slightly greater credence was given to "optimistic" predictions of a coalition victory. However, even this "optimistic" perspective warned that the coalition would pay a relatively high price for their victory, and that it was possible that this might leave Saddam Hussein as the "moral" victor. Neither in the press nor on television were there many who predicted a rapid and overwhelming coalition victory, and even those sufficiently bold to hold to this view in public tended to hedge their bets somewhat.

The "pessimist" appreciation of Iraqi strength resulted partly from a media focus on the sheer size of the Iraqi armed forces. The developing crisis on the Iraqi-Kuwaiti border in 1990 made Iraq front-page news, and information on the Iraqi armed forces – hitherto in the public domain but attracting little interest – acquired a new prominence. Political leaders on both sides of the Atlantic were later reported to be stunned by "the enormous size of the Iraqi military establishment",[9] and even prior to the Iraqi invasion of Kuwait, Saddam Hussein's threats to "scorch half of Israel"[10] were given wide credence in the media. On 5 July, Jim Hoagland in *The Washington Post* interpreted Saddam Hussein's threat to Israel as an "airborne version of Hitler's ovens". In the United States, several newspapers printed articles critical of previous US policy towards Iraq, but these were often couched in terms that reinforced the impression that the Iraqi military machine was formidable. *The New York Times*'s front page of 13 August commented that "[f]or 10 years, as Iraq developed a vast army, chemical weapons, nuclear ambitions and a long record of brutality, the Reagan and Bush administrations quietly courted President Saddam Hussein".

In the days following the Iraqi invasion of Kuwait little was written about the prospects for "liberating" Kuwait. More commonly expressed were the fears that even US military intervention could not defeat an Iraqi invasion of Saudi Arabia. This early pessimism in evaluating the Iraqi threat is clearly demonstrated in an article in *The Sunday Times*, which is worth citing at some length. "One man's army against the world"[11] paints a picture of a formidable Iraqi military machine commanded by a leader who was certainly ruthless and probably mad. The Iraqi armed forces enjoyed the advantage of "formidable size" and "formidable firepower".[12] Of greater importance, however, was the experience of Saddam Hussein's soldiers, for "[t]here is no country in the world that can field a military force with such extensive combat experience".

So formidable was Iraqi military strength, the article speculated, that any attempts by the United States to deploy forces into the area could lead to their facing "main battle tanks skilfully used and the prospect of defeat on the ground". Pentagon experts were also cited who believed that the Iraqis could capture Dhahran and the Saudi oil fields before US forces could deploy. However, the direst scenario focused on the Iraq's ability to use chemical weapons, warning that:

> [w]hat is particularly worrying for any country tackling Iraq is Saddam Hussein's access to chemical weapons. In the wrong hands the effects of chemicals can be as devastating as a nuclear bomb, and there is little doubt that, if facing defeat, Saddam Hussein would order his troops to use chemical weapons.[13]

This analysis of Iraqi military strength was typical of what was both written and voiced in August 1990, and this "pessimist" perspective can be characterised by its focus on the size of the Iraqi forces; on the fire-power at their disposal; on the experience of Iraq in the war with Iran, which ensured that the Iraqi military were "battle-hardened"; on the importance of the "élite" Republican Guard; and on Saddam Hussein's "doomsday" weapons, of which chemical weapons were the prime example.

Expectations that the crisis might escalate during the summer of 1990 proved false, allowing the United States and its allies to build up their forces in Saudi Arabia. Time to reflect and research, and the growing military strength of the coalition, produced a more realistic appreciation of Iraq's military prospects in the media, but there still remained a considerable element of "pessimism" in some assessments of the likely results of a clash of arms. The headline on the front page of The Sunday Times on 20 January 1991 still boldly proclaimed that the "ALLIES FACE LONG AND BLOODY WAR". Perhaps the clearest example of the persistence with which the pessimists clung to their views is that provided by Paul Rogers, Professor of Peace Studies at Bradford University. Writing in The Guardian four weeks after the air war began, he stated that "even the most optimistic military pundit has to accept that it is not going according to plan", claimed that "coalition forces have seriously under-estimated Iraqi capabilities", and concluded with a prediction that "[w]e will be lucky if the war is over within six months".

The "optimistic" analysis of Iraqi strength as formidable but capable of being defeated lacked the bold clarity of the "pessimists", and was characterised by reservations that sustained a wide variety of different outcomes. *Newsweek*, for example, on 4 February, while reporting coalition dominance in the air war, suggested that there was "room for a lot of interpretation" concerning the effectiveness of the bombing. Despite expecting victory, the "optimists" in the media "expected [the war] to be bloody", and regarded the most optimistic official estimates of likely coalition casualties (3-5000 killed and wounded) as being too low.[14] A similar caution can be detected in television news: almost invariably the "good" news of the sheer scale of the coalition victory in the air would be followed by warnings that any ground conflict would be far from one-sided. Hopes that coalition losses would be minimal were often pegged upon the air campaign sufficing to force an Iraqi withdrawal, and Yehoshua Saguy (former head of Israeli Military Intelligence) struck a chord when he warned that "soon will come the moment of truth when the Americans must decide if they are ready to pay the price of ground fighting".[15]

The Daily Telegraph took a very similar line and, although it rightly described the Iraqi Army as having "little flair for high-manoeuvre warfare", it estimated that 250 000 of the Iraqi Army "could be considered of a standard approaching that of the American, British and French forces".[16] Despite the fact that this was one of the few newspapers to suggest that the threat from Iraqi chemical weapons had been exaggerated, it predicted on 12 January that "Saddam is almost certain to use them before air attacks destroy his stocks",[17] and suggested that Scud missiles carrying chemical warheads could be used to attack coalition rear areas. Indeed, throughout the air war against Iraq there was a stream of cautionary stories in the Western press: reports that bomb damage assessments suggested that Iraqi forces were bloodied but unbowed;[18] claims that chemical weapons had been supplied to Iraqi forces in Kuwait;[19] and claims that the Pentagon felt its commanders in the theatre were being dangerously optimistic. Indeed, the media seem to have preferred the more cautious attitude of officials in Washington and London to the greater confidence in coalition prospects often expressed by the military commanders in Saudi Arabia.

It might be objected that, in the months prior to the coalition victory in the Gulf, all the military weaknesses of the Iraqis were actually covered by the media; however, such an argument could only be sustained by a very selective recollection of what had been written and said. However, there was a small minority of individuals who accurately predicted that Iraq would be overwhelmed. On 12 January *The Daily Telegraph* Defence Editor, John Keegan, wrote that a war would be won quickly and at modest cost in coalition lives because "[i]n human terms, it [the Iraqi Army] is not up to fighting a Western regular army in any circumstances". In *The Sunday Times* another historian, Norman Stone, also predicted a rapid coalition victory. But these "hyper-optimists" were hardly sufficient in number to counteract the overall feeling that the coalition would pay a high – perhaps unacceptably high – price to defeat the Iraqis.

Indeed, a strictly methodical analysis of the media appreciation of Iraqi military strength is potential misleading. It would be unwise to forget, for example, that newspapers and television are essentially in the business of selling entertainment: dramatic images, crisp sound bites and sensational stories, rather than the dispassionate relaying of information, are the stuff of much popular journalism. When a crisis is news for only a relatively brief period, its newness is in itself entertaining, but the crisis provoked by the invasion of Kuwait lasted months, and in such circumstances those aspects of the situation with "star potential" were likely to become more prominent. It is certainly in the nature of the news media to emphasise the spectacular, which invariably is the spectacularly disastrous, and a tendency of journalists to entertain by focusing on the sensational. This may seem obvious, but it is important to note how these aspects of media practice helped ensure that the image of Iraqi military potency remained the dominant one, even as the ground war started.

In addition to a tendency to sensationalise, we should note an important formal aspect of television news. Striving to maintain a reasonable balance, issues are commonly presented antagonistically – a perspective favouring one side of an argument is succeeded by a contrary view. This practice seems to have been followed when examining military matters in the Gulf, and frequently items on coalition military strength were followed by a contrary piece on the Iraqi forces. Coverage that had (rightly) just stressed coalition strength and comparative Iraqi weakness, if left "unbalanced", would have been assailed as dangerously triumphalist. Such overt presentational impartiality is more important to serious journalists than cynics might believe, because "impartiality [legitimizes] journalistic authority".[20]

One of the unlikely "stars" of the media war was the Scud missile, which received attention that was totally disproportionate to its military effectiveness, helping to give this ageing, inaccurate missile a political significance it did not warrant. A sign of Scud newsworthiness can be seen from *The Times* from 18 to 26 January 1991: six of the eight daily front pages carry Scud stories, four times as a lead story. In August 1990 the Scud was introduced in the newspapers as a deadly weapon – on 19 August

The Sunday Times, for example, directed readers to its "Focus" special looking at "Iraq moves deadly Scud missiles into Kuwait, threatening US troops". In January 1991 Anthony Cordesman, American Broadcasting Corporation's (ABC) resident expert for the duration of the crisis, described the Iraqi Scud as "a horrifying killing mechanism" – which, despite the hyperbole, was an effective television sound bite.[21] On television, pictures of Scud launches regularly filled a space on the prime-time news, and discussion of the Scud's possible role as a delivery system for chemical weapons added an extra sinister touch to the missile's star persona. The success with which the Scud was portrayed as a "chemical threat" was demonstrated by two leading British tabloids, *Today* and *The Sun*, reporting that the first Scuds launched at Israel had carried chemical warheads – information which, it has been suggested, came from the Israeli police radio. The suggestion that the Scud could carry a chemical warhead was a "peak" (reinforced of course by the possibility of showing another Scud launch), but the contrary view that Iraq did not have the capability to modify a Scud in this way (and, in any case, it would not be a particularly effective weapon) was a valley to be ignored.

A similar and related media star was Iraq's chemical, biological and nuclear weapon capability. Unconventional warfare had previously demonstrated its newsworthiness in the Iran-Iraq War, during which *The New York Times* featured 95 main stories on chemical weapons, in comparison to 58 stories on foreign policy and only six on Saddam Hussein.[22] Between August 1990 and March 1991, television regularly showed the film taken of the Kurdish town of Halabja, a victim of an Iraqi gas attack in 1988, with the implication that this was the likely impact of chemical attacks on coalition troops. One of the main unchallenged assumptions concerning chemical weapons was that they were a "poor man's atomic bomb", and virtually no one on television or in print challenged the view that Iraq was likely to resort to these weapons. Iraq's potential to use biological and nuclear weapons received less attention in the media; nevertheless, speculation about these weapon programmes was an important strand in covering the crisis. Headlines in *The Sunday Times* on 19 August 1990, such as "IRAQ'S NUCLEAR CAPABILITY GREATER THAN WE THOUGHT", were sufficiently ambiguous to make the possibility of an Iraqi nuclear weapon a subject for anxious and prolonged debate.

Other prominent "star" stories similarly reinforced the expectation that Iraqi forces would at least fight sufficiently well to cause significant coalition casualties. Frequent references to the "élite" Republican Guard were only infrequently balanced by reports that their capability had been grossly exaggerated. Iraqi attempts to fortify their positions in Kuwait received a similarly respectful treatment, with descriptions of "elaborate fortifications" and rumours of flooding moats with oil being reinforced by reference to "First World War"-style trench warfare waged against Iran from 1980 to 1988. Finally, there was the menace of deliberate or accidental damage to the environment, with the doomsday scenario being a phenomenon similar to a "nuclear winter". The reporting of the environmental aspects of the imminent conflict was sceptical of these doomsday claims, but merely raising the possibility of such a general calamity reinforced the feeling that the clash of arms in Kuwait would be a disaster not just for Iraq. Reported spectacular threats such as these need to be vastly "outweighed" by contrary reports if the image of disaster to come is to be dispelled.

Deliberate decisions to sensationalise news by the media themselves can also be seen as a contributory factor in the exaggeration of Iraqi military capabilities. There is little doubt that such sensationalism lies at the heart of the appeal of the popular press, but it is by no means confined to this section of the media. While spoken commentary and lengthy articles may have some balance, maps and pictures have an immediate impact that often defines the way a situation is perceived. A good example of this is the large photograph placed by *The Sunday Times* at the head of its "Gulf 4-Page Special" of 12 August 1990, showing troops in chemical warfare gear – a dehumanised, sinister and powerful image. Throughout the crisis, newspapers and television produced computer-generated graphics, creating an image that could be easily assimilated of the simple, quantitative balance of forces which was very misleading. BBC 2's *Newsnight* programme used a sand table in a similar way, which, although it lacked the dangerous aura of technological validation imparted by computers, did have the authentic military feel. One of the clearest British examples of deliberate sensationalism was in reporting official assessments of possible casualties. British reporters visiting the commander of British 7th Armoured Brigade, managed to turn a warning that some casualties were inevitable into headlines such as "PREPARE FOR A BLOODBATH"[23] – a distortion that in one form or another found itself into the popular press, the "quality" newspapers and television. This sensationalism was quite deliberate, and one of the reporters even warned the Brigadier that "we have really made a little bit of a saga out of casualties".[24]

It seems reasonable to assume that the media image of Iraqi military strength results partly from common media practices, in terms of the way in which both an audience "consumes" media output and information is presented. Readers and viewers tend to remember "peaks" that suggested the Iraqi military would inflict heavy casualties on the coalition forces, and the media often presented information that reinforced this view. The need for "stars" and audience-boosting sensationalism was also a factor in influencing the nature of the coverage. However, this is only a partial explanation, and misses the critical point that the output of the media also reflected the honest analysis of those covering the story.

It is important to examine how the opinions of those covering news stories are formed, and the type of journalistic research that goes into preparing stories. Some reporters were able to use their previous experience of the region or fall back on their own academic expertise,[25] and a small minority – such as John Keegan – are reputable military historians. However, the sources for obtaining information and developing interpretations dominates the way in which the media picture is developed. The most important of these are official sources, both formal and informal, "independent" experts, and the personal contacts formed by a journalist over the years (this last category is liable to include either an expert or an official who is not releasing information for official purposes). The importance of officials as sources of information is even more pronounced in the United States, and most of the authoritative American reporting on the Middle East crisis came from the Washington "newsbeats".[26] The belief that "reporters overwhelmingly turn to officials as sources for political stories and for framing the policy content of stories" is an established finding of media research, and recent research suggests that this is accentuated in matters of national security.[27]

To admit the importance of official sources to the media does not automatically imply that reporters are inevitably the witting or unwitting dupes of the governing élites. They often find ways to moderate – or mediate – the official line. This is most easily done when the governing élite is divided, and in the United States critical media coverage of policy in dealing with Iraq tended to peak when powerful elements in Congress expressed contrary views to those of the Bush administration. Another source of an alternative perspective is in consulting some sort of expert, and a growing phenomenon of British television is the use of "resident" or frequently appearing academic experts. Since the confrontation with Iraq lasted seven months, the media had time to acquire perspectives other than the official view; many such experts missed out the "middleman" of the journalist and expounded their views directly on television or in print.

However, the view that the media were systematically misled into misrepresenting Iraqi military strength cannot be refuted simply by demonstrating that they were able to balance official perspectives with outside expertise. Many of the experts whose views were sought by the media can hardly be described as independent: "In their spare time, experts are establishing their credentials as experts by advising or taking the counsel of the

138

same government officials that journalists seek out in the first place".[28]

In the United States it is far more common than in Britain for academics to hope to move into a powerful position in public service. Furthermore, with a military clash imminent, many of the experts consulted were either ex-military men or very closely associated with the military. Even those without such a close connection were affected by the pressure not to behave "irresponsibly", and a widespread belief in the malign influence of the press in Vietnam imposed an extra pressure on American journalists to behave patriotically. These pressures on experts and journalists in the United States have an impact on the British media, not only in terms of influencing British journalists, but also directly through newspaper space and television time being given to American experts. A similar perspective concerning Iraqi military strength in both Britain and the United States strengthens the confidence of the media in both countries that their perspective is correct.

It is thus possible to explain the failure (realistically) to appreciate the Iraqi armed forces as an establishment conspiracy, sustained over the months by independent expertise which merely echoed the views of their respective governments. This "conspiracy theory" presumes that it was in the interests of the coalition governments to build up the Iraqi threat in order to justify the use of overwhelming force. It is relatively easy to cast doubt on this explanation by examining the negative consequences for the coalition of exaggerating Iraqi military potential. It has been widely reported that Saddam Hussein told the American Ambassador to Baghdad, April Glaspie, that American society could not accept high casualties from a war, and this echoed a belief widely held in the USA. A deliberate policy of exaggerating Iraqi military strength was just as likely to erode public support for the military option. Indeed, in both the USA and Britain there was a close correlation between opposition to using force against Iraq and predicting high casualties on both sides – it is not unreasonable to assume that in some cases Iraqi strength was exaggerated to support the argument against war, rather than the other way around.

Similarly, it is too simplistic to talk about the collective view of the Bush administration. Not only did different parts of the US government hold different views, but also very contradictory information was been fed into all the coalition governments. A good example of this was the far from coherent picture that the British government and military were obtaining from computer models. The accurate predictions of the Centre for Defence Analysis (CDA)[29] were only one of a number of sources available, and most alternatives were much less optimistic. Indeed, one such computer-generated "game" saw a British tank regiment virtually wiped out in half an hour. Likewise, in the United States different agencies supplying the government with intelligence gave very different estimates of Iraqi strength, and there were significant disagreements on bomb-damage assessment once the war commenced.

The decision taken in October to double American forces in Saudi Arabia says a great deal about divided councils within the Bush administration, and the range of its real assessments of Iraqi strength. It was the politicians, President Bush and Secretary of Defense, Dick Cheney, who contemplated the possibility of taking the offensive against Iraq in 1990; and there were strong political reasons for opting for an earlier offensive if it were a possibility. But the American military strongly opposed what they believed would be a premature offensive (Schwarzkopf was furious about this possibility), and their political masters did not take much convincing on this issue. Clearly, the administration genuinely were convinced that Iraq would put up a formidable resistance, and allowed this military judgment to persuade it to accept the political risks of delay. Advocates of the theory that the US government and others deliberately misled the media about Iraqi strength, seem to have failed to consider the possibility that their governments genuinely believed that Iraq would be a formidable enemy on the battlefield.

The belief that the media was either deceived or was an knowing participant in the deception over the matter of Iraq's military strength also ignores the source of many of the direst warnings in the media. On the whole, it was experts removed from the process of government who were "pessimists", together with those more closely associated with government, such as ex-military personnel, who normally took an "optimistic" line. Similarly, those reporters taking an independent line from the "tame" journalists of the pool did not on the whole accurately assess Iraqi military weakness. One British journalist who dissented from the pool system was *The Independent*'s Robert Fisk, and a piece from his report of 23 January clearly demonstrates that he was not expecting the clash of arms to be totally one-sided:

> Journalists officially accredited...are not brought to this particular forward location...and when you drive into this swamp of mud and water, it is not difficult to see why. For the gathering of allied armies here...bears little relation to those comfortable, efficient scenarios outlined by American and British commanders in Riyadh. The mass of [coalition] troops and armour gathered here for the offensive have had to fight their way through a logistic nightmare, which at times left armoured units unable to find their headquarters.

Indeed, the only group with a significant influence on the media which was more than cautiously optimistic were the senior officers of the coalition forces in Saudi Arabia, whose optimistic assessments once the air war started were questioned both by the media and by officials back home.

The months of intense coverage of Iraq in the media between August 1990 and March 1991 make it easy to forget how much of an unknown quantity Iraq was prior to its invasion of Kuwait. Despite the eight-year war with Iran, "[h]ardly American news stories were datelined Iraq",[30] and it seemed that "Iraq did not fit into the journalistic map of a Near East dominated by Israel...and by Egypt".[31] This lack of interest in Iraq is amply demonstrated by comparing the 4214 stories and editorials relating to Iraq in *The New York Times* and *The Washington Post* between 2 August and 8 November 1990, to the 200 at best that appeared in the same two newspapers throughout the 1980s.[32] An editorial in *The New York Times* as early as 1981 suggested that "chances are Iraq's president, Saddam Hussein, is less a holy warrior than a cautious optimist",[33] and this judgment would sum up the Western attitude to Iraq just prior to its invasion of Kuwait. The view in the Western academic world was not dissimilar, and most specialists in the region made a cautious but optimistic assessment of Iraq's likely intentions once it managed to end the war with Iran. Typical of this trend was the view that in 1988 "[a]rguably...it is a very much more sober and mature regime that has emerged from the war".[34]

It is not unreasonable to assume that in 1988 Western governments, particularly that of the United States, took a similar perspective. Faced with Iranian hostility since 1979, the United States has had little option but to hope that Iraqi self-interest would force them to act as the protector of the Gulf from Iran. Indeed, Ambassador Glaspie's supposed encouragement of Saddam Hussein's aggressive instincts indicates the unavoidable dilemma US foreign policy was in and probably had little influence on Iraqi decision-making. Contributing to the Bush administration's problems were the varied assessments of the different intelligence agencies. The CIA, for example, submitted a position paper to the President the day before Iraq invaded Kuwait predicting a peaceful resolution of the problem. American assessments of Iraqi intentions were poor, partly because of a growing dependence on electronic means of gathering intelligence data and cuts in human intelligence assets.[35] American analysts could detect movements and accurately count numbers, but this did not give them the capacity to understand the nature of the Ba'athist state, or to appreciate the severe limits that existed to its armed forces exploiting their apparent might.

Far more than those outside government would have expected, the US administration (just like those working in the media) found itself attempting to assess a state of which it had little understanding. Iraq was a closed society, and the Western media was to some extent dependent on Iraqi sources; however, the assessment that "[p]eople in general, even habitual followers of foreign affairs, had no ready-made framework from which to derive a reaction"[36] could be extended to those in Western governments reacting to the Iraqi invasion of Kuwait. Indeed, for those in government, particular the United States, the Iraqi invasion disastrously refuted their framework for the region (which envisaged Iraq as a state with whom the West could do business), and it is understandable that the image of an over-mighty Iraq was uncritically accepted in the wake of this sudden vacuum of understanding. In some respects, this vacuum helped the Bush administration, as the Iraqi regime could be quickly demonised; however, it is by no means clear that the media would not have gravitated to this type of perspective of its own volition. The Hitler template was an obvious aid to "understanding" Iraq, and – despite the analogy being inappropriate – the Iraqi regime was indeed both brutal and tyrannical.[37]

Therefore, there was no clear reason for the Bush administration or the other coalition governments to manipulate the media into exaggerating Iraqi military strength. The media formed its perspective of Iraqi military strength largely by drawing deductions from the data[38] and by listening to experts – both officials and others – who held views that cannot logically be explained simply by reference to a sinister conspiracy.

One source for assessments of Iraqi military strength that was an exception, in that it clearly was an attempt to manipulate the media, was Iraq itself. Saddam Hussein repeatedly boasted of the strength of Iraq's military and made a series of dire threats. As early as August, he proclaimed that "[t]he Iraqi people are capable of fighting to the victorious end which god wants...the blood of our martyrs will burn you".[39] The line had not changed even with war imminent. Broadcasting on Baghdad Radio in January 1991, Saddam Hussein's confidence in victory appears undiminished: "The unjust people will be defeated after shedding their foul blood and the severed members of the bodies of their supporters will be left as food for birds of prey".[40] Supporting these confident threats, Iraq could muster an impressive force at least for a parade, and it is difficult to believe that its displays of military "might" did not influence the outside world's assessment.

To a large extent, this Iraqi bombast was countered in the Western media by the analysis in the defence "community", who on the whole took an "optimistic" line. It is understandable that, despite their expertise, they generally erred on the side of caution. Those in or close to Western military establishments do not want to be responsible for encouraging a complacent attitude towards a potential enemy, and the desire to avoid false optimism is very strong.[41] A similar inhibition restrained politicians from taking an upbeat line on coalition military prospects. Not only would it be politically dangerous to be seen as complacent, but also politicians and officials were well aware that the price for their policies may well be the lives of fellow citizens. Indeed, it could be argued that anyone operating in the public domain, including members of the media, is under a moral obligation not to be seen as irresponsibly optimistic.

In the absence of a substantial body of information and understanding on Iraq's military potential (such as existed on the Soviet armed forces during the Cold War), the people best placed to produce an assessment in the crisis should have been those who were to some extent removed from the pressures that affect politicians, journalists and those connected with the military in some fashion.[42] In other words, the crisis provoked by Iraq's invasion of Kuwait should have been an ideal environment in which academic analysis could influence policy. Indeed, the academic world was the only realistic source which could correct the image of Iraqi strength that the raw data, the powerful imagery and the "information vacuum" was allowing to form in the media. In fact, the reverse happened, and the roots of both governmental and media errors can be traced back to a failure of most academic experts to describe accurately Iraq's armed forces.

In contrast to the self-analysis of the media, there has been no angst in the academic world concerning its failings during the crisis in the Gulf. Indeed, one British university department, whose members managed almost without exception to misunderstand the nature of the Iraqi armed forces, has publicly boasted of how frequent appearances on television have boosted its profile. Nevertheless, the record of failure was remarkable: the military analyst, Anthony Cordesman, whose book, *The Lessons of Modern Warfare: The Iran-Iraq War*, is one of the better informed works on this forgotten war, predicted heavy casualties for the coalition, and claimed that the Iraqis would resort to large-scale chemical attacks.[43] Right-wing experts such as Edward Luttwak warned that the United States were obsessed by "fanciful tactics, flashy weapons and promising gadgets that seem fine in peace-time exercises but fail in combat".[44] Professor Paul Wilkinson similarly warned that a conflict with Iraq would be "one of the most lethal wars since 1945...[with] a high possibility of weapons of mass destruction being used".[45] The more left-wing perspective – for example, that of academics in "peace studies" – echoed this view of dire consequences for the coalition and the Iraqis resulting from any war. Very few academics took a position that was neither "optimistic" nor "pessimistic" and, on the whole, opinion veered towards the latter. The academic world, far from countering the image of the Iraqi military emerging in the media in August 1990, actually strengthened this image.

The failure to understand the Iraqi military partly reflected a general reluctance amongst Arabists in the academic world to highlight the weaknesses of Middle Eastern states such as Iraq, often regarded in some senses as a progressive state. This was demonstrated by the initial reaction to Kanan Makiya's *Republic of Fear*, a book treated by Western experts as anti-Iraqi propaganda until Saddam Hussein invaded Kuwait. Furthermore, a problem for political analysts was that the relationship between the Iraqi regime and its armed forces was a product of the structure of the Iraqi state and the totalitarian nature of the regime – failing to recognise this made it harder to evaluate the effectiveness of the military. A more general problem that inhibited the academic world was the low regard in which it holds the study of things military. Neither the United States nor Britain has many universities with specialist war studies departments, and even in those departments that do exist there is a bias towards the "higher" strategic aspects of the subject. There is still a reluctance to regard the study of subjects beneath this level as respectable. It is perhaps not surprising that John Keegan, one of the few experts publicly and accurately to predict the likely course of the conflict, has a good understanding of the operational and tactical levels of warfare.

A lack of expertise in operational and tactical military problems does matter: as one historian stated recently,[46] the results of battles actually do change things. In the case of the Iraqi armed forces, the differing capabilities of T-55 and Abrams or Challenger tanks and the combat skills (or lack of them) of Iraqi soldiers were highly relevant to an understanding of the likely course of a future conflict, and were all in the public domain in 1990. Data from the Iran-Iraq War pointed clearly to Iraq's being very inefficient in using weapons, and performing particularly ineptly in the air, even with huge numerical advantage. Above all, the things that enable armed forces to function – all-arms cooperation, leadership and fighting spirit – were for various reasons absent or weak in the Iraqi military.

The media clearly exaggerated the military strength of Iraq, a tendency which was given added impetus by the nature of both television and print journalism. In doing this, the media were neither the dupe nor the accomplice of government, but were merely reflecting the understanding of the Iraqi forces held by Western governments, military, and other experts. In effect, the media occupied an information vacuum, and those who should have been capable of refining the early assessments of Iraqi military strength reinforced the initial error. The whole timing and nature of the coalition offensive was dominated by the belief that the Iraqi armed forces were stronger than they actually were. Delaying the coalition offensive to enable US VII Corps to be deployed was politically risky; the coalition might not have held together until February, and it was not impossible that Saddam Hussein could have found a way of withdrawing from Kuwait while claiming victory. The military means used against Iraq represented a considerable overkill which might have been avoided; it is by no means impossible that some of the precautions taken by coalition forces against particular Iraqi weapons whose relative ineffectiveness was not appreciated have actually caused casualties. Finally, it is not impossible that the willingness of many in the West to take Saddam Hussein's military strength at face value actually discouraged him from evacuating Kuwait prior to the coalition's recourse to force.

Notes

[1]   W Lance Bennett, "The News about Foreign Policy", in W Lance Bennett and David L Paletz (eds), *Taken By Storm: The Media, Public Opinion, and U.S. Foreign Policy in the Gulf War* (Chicago; London: University of Chicago Press, 1994): 17.

[2]   The British Army Staff College at Camberley is indicative of this trend towards an increased recognition of the power of the media, substantially expanding the time spent on their various courses contemplating the media and the armed forces.

[3]   CNN, in particular, benefited, acquiring a new status and fame directly from its coverage of the conflict.

[4]   Quoted in David L Paletz, "Just Deserts?", in Bennett and Paletz (eds): 282-283.

[5]   These views were expressed to the author in the course of an interview with Mike Evans, Defence Correspondent of *The Times*.

[6]   Michael Morgan, Justin Lewis and Sut Jhally, "More Viewing, Less Knowledge", in Hamid Mowlana, George Gerbner and Herbert I Schiller (eds), *Triumph of the Image: The Media's War in the Persian Gulf – A Global Perspective* (Oxford: Westview Press, 1992): 219, 224.

[7]   Noam Chomsky, "The Media and the War: What War?", in ibid: 52.

[8]   Andre Gunder Frank, "A Third-World War: A Political Economy of the Persian Gulf War and the New World Order", in ibid: 10.

[9]   Mike Evans, *The Times* 12 February 1991.

[10]   A M Rosenthall in *The New York Times* 5 April 1990.

[11]   James Adams, "One man's army against the world", *The Sunday Times* 5 August 1990: 11.

[12] Ibid.

[13] Ibid.

[14] John Zaller, "Elite Leadership of Mass Opinion: New Evidence from the Gulf War", in Bennett and Paletz (eds): 198-199.

[15] Quoted in *Newsweek* 4 February 1991.

[16] Unattributable clipping.

[17] Unattributable clipping.

[18] For example, in *Newsweek* 4 February 1991.

[19] In *The Times* 21 February 1991.

[20] Timothy E Cook, "Domesticating a Crisis: Washington Newsbeats and Network News after the Iraqi Invasion of Kuwait", in Bennett and Paletz (eds): 108.

[21] John R MacArthur, *Second Front: Censorship and Propaganda in the Gulf War* (New York: Hill and Wang, 1992): 111.

[22] Gladys Engel Lang and Kurt Lang, "The Press as Prologue: Media Coverage of Saddam's Iraq, 1979-1990", in Bennett and Paletz (eds): 47.

[23] Brigadier [now Major-General] Patrick Cordingley DSO, "Future Commanders – be warned!", *Despatches* 3 (1992): 17.

[24] Ibid.

[25] Some reporters actively pursue explicitly academic projects, for example, Channel 4 Television's Nik Gowing has taken a sabbatical at the Harvard School of Government, and in a similar fashion Edward Mortimer of *The Financial Times* has had a period at the International Institute for Strategic Studies.

[26] Cook: 112.

[27] Bennett: 23-24.

[28] Ibid: 29.

[29] Featured in the Channel 4 *Equinox* programme, "Technology and the Gulf War".

[30] Lang and Lang: 51.

[31] Ibid: 59.

[32] William A Dorman and Steven Livingston, "News and Historical Content: The Establishing Phase of the Persian Gulf Policy Debate",

in Bennett and Paletz (eds): 67.

[33]   Lang and Lang: 49.

[34]   Philip Robins, "Iraq in the Gulf war: objectives, strategies and problems", in Hanns W Maull and Otto Pick (eds), *The Gulf War: Regional and International Dimensions* (London: Pinter Publishers, 1989): 57.

[35]   Norman Friedman suggested in *Desert Victory: The War for Kuwait* (Annapolis, MD: Naval Institute Press, 1991) that the absence of any American human intelligence sources in Iraq left an information vacuum that was filled by the media.

[36]   Lang and Lang: 43.

[37]   Sean McKnight, "The Failure of the Iraqi Forces", in John Pimlott and Stephen Badsey (eds), *The Gulf War Assessed* (London: Arms and Armour Press, 1992): 173.

[38]   According to Mike Evans, Defence Correspondent of *The (London) Times*, initial impressions of the Iraqi armed forces were formed largely by consulting the IISS *The Military Balance*.

[39]   Unattributable clipping.

[40]   "What they said would happen", *The Daily Telegraph* 1 March 1991: 19.

[41]   As the author found while briefing British 7th Armoured Brigade as part of a team from the Royal Military Academy Sandhurst's War Studies Department. Challenged by the chemical warfare officer of 40 Field Artillery Regiment, it was not easy to persist in maintaining that Iraq was unlikely to use chemical weapons, and that they would be very ineffective if it did.

[42]   Academics who expressed views in the media have been treated as quasi-journalists, and this section of the essay is primarily focused on academic research which was not intended for a wider public. Work produced within the protection of an "ivory tower" is produced to a different format and in a different environment.

[43]   Cordesman was the ABC's resident military historian for the crisis, but this prediction was given at a briefing attended by Edward Mortimer of *The Financial Times* (interviewed by the author).

[44]   Edward Luttwak, "Blood for Oil", *The Independent* 27 August 1990.

[45]   Quoted in P Towle, "Pundits and Patriots", *Institute for European Defence and Strategic Studies* Occasional Paper 50 (1991): 11.

[46]   Matthew Bennett, in Anne Curry and Michael Hughes (eds), *Arms, Armies and Fortifications in the Hundred Years War* (Woodbridge: The Boydell Press, 1994).

From Morse to modem: developments in transmission technologies and their impact upon the military-media relationship
John Allen

> Nothing is more dangerous in Wartime than to live in the temperamental atmosphere of a Gallup Poll, always feeling one's pulse and taking one's own temperature. (Sir Winston Churchill)[1]

The purpose of this essay is to illustrate how changes in transmission technologies and their consequent effect on news-gathering and reporting have in turn produced changes, at times significant, in the British military-media relationship. The contention will be that as transmission technologies have progressed, so has the relative importance of the media as an aspect of war.[2] For the purpose of this essay, "transmission technology" will mean primarily the *means* by which information is sent, using cable and electricity, or making use of the electro-magnetic spectrum. The form in which information is sent – whether print, word of voice, photographic images or digitised code – will also be considered. Consequently, attention will be focused on the telegraph, telephone and radio, cameras, newsroom computers, satellite transmitters and the telephone-modem-computer triad known as the Internet.

The military-media relationship, one that historically has been complex and problematical, is naturally affected by many factors other than technologies. However, the relationship has been increasingly based on the military needing the media to build up and sustain support for its activities and actions, whether in peacetime or war, whereas the media, particularly in the latter part of the 20th century, needs the military to increase audience and readership size and to sustain corporate aims, whether they related to ratings, charters or profit. The ebb and flow of this relationship will be charted as we consider the impact that the development of those technologies has had. In the final section we shall speculate as to the probable challenges for the military-media relationship with the advent of the "Information Highway" or Internet.

The legacy of the Crimean War

The mid-19th century witnessed the technological application of many scientific discoveries related mainly to steam power and electricity. Similarly, an increasingly sophisticated and literate society was slowly developing with an associated desire for information and "news". In the 1830s the first modern newspapers began to appear, the circulation of quality newspapers such as *The Times* increased, and printing processes became more reliable and advanced.[3] The late 1840s and early 1850s saw the practical development of the electric telegraph, and alongside the advent of the telegraph there gradually developed a global network of lines and cables. A social and commercial consequence of this technology was the genesis of news agencies such as Reuters. As a result, more accurate, rapid and up-to-date foreign and international news was available to a widening circulation of newspaper readers with its consequent effect on their political literacy, understanding and opinion.

It is against this background that we must consider the reporting of the Crimean War (1852-54) and what may be perceived as the birth of the modern military-media relationship. The form of reporting the war and its consequent effect on military-media relations have largely been attributed to W H Russell of *The Times*. As Phillip Knightley has commented, "Russell's coverage of the Crimean War marked the beginning of an organised effort to report a war to the civilian population at home using the services of a civilian reporter".[4] Prior to the Crimean War, editors had employed junior army officers in an epistolary role to send letters from the battle-front. However, as Knightley has pointed out, these military correspondents were highly selective in their reports; they were soldiers first and correspondents second, and they had little conception of what constituted news.[5] Editors also took news from foreign newspapers in preference to no news at all. (History perhaps repeated itself in the Falklands Campaign in 1982, when television news editors, short of British campaign footage, used Argentine news film.)

Russell's reporting of the Crimean War was characterised by very critical copy. He criticised the inefficient and outdated military system, and he made public much information that was perceived to have been of aid, albeit unintentionally, to the Russians. Indeed, it is alleged that the Tsar boasted on one occasion: "We have no need of spies, we have The Times".[6] Not surprisingly, the military felt that *The Times*, with Russell's reports and Delane's editorials, wanted to see them beaten.

It was the ability to send Russell's despatches to London within days rather than weeks and months (using mail, couriers and steamships) that augmented their impact and exacerbated tensions between the military and the press. While the form of the information (written reports) was not of direct significance, the main method of transport (steamship) certainly was.[7]

What therefore were the consequences for the press of the

activities of Russell and other journalists during the Crimean War?[8] Political reaction was characterised by the former Secretary for War, Sidney Herbert, in his declaration, "I trust the Army will lynch *The Times* Correspondent".[9] Prince Albert spoke for the Palace by describing Russell as a "miserable scribbler".[10] These political broadsides provided Sir William Codrington, the new Commander-in-Chief, with the *raison d'être* for instituting some system of restraint upon the press. This was officially incorporated into a General Order issue on 25 February 1856 forbidding the publication of detail deemed of value to the enemy; it also authorised the ejection of a correspondent who it was alleged had published such details, and threatened future offenders with the same punishment.[11] This order has been cited as the origin of direct official military censorship.[12]

hile   the advent of official military censorship marked a significant watershed in the military relationship with the press, it did not necessarily improve the public's opinion and confidence in the Army. However, perhaps an early example of "public perception management" was the despatching of Roger Fenton to the Crimea. Fenton, an unsuccessful painter and founder member of the Royal Photographic Society, was sent out by the authorities to photograph the war and provide a visual counterblast to Russell's literary exposures. Fenton's photographs were antiseptic and anodyne, creating a new adage that "the camera does lie", indirectly by omission. Similarly, his activities set a precedent and tension that exist to this day – namely the dissemination and broadcasting of "official" war photographs, film and video that assist the military in dictating the story to the media and conveying their version of reality. Perspective, as well as truth, is perhaps a casualty of war.

Telegraph to newsreel: from the Crimea to the Boer War

Technologically, the latter half of the 19th century witnessed further developments in the telegraph system,[13] the advent of the telephone and of cinematography, plus refinements in stills photography, printing and modes of transport.[14] Socially, Britain was developing into the formative stages of the mass consumer society. In 1870 Forster's Elementary Education Act was passed, and in 1896 *The Daily Mail* was founded as the world's first mass-circulation newspaper. A whole new stratum of public opinion was now open to influence.

There were many wars and military events to cover. The Indian Mutiny (1857), the American Civil War (1861-65) and the Boer War (1899-1902) signpost the road from the Crimea to the end of the century. How did changes in the technologies of news-gathering and reporting affect the press–military relationship? The increasingly global nature of the telegraph network and with it the increased coverage of military conflict in general served to increase the friction between the military and the press. The press became increasingly professional and more powerful in their effect on the widening pool of public opinion.[15] The military for their part were slow to realise the potential power of this newly arisen section of public opinion:

> To the military authorities war correspondents were 'newly-invented curses to armies' and it took time for them to realize that newspapers could make valuable allies. In other words, both government and press had to learn to unite in support of the same cause if a national propaganda campaign in wartime was to be effective.[16]

The military restrictions placed on reports during the Sudan Campaign (1898) reflect this point: Kitchener limited the telegraphic facilities to 200 words a day, and there were no briefings or guidance and little courtesy. Knightley comments that the Army felt that they were being denied the glory of reporting their own victories.[17]

The Boer War, although its reporting was restricted by field censorship, did reflect a change in attitude towards the press corps in some officers. General Roberts, for example, believed in the pen as a weapon of war and had always given good relations with the press a high priority. Significantly, the British press became increasingly jingoistic in their reporting of this war. While the main method of news-reporting was still written copy and the telegraph, the Boer War also initiated the first cine-camera coverage by recently formed newsreel companies, thus laying the cornerstone of the modern military-*media* relationship.

Newsreel to television: the First World War to Vietnam

At the turn of the century the telephone was in general use in Britain, underwater telephone cables were being laid, the popular press was established, and the cinema was about to launch itself upon a wider public. Furthermore, in 1904 the Russo-Japanese War became the first conflict to be reported by radio. Would these new technologies produce significant changes in the military-media relationship?

Reporting in the First World War was restricted and censored. Consequently, despite the use of telephoned news reports,[18] increased use of newsreel and still photographs, the regulations and rules of field censorship precluded any discernible change in the relationship. Indeed, the relationship improved: the media provided "colourful stories of heroism and glory calculated to sustain enthusiasm for the war and ensure a supply of recruits for the front".[19] Indeed, in 1914 reports of casualties were not mentioned in British newspapers, because the authorities did not want to dishearten the population; similarly, propaganda[20] and atrocity stories were written up in the press.

The Second World War was characterised by a very thorough and controlled censorship system. All dispatches and reports – whether in print, telephone, radio or film form – were censored. By mid-1940, after some initial problems, the system was in place, and all news was censored at source.[21] Journalists who were attached to the Armed Forces in tightly managed pools under the supervision of a military escort officer had their reports checked. Filmed news and feature documentaries were propagandist in nature, and no filmed material could appear without Ministry of Information approval[22] or a British Board of Film Censors (BBFC) certificate. Radio war reporting, voice reports and recordings that were used in bulletins all remained within the limits of military censorship.[23] Indeed, the War Reporting Units set up in May 1943 underwent special training in military knowledge, censorship awareness and survival tactics, similar to that of the Media Response Teams set up in the Gulf War of 1991.

As with the First World War, the government controlled the transmission technologies; however, both the government and the media had the same fundamental objective – to beat Nazi Germany and the Axis powers – and had therefore a joint understanding and acknowledgement of the operating parameters involved, although, as Taylor comments, "the MOI soon learned that it was better to leave news communications to the experienced professionals and that the credibility and integrity of their coverage could only be enhanced by an outward appearance of independence".[24]

The BBC radio transmission technologies themselves improved steadily throughout the war. The BBC moved from Blatternerphones (devices which recorded magnetically onto a large reel of steel tape) to disc recording machines. Similar in design to gramophone players, these machines cut grooves in acetate-covered aluminium discs that were instantly ready for playing. Early in 1944, midget disc recorders were available, weighing only 42 pounds, thus enabling reporters more mobility and greater scope – i.e. allowing reporting directly from trenches. Vehicles were adapted to accommodate both Blatternerphones and disc recorders. Completed discs and tapes were then transported to telephones or radio transmitters, sent to London and played on the radio. These developments, combined with the advent of mobile transmitters (used "to follow the war" after D-Day) and the ability to disguise signals from fixed transmitters in order not to aid enemy aircraft,[25] provided BBC Radio with a mobile worldwide reporting ability. Thus, they were able to produce programmes that were fundamental to both military and domestic morale.[26] Indeed, Montgomery considered broadcasting as the fourth arm of warfare, seeing it as a way of communicating not only with all his soldiers, but also with their families at home.

The Korean War (1950-53) was the last major war to have formal censorship and, given the unfamiliar terrain, the media relied entirely on the Army for communication and logistic support.[27] Consequently, facilities such as telephone lines were provided when official versions of events – for example, the Inchon Landings – required expeditious distribution. The threat of denial of transmission facilities to journalists reduced attempts to bypass official channels of communication. As the war developed, particularly after the Chinese entered the war and the United Nations' front finally stabilised south of the 38th Parallel, journalists began more to question the war, and photographs appeared in *Life* magazine and other newspapers capturing the deplorable conditions. Film and radio reports began to question the very rationale of the war, and disillusionment set in. As a result, the voluntary censorship ended and full military censorship was imposed on news broadcasts – radio, television and film reports – as well as magazine articles and photographs. Restrictions on correspondents were further tightened in January 1951 – all evidence of a backlash by the military, critical of the film and copy leaving Korea. Despite the ability to send photographs "over the wire" and fly back filmed reports that would appear both in the cinema and more significantly on television – those improvements in transmission did not provoke any significant change in the military-media relationship. Censorship and the willingness of most journalists to follow the "official line" stopped any notable challenge to the conduct of the war or to its political aims. A challenge which, if taken up, would have been made all the more powerful by the advent of television and the mass audience.

Korea was the first war on television, but not the first television war[28] – that was the other Asian war, Vietnam (1960-75).[29] This was a war which, despite no military involvement, changed British military perception about the power of the media. Vietnam coverage was characterised by two factors: self-censorship and international television coverage. Television crews were allowed to go virtually anywhere and film anything. As a result, images of war, never seen before by a mass audience, began to unfold on television screens within a couple of days of the events taking place. In the competition and pressure for ratings, newscasts needed to be sharp, and crisply edited and presented; television required visually exciting material – sometimes at the expense of sacrificing the context for that material. As studio and camera technology improved, image and expression in some cases overtook content and substance. The relationship between the American military and the media began to change due to the perceived nature of press and particularly television coverage. The Army became distrustful of the media, seeing its reporting as biased, selective, unfair and untrue. General Westmorland's comments on the media reporting of the Tet Offensive in 1968 serve to illustrate the point:

> The American media had misled the American people about the Tet offensive and when they realized they had misjudged the situation – that in fact it was an American victory – they didn't have the courage or the integrity to admit it.[30]

Similar criticism was levelled against media coverage of Kay Sanh and the search-and-destroy missions in the Central Highlands.

Gradually the "stab in the back" theory began to develop, that the war had been lost in the living rooms of Chicago through biased, inaccurate reporting turning public opinion against the war: "What the media reflected in their coverage was not so much the horror of war as the mood of the country".[31] People's attitudes changed towards the war; as people became more critical and less enthusiastic, so did the reporting. Television did not turn public opinion against the war; television was a follower and not a leader in US public opinion. Indeed, a *Newsweek* survey conducted in 1967 suggested that initially television encouraged a majority of viewers to support the war – people formed their own conclusions from what they saw in news reports, and television reinforced existing views. As Nicholas Hopkinson succinctly puts it, "US public opinion turned against the Vietnam war because it was long, unsuccessful, costly in terms of human life and expenditure, and because it was hard to connect Vietnam to vital national security interests".[32]

How, therefore, did the television coverage of the Vietnam War alter the British military's perception of the media? Television was seen by some to have been responsible for the collapse of morale in Vietnam. The liberal and wide-ranging television coverage was also criticised: it was felt that it had the potential to jeopardise a democracy's ability and resolution to prosecute a war effectively. It was also felt that the whole idea of allowing cameras onto the battlefield was now open to question.[33] Certainly, the use of television in Vietnam had concentrated the military's mind and heightened the debate, not only about the potential power of the medium, but also about its control and use.

This debate achieved its first practical applications when the British Army was sent to Northern Ireland in 1969 in support of the civil power. As Schlesinger states, the BBC in its reporting of Northern Ireland has fought a continuous battle against censorship, control, regulation and intervention from outside.[34]

Television, in particular, as a medium provides the "oxygen of publicity" for all sides in the dispute. All sides are aware of the immediacy of television, the live link and the effect of instant feedback for soldier, politician and terrorist alike. The BBC and ITV especially have found this power problematic, for, as Schlesinger says, "[to] report on matters adverse to the army is particularly difficult for the broadcast media given their relationship to the state".[35] Throughout the conflict, the military-media relationship had fluctuated between criticism and praise for coverage – with some sections of the media receiving more criticism than others, particularly in the field of investigative journalism (*Death on the Rock*), current affairs (*A Question of Ulster*) and interviews with terrorists (BBC's *Panorama* and *Newsnight*). However, again to quote Schlesinger, "any ideology of mass communication stressing the transmission of wide and versatile spectrum of information when honestly applied is bound to be partial in favour of suppressed interests in society".[36]

Satellite dishes and newsroom automation: from the Falklands to the Gulf

The Falklands War (1982) was conducted in the age of satellites and transmission dishes, but was not itself a "dish" war. The Ministry of Defence (MoD), ever mindful of the perceived power of television, wanted total obedience from the press, as if it were total war.[37] Access to the war zone was controlled; no reporters other than British ones were allowed to accompany the Task Force; and the seventeen eventually accredited correspondents worked in a pool system and had to sign a declaration accepting specific reporting rules and restrictions. The broadcasters were unable to use satellite technology; consequently, it took up to twenty days for film and video material to reach Britain. This lack of television coverage was very contentious. In the aftermath of the campaign, much criticism was directed at the military for their lack of cooperation – indeed, Knightley maintains that the MoD controlled the media through censorship, suppression and delay.[38] However, later studies reveal a wholly more complex situation.[39] The broadcasters were dependent on military satellites and terminals because they were technically unable to use commercial satellites from ships, and there were no ground stations or terminals designed for transmission. It was technically possible to use military satellites for television transmission; however, to adapt these satellites for television pictures would have meant that they could not be used for anything else, including military traffic. Written despatches were transmitted through commercial and military channels, voice reports through commercial channels. In the later stages of the war, still photographs were transmitted by wire machines on commercial links; access to these channels was controlled by the military.

The media accepted that some form of control was inevitable and during the conflict itself were very supportive: very few newspapers or television programmes at the time expressed the slightest reservation or dissent about Britain's actions. It was only in retrospect after victory that media criticism was levelled at the MoD for its control of the information war and its less than cooperative attitude towards the provision of communication facilities.[40] However, if the facts about general communication difficulties had been explained at the time, this might have prevented some of the subsequent rancour.

During the 1980s, with the improvements in satellites and portable transmission dishes, the rise of international communication corporations, and the development of global television news, satellite telephones and newsroom automation, it was becoming obvious that traditional control of the media through censorship and restriction was becoming increasingly untenable, both politically and technically. By the end of the decade, the British military had concluded that control over the media would have to be institutional (letters of accreditation, pooling arrangements, and so on) and based on cooperation.[41]

What therefore were the implications of these new technologies for the military-media relationship? Given that it is now politically inappropriate to censor and that portable transmission dishes and satellite telephones are difficult to control militarily,[42] operating agreements and codes of conduct have to be negotiated. Similarly, the time factor, whether the pressure of a real-time television report or the twenty minutes from editing to newsroom via satellite, negates "third party" control. The equipment itself determines where reporters go, what they do and how they do it. The reportage has changed together with the technology; live television's sheer speed erodes the capacity to reflect, interpret, sift and edit information. The imperative is to get the story on air and, as a result, it can produce a careless type of journalism. Live television tends to confuse rather than enlighten, and journalists ignorant of military matters are under pressure to give instant analysis.[43] There can be a propensity for trivialisation and "infotainment". Real-time television empowers the media in a new way: it has been alleged that it forces governments to "catch-up" and respond to events – a concept known as "tele-diplomacy".[44]

Not unnaturally, this creates a tension with the military, who are aware of the media's power and what it can do for them, and yet in specific circumstances would prefer a considered coverage with more context, reflection and perspective. Image and information on television is now part of war, and it is an organisational imperative that the military convey their version of the war. This is an objective complicated not only by the new technologies, but also by the growing power of international corporations such as CNN, Reuters and Associated Press, who do not necessarily reflect a British "national interest", unlike the state-sponsored BBC.[45]

Newsroom automation and associated technology trends similarly have implications for the military-media relationship. Newsroom computers now provide the journalist with quicker access to sources; they can see copy coming in constantly and can therefore respond more quickly to breaking stories, thus producing shorter lead times and later deadlines. With satellite communications it is possible to be on-line to the studio and view studio computers. Tape formats are now smaller, lighter, faster and more efficient. With mobile/portable terrestrial links, 85% of the world can now be covered by satellite.

The transition from analogue to digital tape means that images can be stored as data. The ability to compress digital video negates the need for vast storage capacity. It is now possible to compress the wavelength of a video signal, transmit it, and then widen the band at point of delivery. This video data can be sent down a modern telephone line. Fibre optic cables will enable an almost limitless supply of data to be sent.

Technology will make archiving more comprehensive and quicker. Digital video and computers will make "rolling news" (24-hour news) and recycling much easier, thus enabling menus to be available to the viewer who can browse, interact and select his/her own items. The globalisation of television and the new distribution networks, such as Visnews, CNN and the European News Exchange, plus the various cable systems and providers, mean that images can move around the world very quickly.

The implications of these newsroom technologies are profound. Digitised video editing is cheap, more material is available, and costs can be reduced. As a consequence, more communication companies will be formed with potential for less control, particularly in times of crisis. More consumer choice and less consumer-passive news – with the distinct prospect of news on demand, interactive news and viewer selectivity – will pose challenges. Control, attracting viewers, retaining their attention, news-management, reaction and response to stories and coveying your point of view will all become more daunting for the military. Yet, almost in the sense of a double bind, the globalisation of television means the medium will assume a more significant role in the construction of world opinion.

Many of the technological trends outlined here, while still on the horizon, are a technical probability.[46] How did the military deal with the satellite and transmission technologies that now exist? The Gulf War of 1991 provides a valuable perspective. As already discussed, in military circles understanding the media and its role is essential for any commander, since image and information on television are now part of war. As Major-General Patrick Cordingley said, "very soon media was not third on my list of priorities but first on the agenda of the daily conference".[47] How, therefore, were the media accommodated?

Journalists and broadcasters were invited to join the British Army pools known as MRTs (Media Response Teams). The media who joined were deliberately socialised and made part of the military organisation – they exchanged independence for information. In return, they had to sign a declaration that they were subject to military discipline, and they were given specific reporting rules and restrictions. The ethos was one of cooperation and common sense; the ultimate deterrent as with all journalists – pool or independents – was the loss of letters of accreditation and the subsequent expulsion from Kuwait. In return, the Army provided good filming opportunities and copy, plus transmission facilities so that the pool material would be in London within the hour. Once the land war started, Forward Transmission Units (FTUs) were set up with Army permission and assistance to enable journalists to "follow" the war. It was in this way that the military and media arrived at mutual accommodation. The journalists obtained access to the battlefield and the military were able to provide the copy that they wanted in order to fulfil their own media aims of maintaining morale and public support for the war. Naturally, the media, never a collective entity, were not all supportive of the pool system. Non-pool members were cynical about their colleagues integrating and identifying with the military, and saw the pool system as a public relations service for the Allies. However, of all the major networks, only ABC rejected the pool system. From a military point of view, the pool worked well, but their critics alleged that the media were, in fact, crippled and rendered unable to provide the public with a credible picture of what the war was actually like, and that the pool was used not to facilitate news coverage, but to control it.[48]

The use of video material in military press briefings was for many a new departure.[49] In his briefings from the ballroom of the hotel in Riyadh, General Schwarzkopf played edited videotapes (available to the press) showing the effects of precision-guided weapons on various targets. In retrospect, many journalists felt that they were led a merry dance, and that the use of the tapes allowed the military to dictate the story to the media:

> The medium's pathological need for moving pictures delivered it into the hands of those who controlled access. Lack of knowledge about the air-land battle forced reliance on military briefings. The US military knew what they were doing when they produced irresistible footage of a Laser Guided Bomb going down a ventilation shaft. What got lost was a kind of scepticism that serious journalism demands

– no-one asked if this footage was statistically representative of the aerial assault.[50]

The British also produced footage of their own aerial assaults. This carefully selected footage worked – most journalists accepted it – but will it work in the future? Many journalists and media commentators have expressed doubts.

The Gulf War illustrated from a British point of view that the military had come of age in a media sense, with the absence of source censorship. They made adequate provision for "pool" journalists; they provided necessary assistance in the establishment of transmission facilities; good "copy" and information were made available; and officers and soldiers alike were proactive and media-aware, *and encouraged to develop a trusting and good relationship*. However, this organisational awareness did in no way consummate the military-media relationship. The critical presence of the "independents" and the post-Gulf scepticism regarding media management have ensured that creative tensions remain.

Towards the Information War: speculation about the Internet

The Internet is essentially a marriage between the computer and telephone, with a modem acting as a go-between. This means that one can access other computers and databases which have subscribed to the Internet. This network of networks is also known as the Information (Super-)Highway. The Internet therefore facilitates the global exchange of massive amounts of information – virtually free and unregulated (at the time of writing).[51] The Internet can offer a variety of functions, including electronic mail and mailing lists that enable one to join in group discussion and exchange information, and mail servers, which allow one to retrieve database information mainly from Bulletin Board Networks and their commercial equivalent, Content Providers. Of the Bulletin Board systems, Usenet is one of the most popular. Every Usenet site ships a copy of messages it has received to all its neighbours several times a day. Every day, 30 000 messages appear at a typical well-connected news machine. These messages are assigned to news groups or topic headings, and these topic headings are arranged into hierarchies. The news hierarchies range from world affairs to specialised areas such as science and the military.

The Internet can now be considered as part of the media.[52] What challenges does it pose to the military-media relationship? No one can really say where the highway will take us; it is still being built, but we can indulge ourselves with some provisional remarks and speculative questions. Certainly, the military should become aware of the potential – both good and bad – of the Net.

Censorship will be virtually impossible,[53] and there will be wide freedom to publish information. Access to news bulletins, alternative new sources and databases will therefore confront the military with a decision as to how to react to critical bulletins and information reports. They will have to make value judgments about the power and potential influence of the Net. To what extent will public perception of the military and its policies be shaped by the Internet?[54] Certainly interactivity and debate will ensure multiple sources of information and opinion with a constant infusion of new ideas – but how will this affect public opinion? To what extent will the traditional print media change? Will it adapt to this new world, or will it shrink and become more specialised and focused? What implications might this have for the military? Similarly, will broadcast media become marginalised in terms of conventional newscasts? Will they change to being providers of live, major-event coverage and in-depth special reports? Again, how will the military adapt to this?

The Internet itself may become part of the battleground – already Bosnians and Serbs exchange and debate over the Net. In Mexico the Zapatista rebels word-process press statements and situation reports, and send them to sympathisers on the Net, who disseminate the reports on the Net and fax foreign embassies and public figures. Information will become a very powerful weapon. Perhaps in the future, to amend Mao's dictum, political power will come out of a floppy disc. In the past, territory and resources have been fought over – will the Net imply the partial eradication of national boundaries and roles, or will control of information now become another means to enhance a state's power? And, as a consequence, will the nature of military power itself change, and with it the whole rationale of the military-media relationship?

Conclusion

As we have seen over the last 150 years, and particularly in the latter part of the 20th century, communication technology has been riding ahead, and in its wake producing changes in the way in which the military and the media have interacted. Censorship always limited the impact of technology; however, satellite technology and automation proved to be the *deus ex machina*, and, with the genie out of its bottle, a relationship quickly developed based on mutual cooperation and understanding. The Information Age of the 21st century may produce the most profound changes yet, affecting the very nature and form of military and media organisations. However, one fundamental tension may remain – the conflict between the public's right to know and the right of a soldier to survive through the secrecy of the operation.[55]

[1] Speech in the House of Commons, 30 September 1941. Quoted in Charles Eade, *The War Speeches of the Right Honourable Winston S Churchill*, volume 2 (London, 1952): 89-90.

[2] The term "media" is here used to include press, radio, television, cable, satellite and computer/telephone-based broadcasting systems. Until the advent of cinematography, we will refer to the "press-military relationship".

[3] Between 1840 and 1852 the circulation of *The Times* increased from 10 000 to 40 000.

[4] Phillip Knightley, *The First Casualty. From the Crimea to Vietnam: The War Correspondent as Hero, Propagandist, and Myth Maker* (London: Pan Books, 1975): 4.

[5] Ibid.

[6] Geoffrey Regan, *The Guinness Book of Military Blunders* (Enfield: Guinness, 1991): 171.

[7] It is salutary to note that the first successful telegraph cable from Dover to Calais was laid in 1851.

[8] Russell was not the only journalist dismissive of the British in the Crimea. Edwin Godkin (*London Daily News*) and Thomas Chenery (*The Times*) were equally critical: Chenery provided graphic descriptions of the conditions at Scutari.

[9] Knightley: 15.

[10] Ibid.

[11] UK Public Records Office WO 28/131, quoted in Knightley: 16.

[12] The precursor to this direct bureaucratic control had been army commanders refusing to allow civilian reporters near the battlefield. To overcome this hurdle, reporters resorted to a variety of deceptions and disguises. Similarly, one would suspect, to the tricks and stratagems used by non-pool journalists to enter the battle area during the Gulf War (1991).

[13] In 1866, a regular cable service was established between Britain and North America.

[14] In 1884, Parsons's first steam turbine was developed.

[15] The requirement to use a telegraph key and Morse code produced a crisper approach to journalism, anticipating and

answering questions efficiently.

[16]   Philip M Taylor, *Munitions of the Mind: War propaganda from the ancient world to the nuclear age* (London: Patrick Stephens, 1990): 157.

[17]   Knightley: 54.

[18]   Britain controlled the cable links between both Europe and the United States.

[19]   Knightley: 97.

[20]   Propaganda became increasingly sophisticated, due mainly to improvements in photographs and print development.

[21]   The cable system to the Press Association and Reuters, which supplied domestic and international news respectively, was intercepted (both cables passing conveniently through the headquarters of the Press Association), and therefore most news was pre-censored before it actually reached the press. See Taylor: 192.

[22]   Celluloid which was classified as a vital war material was controlled by the Board of Trade. Therefore, no film could be physically made without government approval. Priority was given to the five newsreel companies: Pathé, Universal, Gaumont-British, British Movietone and Paramount. See Taylor: 196.

[23]   In 1939, Richard Dimbleby and David Howarth provided the first "on-the-spot" reports from France using "an ordinary car with recording gear on the back seat". See Philip Schlesinger, *Putting 'reality' together* (London: Routledge, 1992): 22.

[24]   Taylor: 199.

[25]   For further technical details, see Tom Hickman, *What did you do in the War, Auntie?* (London: BBC Books, 1995): 141-142, 146-196.

[26]   Eye witness reports, battle descriptions and sounds, soldiers talking and news talks were all available and incorporated into programmes such as "Combat Diary", "War Report" and "Radio News Reel". For examples of "War Report", see Hickman: 180-196.

[27]   Initially, there was no censorship, only a voluntary code which was unclear and unsatisfactory. See Knightley: 337.

[28]   At the time of the Korean War there were ten million television sets in the United States; at the peak of the Vietnam War it was approximately 65 million. Melvin L DeFleur and Everette E Dennis, *Understanding Mass Communication: A Liberal Arts Perspective* (Boston: Houghton Mifflin, 1994): 220.

29   It was from television that approximately 90% of the American population obtained its news. Quoted in ibid: 220.

30   Quoted in Taylor: 226.

31   Nicholas Hopkinson, "War and the Media", *Wilton Park Paper* 55 (London: HMSO, 1992): 6-7.

32   Ibid: 7.

33   All views expressed at the Royal United Services Institute seminar in London, 13 October 1970 and quoted in Knightley: 411.

34   Schlesinger: 205-243.

35   Ibid: 223.

36   Quoted in ibid: 245.

37   A point made by Stephen Badsey in a lecture to Staff College, Camberley, April 1994.

38   Knightley: 436.

39   For a very detailed explanation of the situation as regards satellite transmission, see Derrik Mercer, Geoff Mungham and Kevin Williams, *The Fog of War: The Media on the Battlefield* (London: Heinemann, 1987). Mercer's "The Falklands War" (145-156) provides a full understanding of the communication difficulties faced by the military and their effect on the media.

40   It was also felt that a lack of foreign reporters, as well as of television coverage, handicapped British credibility overseas.

41   A point made by Stephen Badsey in "The Media War", in John Pimlott and Stephen Badsey (eds), *The Gulf War Assessed* (London: Arms and Armour Press, 1992): 229.

42   No longer is it necessary to get the story back to a "feeding point", a capital city or a telephone that works, where access could be controlled by the military; similarly, transmission jamming or shooting down satellites is a wholly inappropriate option for a mature democracy.

43   Points eloquently made by Jason Murdoch, *The Gulf War*, MA dissertation (Canberra: Australian National University, 1994): 251.

44   The reports on the Amiriyah bomb shelter and the Basra highway "massacre" may have influenced Bush to stop the coalition's advance into Iraq.

[45]   Indeed, CNN reported from both sides during the Gulf War – it had Peter Arnett with a portable satellite transmitter in Baghdad. Similarly, it is alleged that Clinton's decision to withdraw the United States from Operation Restore Hope (Somalia) was based on CNN film of a dead American helicopter pilot being dragged around Mogadishu. The graphic footage of Kurdish families fleeing Saddam Hussein in early 1992 may have forced both Britain and the United States to help create enclaves for the refugees.

[46]   I am indebted to Adrian Scott, Broadcast Market Manager, Avid Technology, for his observations and information, based on a lecture he delivered on the impact of new technology on television news at the Wilton Park Conference, November 1994.

[47]   As a Brigadier, Patrick Cordingley was a Brigade Commander during the Gulf War. Brigadier [now Major-General] Patrick Cordingley DSO, "Future Commanders – be warned!", *Despatches* 3 (1992): 16.

[48]   Murdoch: 249.

[49]   However, the British Army had been making videotapes available as news releases in Northern Ireland.

[50]   Murdoch: 253.

[51]   The origins of the Internet are military: it started as ARPANET (Advanced Research Projects Administration), a project started by the US Department of Defense in 1969, both as an experiment in reliable networking and to link the Department with military research contractors.

[52]   While the traditional media were fairly late converts to the Internet, media organisations, ranging from television to newspapers, are now logging on to communicate interactively with each other or their sources.

[53]   Regulation and control will probably mainly be directed on pornography.

[54]   The British Army is planning to issue an abbreviated form of its core public presentation on the World Wide Web. Pages of text, graphics, audio and video clips about the Army will be interlinked throughout the world on the Internet.

[55]   A point made by Kate Adie in a lecture to the RMA Sandhurst, November 1994.

The meanings of war-toys and war-games
Jonathan Bignell

This essay is written from the perspective of cultural studies, the branch of the academic study of social life which, as one of its main currents, has focused on the ideological meanings of everyday objects and practices.[1] The theory of ideology, classically outlined by Louis Althusser and subsequently refined, argues that the individual human subject takes up a place marked out for him/her within a world of meanings constructed by the institutions and practices of culture.[2] Language offers the position of "I" from which to speak and conceptualise oneself as a unique and coherent identity. Institutions such as the toy industry, the school, the family and the media reproduce representations of the world in which the individual subject recognises himself/herself as masculine, feminine, child, adult, and so on. These social structures are ideological in that they are not natural, eternal or accidental, but instead cultural, contingent and suited to the continuance of the economic and political form of the society in which they exist. Some of the cultural meanings of war-toys which can be analysed from this perspective include their role in the construction of masculine identity, their representation of particular wars and warlikeness in general, and their relationship to consumer society.

But that which counts as a war-toy or a war-game for this analysis is less easy to define than it might at first appear. There are toy guns, toy soldiers, military vehicles, aeroplanes, forts, and so on, together with the games that can be played with them. But only some of these toys are representations of existing war equipment or armies, either in the past or in the present. There are war-toys based on television fiction or cinema narratives, for example, such as the range of toys related to the science-fiction film, *Stargate*. Although the film and the toys which spin off from it are set in a fictional futuristic scenario, the weapons, uniforms, vehicles and rank structure of the human characters are recognisably taken from the contemporary American military. The film and the toys are based upon a military conflict between the familiar (contemporary characters, equipment and behaviour) and the unfamiliar (alien races, equipment and behaviour).

The *Stargate* film and the range of toys establish a fictional world whose value-system is consonant with contemporary ideology. The "good" characters in the *Stargate* world include a mild-mannered archaeologist, trustworthy American soldiers, and a woman who is rescued from the aliens by the enamoured archaeologist through the competent use of war technology. The "evil" characters include an ambiguously gendered and perverse alien dictator, his brutal henchmen, and a traitorous human military commander who is redeemed by his relationship with a child. Despite the science-fiction trappings of the film and the toys, they set their war scenario firmly within a moral structure which values loyalty, altruism, competence, heterosexual romance and family values. One argument of this essay is that war-toys, whether "realistic" or "unrealistic", are always enfolded in meanings which support a dominant ideology, although this ideology may itself contain contradictory values.

I am discussing toys which are representations of actual war equipment and also toys which are presented, by name or by images on their packaging, as representations of fictional war equipment. Therefore, ACTION MAN and his miniature "realistic" weaponry are war-toys, as are the *Mighty Morphin' Power Rangers*, whose warlike equipment is used in fictional futuristic battles with alien supervillains. Similarly, the war-games discussed here are those based on actual wars, like war-games replaying elements of Second World War conflicts, as well as games which are warlike but based on fictional narratives, such as *Spectre Supreme*, a computer game based on tank battle, which, however, is set in a fictional futuristic environment.

In terms of the representation of war, these "realistic" and fictional war-game scenarios share a number of characteristics. They have a delimited field of play, whether it is the Normandy countryside for a Second World War game, or Cybernet (a simulated three-dimensional landscape) in *Spectre Supreme*. In both cases, a fundamental knowability of the scenario is offered by the games: the player has a "bird's-eye view" of the action which allows control of the play and strategic planning. In war-games played with model vehicles and/or figures, and in computer games, there are elaborate rules which define possible actions. These rules specify the characteristics of the combatants' equipment (speed, strength of armour, ammunition available, and so on) in quantitative terms, and determine how success or failure in the game is evaluated. War in the context of these games is a rule-governed and rational activity, in which chance, politics and morality play a minor role, and this corresponds to one of the major conceptualisations of actual war in contemporary culture (although it is not necessarily "true"). As actual modern war is mythically believed to be, war-games are about the calculated management of risk and the competent deployment of technological resources. Despite their differences in terms of the medium of play, "realism", or historical basis, war-games implicitly value particular attributes in the player. These include the ability to plan strategically, to balance risk against benefit, to quantify potentials, to follow detailed and often bureaucratic procedures, and to attain victory by effective management of resources. War-games share in the contemporary ideological representation of militariness (in recruitment advertising, for example) as professionalised and technological.

In their research on children's and adults' games, John Roberts, Robert Kozelka and Brian Sutton-Smith have suggested that games of strategy and combat such as these are prevalent in societies such as those in Europe and the United States (and not in agrarian or non-consumer societies), because these societies train children in obedience and independence in the context of a highly stratified and complex competitive culture.[3] The demands for the child's obedience to elaborate rules and social conventions are pressing, and the frustration experienced as a result of this is expressed in unreal combat. War-games mirror the ideology of Western culture in their elaborate organisation, their complex rules and their quantitative and evaluative character. The notion of the play-space as a microcosmic world supports this notion of a parallel but alternate reality. However, because the game is bound by knowable rules, delimited in real time and space, and provides a system for defining and attaining success, it is both comprehensible and satisfying where the world beyond the game may not be.

The second feature of societies such as ours which Roberts, Kozelka and Sutton-Smith relate to game-playing is games' emphasis on personal achievement and success, which are highly valued in contemporary culture. The result of this, they suggest, is that children's games emphasise physical skill. Computer-based war-games very commonly demand physical skill from the player, and the games provide a figure representing the player whose task is to win by using physical skill. Insufficient skill results in the "death" of the player's representative in the game, and repeated "deaths" will end the game, whereas the ability to remain "alive" will reward the player with further games, more complex levels of play, and points or some other reward. One of the most popular games for the Sega Mastersystem games computer is *Desert Strike*, based on the Gulf War and involving a helicopter mission plotline. The package text invites the player:

Pilot your A64 Apache helicopter through 27 in depth missions. Destroy Scuds, tanks, nuclear reactors, and rescue vital personnel in this all action test of speed and skill.

The reference to the Gulf War functions here only as a setting, rather than as the realised historical representation found in some more elaborate figure and rule-book war-games. The mention of "Apache" and "Scuds" triggers mythic knowledge about the scenario, as do the game's visuals, which are similar to flight-simulator images or televised footage of actual missions. But the appeal of the game is located much more in the customary combination of a task, a narrative structure, technical competence in playing the game, physical dexterity and reward for success.

Research by Thomas Malone on computer games played by American schoolchildren has shown that the presence of moving visual imagery and of a goal was the most important factor in computer games' popularity among a group of children aged 5-13.[4] Other features which children rated highly were the presence of audio effects, automatic score-keeping, randomness in the operation of the game, and the importance of speed in the game. These features all appear in *Desert Strike*. Video games have tended to challenge watching television as the dominant activity for children because they are interactive rather than passive. As in the case of war-toys, computer combat games "do something" and encourage the child to play actively, but their war scenarios support the positive valuation of particular individual attributes (such as rational planning) and particular attributes of war (such as its excitingness and heroism).

From an ideological viewpoint, computer games depend on an interaction with a pre-existing scenario generated by their programming, and therefore repeat the double-bind of ideology in general. The player, like the individual subject of ideology, is the hero of the scenario, a positively presented unique individual, and yet anyone can occupy this role. Success in the game depends on the virtues of physical dexterity, competence within the rules, and correct internalisation of the moral framework of the game (you must not shoot down your own comrades, for example). This values individual performance, effectiveness and conformity with the pre-existing moral framework. As in society in general, freedom and choice exist within an apparatus which precedes the individual and determines the range of possible actions. Freedom of action, as in *Desert Strike*, means only the freedom to live or die by preordained rules which are beyond the individual's control. As Althusser argued about ideology in general, the ideology of *Desert Strike* positions the individual as a freely acting subject, but imposes on him/her the definitions of reality and subjectivity which ideology proposes.

By increasing their consumer's familiarity with computer technology, computer war-games, unlike traditional war-gaming with figures and models, are in themselves part of the technologization of leisure in contemporary culture. Like television, video and computer games reduce the amount of prosocial play in the children using them, and there is some evidence that aggressive or violent single-player games (not only

168

games where violence is the content or scenario) increase the propensity for aggression in their players.[5] Nevertheless, there are some multi-player war-based computer games, and whatever their aggressive or violent content, these have been found to reduce aggression in the players, and of course they involve social interaction in the play itself. This issue of aggressivity can be further investigated in relation to the gendering of war-toys and war-games.

Masculinity in war-toys and war-games

One of the key cultural meanings of war-toys and war-games is in their relationship to gender roles. Researchers have found that boys are much more likely to play war-based games involving shooting, capturing and chasing than girls, but have been unable to decide whether toy or game preferences arise from inborn gender characteristics or are determined by social convention.[6] This dilemma is, in any case, a false one, since it is in principle impossible to isolate play practices from their social context. War-toys are presented as products with a gendered consumer already encoded by their package images, text, colour system and placing in toy shops. War-toys are used by children in the context of their role in the family, which is a gendered role, and in the context of their social relations with other children and with adults, which are also structured by gender. Assumptions about gender have a very important role, since parents discourage boys from playing with dolls (unless they are ACTION MAN or toy soldiers), and discourage girls from aggressive play (although girls do mutilate and dismember dolls). War-toys are advertised by using gendered images, and their physical forms and themes are complexly related to a range of media representations of war (in films, television, comics, and so on), which have their own gender-coding.

Warlike play legitimates masculine roles for boys, and is used as a way of marking their difference from girls. The theorist of children's games, Brian Sutton-Smith, remarks that games are

> models of power, by which we mean that they are buffered learning situations through which the child gains acquaintance and experience at the power stratagems relevant to some of the major parameters of influence within his own culture.[7]

Play in this context is an anticipation and modelling of social life in the adult world, or, as Sutton-Smith states, "a form of war which can only occur between those who are at peace".[8] War-toys such as guns and swords support the construction of masculinity as active, while the toys sold specifically for girls restrict activity to collecting, nurturing or crafting, for example, reflecting the division of powers inside or outside the home for adult men and women. Some interesting information can be found by investigating the available range of war-toys and games in the toy superstores which now exist in most British towns. How the toys are presented and where they are found in the shop can tell us much about how manufacturers and retailers imagine toys and games will be used, and by whom. Boys' toys for active play, like toy guns, can be used in the world outside the home, while the packages of girls' toys show them being played within a domestic space.

The toy gun section of my local toy superstore contains about twenty different types of rifle, pistol, revolver and machine-gun. They differ widely in their level of "realistic" accuracy and in their relationship to the actual size of real guns or adult-sized fictional weapons. Significantly, all the guns do something – either firing caps, making an electronically generated noise, shooting water or plastic balls, or changing to alternate configurations. They are designed for active play, probably in a space outside the home.[9] In reality, not only do war activities take place in the outside (command and control functions, for example, may not), but also this fact is not reflected in the nature of the toys, which are vehicles and weapons used in the field. War-toys enable boys to be active, to colonise the extra-domestic space. War-toys and games shape masculine roles for boys, but masculinity itself is a diffuse social construct which already exists and is activated by war-toys and games in particular ways which remain consonant with its general features. War-toys exist for children, parents and other adults, and for the toy industry, in the social context of binary divisions between masculine and feminine roles, products, spheres of influence and activities.

Toy guns present the technology of violence, and the power which violence represents, as attributes belonging to masculine proficiency. This is the same ideological meaning that guns have in adult culture.[10] One of the uses of toy guns is to confer imaginary status, power and proficiency because of their imitative visual and tactile relationship with real guns, and because of the fact that toy guns resemble real guns in terms of functionality: they fire something. Toy guns provide supporting props for chasing, running, scrambling and other physical activities because these can be included as part of a war-play scenario, and the association of war, physical prowess and aggressivity with masculine identity is thereby confirmed. The fact that toy guns do something shows not only that they are valued as representations of guns *per se*, but also that they allow certain types of game to be played. The firing noises of caps or sound effects mark the act of shooting, the central activity in war-play, and the toy's noises supply sounds which children would otherwise make for themselves. Shooting noises are evidence of the fact that "I shot you", as well as increasing tension and excitement by providing a "realistic" soundtrack to war-games. Guns that fire something are useful for war-play since it becomes even more evident that "I shot you" because "my" water, ball or whatever actually hit "you". Toy guns not only carry cultural meanings as objects, but also have a number of specific functions which enable or enrich physical activeness in the context of masculine aggressivity.

War-toys intensify aggressive play, provide scenarios and roles which give aggressive play a structure, and provide attractive narrative roles to boys. Because the toy is an enabling device for the expression of masculine characteristics, rather than a cause of these characteristics, discrimination against war-toys as a way of altering the forms of masculinity taken up by boys faces a number of problems. If toy weapons such as *Power Ranger* guns and swords were banned from the school playground because they seem to intensify aggressive play among boys, it would also be necessary to prohibit children from making gun finger-shapes and gestures because of their role in make-believe war-play. But the problem of gun gestures demonstrates that war-toys themselves are simply products which concretize and facilitate existing play aims deriving from the social construction of gender roles in the media, the family or other social institutions. The toy gun and the gun finger-shape are both physical representations which function as signs supporting the enactment of a masculine role. War-play for boys fulfils the function of enacting their developing masculinity and choosing to play war is also a choice not to play some other, less masculine game. War-games both express masculinity and ward off the expression of non-masculine roles:

> Masculinity or the male identity is achieved by the constant process of warding off threats to it. It is precariously achieved by the rejection of femininity and of homosexuality. Male violence against women, and the taboo against male homosexuality may both be understood as effects of this fragile sense of identity, rooted both in the psychic traumas of childhood (in which boys must break their identification with women in order to become 'men') and in the historical norms which have defined male identity as counterposed to the moral chaos of homosexuality.[11]

As psychoanalytic practitioners have discovered, gender characteristics are progressively acquired through socialisation, of which war-play is a part.[12] But, while gender roles are fluid and changing throughout life, they only become adopted as differential masculine or feminine identities when the child is able to symbolise himself/herself in language, by speaking, and to use

171

objects symbolically to represent something. Toy guns, whether "realistic" or not, are used symbolically by children: they represent real guns. The games played with toy guns are also symbolic representations of the activities associated with real or fictional wars. By using toy guns and playing war-games, boys play masculine roles and distance themselves from feminine roles. The association of war with a masculine gender role, perceived by adults and children and evaluated as either proper or improper for boys or girls, is part of the gendering of the child. In a society in which war-play is proper for boys but not for girls, war-play itself is one of the arenas in which the child is subjected (made into a masculine or feminine subject, and made subject to this identity), according to prevailing ideologies of gender.

Toys and games often involve the use of positive and negative characterisations: heroes and villains, us and them. Ideologically, these figures function as representations of insiders and outsiders as the child learns to identify himself/herself with a gendered, national, cultural or subcultural identity. Identification with another person is a key aspect of the process of taking on a sense of self, the development of subjectivity which has been described by psychoanalytic theory.[13] The positively valued person with whom the individual identifies is the "ego-ideal", representing the self which the individual subject would like to become. But identification never stops with the subject's alignment with a positive role. The figure of the other, the outsider, the enemy, represents the otherness that is within the subject: the repudiated part of the self or the aspects of his/her personality which cannot be accepted without guilt and shame. Identification shifts around in children's play scenarios from identification with the one representing the desired self to identification with the other who represents some other, negative aspect of the self. Play offers an arena for negotiating between these versions of the child's identity. Games also teach discrimination between right and wrong, in others and in the child, promoting the development of the superego, the mental agency that watches critically over the ego's demands and judges it. Games allow the player a certain autonomy of action and the sanctioning of experiments in positive or negative behaviour, but are safely bound in time and space and by rules. The ACTION MAN range of war-toys illustrates the function of the ego-ideal and identification in a war-toy context.

ACTION MAN and other 12" toy figures sharing his war-toy theme occupy nearly an entire aisle in my local toy superstore. Either ACTION MAN is sold as a boxed figure with accessories, under a specific title, or his accessories only are sold under the same title as the with-figure version. He has articulated limbs, posed and flexible hands for holding accessories, short-cropped, dark hair, a pale but rather stubbly face, and a determined, gritted-teeth expression. His opponent, DR X, is also available, dressed in a fantastical blue and white outfit, with a battery-operated "laser eye" and "computer brain" exposed on the side of his head. DR X has a spiky Mohican haircut, a savage expression and a pasty, white skin. The iconography of ACTION MAN (his expression, clothing, equipment and even his name) shows him to be an ego-ideal in the context of the representation of war and its masculine ideological characteristics. DR X, in terms of his contrasting physical attributes, is evidently an "other", a negatively represented alien figure, although also exhibiting masculine characteristics.

While ACTION MAN is a war-toy in the most obvious sense, modelled on a stereotypical soldier hero familiar from traditional war comics or animated television fiction, DR X is more like the supervillain or evil android of science-fiction fantasy. It would seem that although the positive role-model offered by ACTION MAN can draw on a long history of fictional war heroes, his opponent has to be drawn from mythical fantasy narratives because of the contingency of real wartime enemies and the need to make him fittingly alien, fearful and powerful. These two opposed versions of masculine identity mark the extremes to which identification might go in make-believe war-play scenarios, where ideologically approved masculine roles are focused on ACTION MAN himself, and all that is alien, other and devalued in masculine heterosexuality is located in DR X. These war-toy figures provide an arena for the boy to dramatise and explore his gendered identity while loading the drama with already constructed social values.

The majority of ACTION MAN's incarnations are as a soldier with uniforms and weapons based on actual NATO equipment. In the "Basic Training" pack he sports a red T-shirt, backpack and rifle; in "Battle Force" he is an infantryman; in "Rapid Fire" a more heavily armed assault trooper; and in "Special Forces" an SAS-style commando with a rope to slide along. Each figure package displays an illustration of ACTION MAN in the relevant uniform engaged in combat, in the visual style of war comic images, and the reverse of the pack includes a "Mission Profile" detailing a scenario in which he is charged with an adventurous solo mission against all the odds. These missions include rescuing a top scientist held hostage by DR X, and defeating DR X's plan to sabotage a vital installation. In a contemporary variation on this theme, *Operation Tiger* offers ACTION MAN in jungle camouflage and tiger tattoos, on a mission to stop DR X from poisoning the rain forest. Clearly, ACTION MAN's appeal rests on his triggering of war adventure narratives in a range of media, including films, television and comics, for example, and on the positive attributes of masculine military heroism which these supply.

ACTION MAN is a toy which has been designed to appeal to

173

children in a variety of ways. As his name suggests, he is constructed in a manner which allows his body to be posed statically or in motion in action-play scenarios (shooting, climbing, fighting, and so on). The package's "Mission Profile" suggests a range of warlike scenarios that can be elaborated on by the child, who might supply speech, sounds and settings for ACTION MAN to perform a wide range of roles as the hero of a make-believe fantasy. As a highly competent and well-equipped soldier, ACTION MAN offers a masculine ego-ideal, which is given form by his facial expression, bodily development and the images and text on the packaging. He is a figure of identification for the child, a superhero like James Bond, but he is also linked through the realism of his equipment to warlike narratives based on real events. Ideologically, this masculine image is part of a mythology of military heroism and a simple version of recent military history in which NATO forces are the positively presented "good guys". Furthermore, the collectability of the themed figures and accessories encourages further buying of the product range and a desire for the complete ACTION MAN world of products. In this sense, ACTION MAN is very similar to the themed figures and accessories of the BARBIE doll or SINDY doll world. But the crucial difference between the boys' toy, such as ACTION MAN, and the girls' toy, such as SINDY, is that the former is equipped mainly for active and goal-directed individual action, whereas the latter is a passive figure equipped largely for dressing, haircare and domestic leisure. The boys' doll and the girls' doll represent a simplified version of the binary division in ideology between masculinity and femininity. The success of ACTION MAN, his suitability as a masculine ego-ideal for boys, can be seen by the number of parallel or imitative products, such as *Rapid Deployment Force* and *GI Joe*, which are presented in very similar ways.

Wars in war-toys and war-games

It is revealing to note which actual wars and conflicts have toys and games based on them, and there have been major shifts of emphasis in the last twenty years or so. There are still toy soldiers, guns, model kits and war-games deriving from the Second World War, but comparatively few from any earlier wars. This is probably because of the fetishization of technology in toys in general, and in war-toys in particular. Toys representing technological equipment (such as helicopters or tanks) and technological toys (such as sound-generating guns or computer games) comprise the majority of toys for boys. But there are few toys or games relating to the Vietnam War or to the Falklands War, for example, although these offer opportunities for the production of technological toys. It is self-evident that, in Britain at least, these wars have lost cultural visibility because of their political sensitivity in comparison to the apparently more clear-cut issues involved in the Gulf War and the Second World War. There are toy weapons, computer games and model vehicles and aircraft representing aspects of the Gulf War, and interestingly some representing the United Nations Peacekeeping Force.

One of the toys in the *My Toy* range of cheaper plastic toys is "Peacekeeper". This is an ensemble of toys in a single package containing a black plastic machine-gun, a military-style watch, a walkie-talkie and two dog-tags. The packaging shows an illustration of a tank. Despite the fact that the toy itself is in no specific way related to UN Peacekeeping except in name, and is physically similar to any number of war-toys not associated with the UN, it claims a form of legitimacy and acceptability by referring to UN Peacekeeping Forces, which are not only "our side", but also keeping the peace. In each case of the toy figures representing combatants in actual wars, there is a greater variety of different infantrymen, tanks, aeroplanes, etc. on "our" side than on the side of the Axis powers, Iraq or other "enemies". This is notable in the case of the UN Peacekeeping troops and their enemies, manufactured by the company, Britains, under the "Task Force" logo. The "Peacekeeper"'s enemies are costumed in non-specific camouflage uniforms, equipped with Soviet-made arms, and their skin colour is noticeably darker than the usual pink of the UN troops. It seems that the "enemy" in this case is simply "other", different from "our side", rather than nationally specified in the detail which is found in the plastic figures representing Axis forces, which are specifically German, Japanese, and so on.

The statically-posed plastic soldiers made by Britains under the "Task Force" brand are explicitly offered as representational and realistic, using the same mixture of fantasy-adventure and a link to contemporary war as found in ACTION MAN. "Task Force" sets contain several figures in combat poses, together with an artillery-piece, boat or helicopter. The product name seems to allude to the Falklands War and to UN Task Forces, and pack illustrations show a scene in which the relevant assault team are entering occupied territory. The package text shared by the sets invites us to:

> Join the Task Force and be ready for the thrills and adventures in the exciting world of modern combat. On land, in the air, at sea – the Task Force are ready to face the modern military challenge. Task Force action figures – put them to the test.

These figures invite identification with "our side" and with contemporary military operations in general. The package illustrations suggest a way of playing with the figures in which a static diorama is constructed, or a simple war-game is devised. Unlike the case of ACTION MAN, physical play is difficult with these small static figures, and there is no central character in the fictional scenario. However, like ACTION MAN, the "Task Force" figure sets represent war similarly as "thrills" and "adventure", and as active, challenging and masculinised.

"Task Force" figures are differentiated from other Britains figures representing ceremonial uniformed figures (such as a Changing of the Guard set) by price, name and packaging, and in my local toy superstore by a sign which informs the shopper that the ceremonial figures are "collectable models and not toys". The "Task Force" figures representing recent military conflicts reflect the ideological opposition between "us" and "them", and the unspoken positive valuation of combat in general, while the ceremonial figures confirm the "heritage" role of the military in Britain. This heritage role legitimates the centrality of the Army to the notion of Britishness and refers to the mythic solidity and continuity of our hierarchical social system. The value of this heritage is reflected in the relatively high monetary cost of the figures, and the implication that they are to be collected and admired as valued possessions.

As in the case of war-toys, video and computer games based on fictional wars or on versions of actual wars are varied, but show interesting similarities in theme, presentation and possible ways of being played. The presence of an explicit war theme in computer games promotes a naturalisation of war as an activity, and of the simplified ideological representation of particular historical conflicts. Games produced for the Sega Mastersystem games console, for example, are mostly warlike in character, but there are many more games based on fantasy scenarios such as dungeons and dragons, space combat or science-fiction film spin-offs (the *Terminator 2* game, for example) than on historical wars. Computer games are of course technological in themselves, but the war-games based on actual conflicts emphasise the technological nature of the recent wars represented in the game.

This is particularly evident in the package text accompanying the IBM PC version of *Desert Strike*, entitled "Desert Strike: Return to the Gulf". The scenario is described in a highly melodramatic form: "The whole world holds its breath as Armageddon threatens. The location is the Middle East: a melting pot of religions, races and conflicting arguments." The key themes here are the urgency of the scenario, the otherness and the inscrutability of the causes of the crisis. It is evident that there is no need or advantage in understanding the crisis historically or politically. Instead, the immediate military situation is what is important, and the description of the game moves at once to the technological sophistication of the conflict:

Without warning, a madman has emerged, the mysterious 'General' Kilbaba. His armies have swept into a tiny neighbouring emirate and are even now holding the country to ransom. Little information is available on this dictator and his regime but we suspect an arsenal of lethal conventional chemical and maybe even nuclear weapons are at his disposal.

The player's overall opponent is a mad dictator, functioning simply as a demonised other who clearly must be destroyed. The situation is interestingly similar to ACTION MAN's opponent, DR X, although here the popular press's representation of Saddam Hussein is called on to justify the fictional scenario. As in the case of ACTION MAN and his "Mission Profile", the player is a lone hero on a vital mission, legitimated by a higher power. "Our side" in this case is the United States:

The President has chosen you to fly a series of dangerous missions in an Apache attack helicopter with the aim of striking at the very heart of this evil empire. Time is not on our side. Your helicopter is fully armed and waiting so head straight for the war zone. You'll need the right strategy, nerves of steel and a steady hand under fire to succeed. Fortunately you've got some state-of-the-art weaponry to unleash – and you're going to need it! Good luck, the free world is counting on you!

The narrative voice here moves from establishing the enemy as inscrutable, irrational and evil (borrowing the "evil empire" reference from President Reagan's description of the Soviet Union, which itself referred back to the fictional war narrative of *Star Wars*) to the competencies needed to succeed in the game. The means used to win the game are finally more significant than the end proposed by the outline scenario, and the relationship between "striking" at the "evil empire" and strategic war aims is left unclear.

The text uses a series of discursive tags or triggers borrowed from representations of actual and fictional wars as a confused but effective way of defining "us" and "them", good and evil, in the game scenario. We might suggest that the same was true of the language used about the Gulf War itself, where the imperative to do something active and competent appeared to be more significant than pursuing a clearly-defined objective, and demonization of the opponent took the place of debate about strategic reasons for fighting. The game's narrative discourse uncannily reproduces the language in which the Gulf War was discussed in actuality. The visual representation of battle in the game itself reproduces the form of the television coverage of the war, where, for example, BBC Television's *Newsnight* programme

177

used a sandpit diorama to represent battle positions, and nightly televised briefings by General Colin Powell used video pictures from air missions, where "state-of-the-art weaponry" was shown being unleashed. Like a computer game, the war was represented as "clean", dehumanised and well-managed. While the ideological coding of the *Desert Strike* game reproduces the terms of the ideological coding of the Gulf War, the Gulf War reproduced the terms of computer war-games. The actual war and its representation in the game mutually legitimate and confirm each other.

On another level, these war-toys and games perform the significant function of rendering war itself a natural phenomenon of the real world, the world of adulthood which children are about to enter. As the French cultural critic, Roland Barthes, wrote in an essay on toys nearly 40 years ago:

> French toys *always mean something*, and this something is always entirely socialized, constituted by the myths or the techniques of modern adult life: the Army, Broadcasting, the Post Office, Medicine,...School, Hair-Styling...Transport... Science...[14]

Toys are particularly important because they are part of social development for children, introducing them into the ideology and social structures of adult culture. Rather than war being a contingent part of our culture, with a specific place in our political, economic and historical sense of our national identity, war appears to the child as natural, part of the greater order of unchanging human nature.

The cultural function of war-toys is not crudely to inculcate national and cultural stereotypes (although toys also do this), but to make the concept of war both natural and eternal. Playing war, which involves the imitation of warlike activities and also the adoption of ideological stereotypes about the combatants, introduces to the child a range of ideas about the adult world which are already circulating culturally. As Millar remarks:

> Imitative play apes the adult world to a large extent because the child must be active in some way and has few or no ideas or sustained aims of his own as yet. The battles and wars of one generation are the games of the next. Toy soldiers are dressed and named according to the most impressive or latest adult tale.[15]

War-toys and war-games represent a world in which adult activities such as war are already meaningful and accepted, with relatively clear demarcations between heroes and villains, and between acceptable and unacceptable actions. The child uses the materials and ideas of this miniature, simplified world in play, and toys set limits to the creativity and originality of play. No matter how elaborate or original the child's games and fantasies, they must by definition exist within the terrain of the thinkable ideas that exist in the child's cultural environment. The meaningfulness of war-toys and war-games for the child can only exist in relation to, as part of, or as a resistance to the ideological representations that already exist around him/her.

As Barthes comments, toys of all kinds prepare the child to be a consumer of ideological myths, in addition to a consumer of products, and thus toys perpetuate the ideological terms in which society is structured as meaningful, whatever the nature of the particular toys which are played with:

> the child can only identify himself as owner, as user, never as creator; he does not invent the world, he uses it; there are, prepared for him, actions without adventure, without wonder, without joy.[16]

This is a form of apprenticeship for adulthood, in which lived reality appears to be mostly unalterable in its form and character, and where "reality" "naturally" lays out a limited set of roles for the individual to take up.

It has always been the case that the forms and popularity of toys are related to the ideology of the culture which consumes them, the obvious example in Britain being the long history of the aptly named Britains toys, reflecting the imperial scope and ambitions of the British Empire in its toy soldiers. Since modern toys are mass-produced products, commodities made cheaply and sold in large numbers, their production has been exported to the low-wage economies of the Far East, although the toys themselves represent the conflicts engaged in by the Western powers. The toy economy is itself a form of cultural imperialism, practised not by war but by trade. What war-toys are available and the specific details of those war-toys unsurprisingly reinforce cultural and political stereotypes about "our side" vs. "the enemy", which derive from the dominant players in the "New World Order". But children playing with war-toys are not only consumers of ideas about war – which are circulating mostly beyond the control of the adults who buy toys, as well as of the children who play with them – but also consumers of toy products bought for them in a commercial and industrial context.

War-toys and consumer culture

Branches of the well-known toy superstore, "Toys Я Us"®, are divided into sections corresponding to the types of goods on sale. The design is very similar to that of a food supermarket, with aisles of particular types of goods. Like supermarket shoppers, customers use the same wire baskets and trolleys in the toy store. This design contrasts with Early Learning Centre shops, for example, which contain no war-toys, are arranged more by age group than by toy category, and have toys for young children only. War-toys and games, like the other toys in "Toys Я Us"®, are presented as commodities, rather than as aids to child development, as in the Early Learning Centres. The majority of shopping space in "Toys Я Us"® is given over to categorised toys for children aged approximately 4-11. Separate sections display toy vehicles, guns, plastic figures, model kits, sports toys, cuddly toys, dolls and "girls' toys", collectables, bikes, prams and baby equipment, videos and computer games. Despite the categorisation of the main area of the store, war-toys can be found in every toy section except in the cuddly toys or girls' toys areas. War-toys are conceived by retailers as just another kind of toy, although they are not legitimated by their role in children's learning.

There are obvious differences in colour of packaging between girls' toys, which are predominantly pink, pale blue and other pastel shades, and the (much greater number of) toys for boys which have darker, stronger colours. The photographs and illustrations on these boys' toy packages often show an excited child (aged about 6-8), and the illustrations usually give an indication of how the toy should be played with by portraying an action scenario involving the toy. These differences between toys according to gender and the activeness represented by boys' toys have already been discussed. But the function of war-toy presentation is not only to show and define the toy, but also to stimulate a desire for it. In effect, toy packaging is a form of advertising. The way that package images stimulate the desire to buy and own them in children is by presenting the toy as an attribute of an ego-ideal. As Judith Williamson comments in her study of advertising, the role of an advertising image is "to signify, to represent to us, the *object* of desire".[17] Since the desired object is desired because it promises the subject fulfilment, the attainment of an ego-ideal, the image of the war-toy or of the happy child playing with the war-toy on the package is an image of a desired self or an attribute of one. As Williamson argues, "while ensnaring/creating the subject through his or her exchange of signs, the advertisement is actually feeding off that subject's own desire for coherence and meaning in him or her self".[18]

War-toys, therefore, like any other consumer commodity, do not supply any basic human need, but are desired because they promise to give satisfaction to a sense that something is lacking in the subject's notion of his/her identity. As we have seen, war-toys are active and not passive; they are masculine and not feminine. The meaning of war-toys and war-games depends on their ideological role in setting up a binary division between a positively represented meaning and a negatively represented one. War-toys establish an ideological field of meanings in which the toy consumer is subjected to a masculine, active identity defined by the repudiation of feminine, passive roles. However, because this construction of subjective identity can never be complete and finished, there always remains a lack in its structure, a further emptiness which calls to be filled. Because of this lack in being, there always remains a desire for further confirmation of the ideal masculine identity. By representing war-toys as objects which promise the attainment of an ego-ideal, the unfulfilled desire of the child unconsciously takes the acquisition of more toys to be the means to complete and confirm his/her identity. Since no one can escape the ideological field of meanings which define his/her identity but leave this identity perpetually uncompleted, there is always a desire to possess more commodities, to consume more products. The desire for war-toys is one aspect of the desire for a coherent masculine identity for the male child, and it is this imaginary identity which is being sold.

Children learn to play in their families, where adults may have all kinds of reasons for encouraging or discouraging the consumption of certain types of toys or games, perhaps including war-toys. But children learn also to play outside the home, in groups of other children, where different rules and prohibitions will be in play. Children are also exposed to television, cinema, advertising, books and comics, which not only include explicit war-toy and war-game merchandising opportunities, but also support more abstract ideological meanings promoting aggression, competition and the other components of masculine identity which war-toys reproduce. As Cohen reports in his book on play:

> When both our sons were young, we were determined in best *Guardian* reader style not to encourage aggressive impulses in our boys. No guns, more dolls. We found we couldn't stick to this ideal because the boys insisted on having all kinds of space weaponry especially after *Star Wars*.[19]

It is probably impossible to prevent a desire for war-toys in a culture which invests them with significance and offers them as attractive consumer products.

One of the most successful recent war-toy ranges is the *Mighty Morphin' Power Rangers* brand. In addition, there are toys clearly imitating the *Power Ranger* brand by using similar names, colours and product designs. *Power Ranger* toys include a plastic sword about 12" long, at once oriental and futuristic, whose blade lights up, and a plastic pistol in the same sci-fi style. Like the other branded television spin-off toys, which include miniature figures as well as action toys and collectable accessories, what is being sold is a whole "*Power Rangers* world", a selection of products with which the child can re-enact narratives from the television series using the toys, and create new narratives for himself/herself. The pleasure in using the toys comes largely from their function as props in make-believe play, a dramatised role-play war-game.

Like the rather similar phenomenon of the *Teenage Mutant Ninja Hero Turtles* a few years ago (these toys are still on sale, but in lesser numbers), the *Power Rangers*' fictional narrative world includes toy commodities which can be collected, repeated plot scenarios which can form the basis for make-believe identificatory play, and distinctive character movements involving physical prowess (a mixture of eastern martial arts, fist-fighting and armed combat) which can be imitated in aggressive physical play. Clearly, these toys activate similar meanings in relation to masculine identity as other toys discussed above. But, as in the case of ACTION MAN, for example, the themed range of toys sharing the same logo, design features and name provides an explicit opportunity for the desire to amass all the products in the range. This stimulates the desire to consume, and the desire to attain peer-group prestige by possessing toys which have become indicators of social standing by virtue of successful marketing. Like all the war-toys and war-games discussed here, these toys fulfil a range of ideological functions in relation to masculinity, war and consumerism.

Further research on how toys such as these are played with might reveal that children negotiate with the dominant ideological meanings of war-toys and war-games in the context of their own lives. Some children might use *Power Rangers* toys or ACTION MAN, for example, in ways which challenge their role as legitimators of an active and aggressive masculinity. Just as some adults are able to articulate views about war that are alternative or resistant to the dominant representations of war in our culture, children too may consciously or unconsciously find ways of positioning themselves differently from the ways in which they are positioned by the discourses of war-toys and war-games. While ideology determines the common sense and "natural" attitudes which make up our reality, it is never entirely consistent, coherent or eternal.

There is a limited amount of published research on war-toys and war-games of any kind, and much of the work that has been done on children's toys and play (which does not discuss war-toys or games) concerns children younger than those to whom the toys discussed here are marketed. This essay has aimed to outline some of the significant ideological meanings of war-toys and war-games, and to suggest that war-toys and war-games are culturally significant. One of the most productive ways in which the study of war-toys and war-games could be developed is to investigate the meanings of particular toys for particular children. This type of ethnographic study would be concerned with which toys and games children enjoy, why they are enjoyed, and how they fit into the lived experience of individual children.[20] Such an approach has been used to study adult culture (television, popular literature and film, for example), and could be adapted for research on children's war-toys and war-games.

Notes

[1]   A useful collection of essays representing the current state of cultural studies as a discipline, together with an account of its evolution, can be found in Ann Gray and Jim McGuigan (eds), *Studying Culture: An Introductory Reader* (London: Edward Arnold, 1993).

[2]   Louis Althusser, "Ideology and Ideological State Apparatuses", in *Lenin and Philosophy and other essays*, translated from the French by Ben Brewster (London: New Left Books, 1971): 121-173.

[3]   Brian Sutton-Smith et al, "Game Involvement in Adults", *Journal of Social Psychology* 60 (1963): 15-30.

[4]   Thomas W Malone, "What Makes Things Fun to Learn? A Study of Intrinsically Motivating Computer Games", paper produced for Cognitive and Instructional Science Series CIS-7, Palo Alto Research Center, California (1980), and Thomas W Malone, "Toward a Theory of Intrinsically Motivating Instruction", *Cognitive Science* 5 (1981): 333-369.

[5]   This issue is discussed in Patricia Marks Greenfield, *Mind and Media: The Effects of Television, Computers and Video Games* (London: Fontana, 1984): 92-94.

[6]   Evidence is surveyed in David Cohen, *The Development of Play* (Beckenham: Croom Helm, 1987), especially 55-59.

[7]   Brian Sutton-Smith, "The Game as a School of Abstraction", in Loyda M Shears and Eli M Bower (eds), *Games in Education and Development* (Springfield, IL: C C Thomas, 1974): 119-127, 122.

[8]   Ibid.

[9]   Some of the toy guns carry warnings that they should not be used in an enclosed space or near other people, implying that they are designed for use outdoors.

[10] Guns as emblems of masculine power and prowess are commonly found in films and television for an adult audience, for example.

[11] Jeffrey Weeks, *Sexuality and Its Discontents: Meanings, Myths & Modern Sexualities* (London: Routledge, 1985): 190.

[12] Sigmund Freud conceived of gender identity as an unstable and evolving process, and this conception lies behind the quotation from Weeks in note 11.

[13] A critical account of the Freudian model can be found in Weeks: 127-181.

[14] Roland Barthes, "Toys", in *Mythologies* (London: Granada, 1973): 53. Emphasis in original.

[15] Susanna Millar, *The Psychology of Play* (London: Penguin, 1971): 174.

[16] Barthes: 54.

[17] Judith Williamson, *Decoding Advertisements: Ideology and Meaning in Advertising* (London: Marion Boyars, 1978): 60. Emphasis in original.

[18] Ibid.

[19] Cohen: 58.

[20] Ethnography is a significant recent contribution to cultural studies. Two significant works taking this approach are Janice A Radway, *Reading the Romance: Women, Patriarchy, and Popular Literature* (London: Verso, 1987) and Ien Ang, *Watching Dallas: Soap Opera and the Melodramatic Imagination*, translated by Della Couling (London; New York: Methuen, 1985).

Postmodernism and military history
Nigel de Lee

We do not know what we know. (Major-General Rupert Smith)[1]

Rupert Smith is the very model of a postmodern Major-General, very well aware of the limitations imposed upon the military thinker by the conventions of modernity. Modernists insist upon the application of rationalism, scepticism, positivism and the bivalent truth theorem to all questions. Postmodernists reject the scientific and liberal views of knowledge and wisdom. Military historians should also reject the modernist method, for it is not a suitable instrument for the consideration and understanding of the most important of military affairs. Military history cannot provide exclusive, absolute, categorical, certain truths, and be comprehensive and honest. Military activity as such is alien to liberal political ideas of individualism and libertarianism; effective military training and operations require a collectivist and highly disciplined attitude.

The modernist student of military history soon encounters the basic problem of evidence. The availability and quality of evidence concerning military activity is often highly dubious, especially testimony about combat. The type of evidence preferred by the modernist – voluminous texts that can be examined and analysed as sources of revealed wisdom with rabbinical precision – is usually not available for combat. This modern evidence is available in profusion concerning the bureaucratic aspects of war, such as administration, planning and conferring. These activities are essential, but only as auxiliaries to the vital business of armies, which is fighting.

Even if the modernist is content to limit his interest to strategic planning, civil-military relations and administration, the documentary sources may be incomplete. In recent decades, many questions have been decided by means of unrecorded telephone conversations, personal meetings at which a nod can signal assent, or by tacit consensus. Many conferences issue partial minutes or papers designed to deceive, for reasons such as the maintenance of security, the avoidance of personal embarrassment, or other causes connected to bureaucratic intrigue. The sources available can be very heavily tainted with falsehood, which the scholar may not be able to detect or purge from his material or from his own fallible and receptive mind.

Few armies in the field are capable of keeping full records of their activities; they have more important and urgent matters to preoccupy them. Armies are inherently mutually destructive and self-consuming; soldiers are expendable and they know it. A defeated army will usually attempt to destroy important papers if it has the time and opportunity. If it has not the leisure, the papers will most likely be scattered to the winds to litter the stricken field. Many a fighting soldier has wondered at the sheer quantity of paper strewn about on the battlefield. Successful armies often achieve victory by direct attacks upon the enemy HQs and chains of command, striking at command centres and communications facilities. These are exactly the places where the records and archives of an army are located. Napoleon even had a mobile library in his train as a source of reference.

Where documents produced by field units and formations do survive, "action documents", such as orders, signals, "sitreps" (situation reports) and so on, they tend to be ephemeral and laconic. They are often based upon assumptions that the recipients will already have a broad background of knowledge; this can mean that they might as well be written in an impenetrable code for any person not reading them in the fleeting context of their original time and place. Although functional, they are also subject to distortion of truth, as they are frequently based on false assumptions about the enemy or friendly forces. As Clausewitz observed, war is the province of uncertainty. The necessities of war ensure that all orders must be speculative, and the requirement to speculate entails a risk of involuntary deception. As Colonel Mosby remarked, "[s]trategy is only another name for deception".[2]

For land operations, an historian can also examine the ground over which armies have fought. This, at least, is solid evidence. But terrain and landscape can change with the effects of seasons and the operations of man. It is often necessary to seek information about the past character of the ground by consulting the folk memory of the settled inhabitants, if there are any. In any case, the influence of the ground on the conduct of operations has to be subjected to *ex-post facto* interpretation; the hills and woods may speak but, as with all language, the meanings of the terms they express can change.

All historians are forced to rely on memory, whether it is collective or individual; military historians consult records of immediate short-term memory, such as after-action reports and post-exercise reports. Memory, never wholly reliable, is often accorded an unjustified authority if presented in written form. Memories of life on campaign or experience in battle are particularly unreliable due to the effects of excitement, tedium, excessive exertion and the fragmentation of collective experience

186

into individualist shards. The soldier has to isolate himself from his comrades to maximise his chances of survival on the modern battlefield. Subsequent experience and the reception of information and ideas taken from other veterans' accounts can cause more distortion and confusion to the individual witness. With the passage of time, memory becomes more comprehensive, but also subjected to the effects of reflection and refraction. Miles Gloriosus rewrites the tale, or his successors in the arts of creative recollection, Falstaff, Pistol, Nym and Bardolph.

Oral history can overcome some of these difficulties. The physical provenance of a document can be tested using the methods of chemistry and physics, but the truth of statements in it cannot. In an interview an informant can be interrogated directly; contrary or contradictory statements can attract supplementary questions; and tone of voice and physical posture will supplement the verbal evidence. It is easier to lie deliberately, by calculation, in a written document than *viva voce*. The interview is a dialogue of fallible parties; it is a subjective method, as is the reading of a piece of paper. But, because it is an exchange of ideas which is active, mutually stimulating and cumulative, it is capable of revealing far more than the most detailed examination of cold print. A document cannot be cross-examined.

Descriptive documents, reports, dispatches and memoirs most often give accounts of action from the witness's point of view. If the losers give their own impressions, they can be influenced to conform to the winners' opinions. Defeated commanders can be especially vulnerable to cajolery, as shown in Liddell Hart's behaviour when interviewing German generals in preparation for "the other side of the hill".

Military historians of the modernist tradition are invariably anxious to be positive and to assert. It is very difficult, if not impossible, to know what happened in a battle; all available forms of evidence are unreliable and fragmentary. Battles are uncertain and messy, hence the tendency to neglect them, as described by John Keegan in *The Face of Battle*.

We may not be able to know with certainty and valid proof what happened in combat, but we can form reasonable beliefs, based upon imagination, about the events, conditions and characteristics of military engagements. The use of imagination, based upon sceptical use of what evidence can be obtained, is more akin to the creative work of the artist, than the analysis of a chemist or the calculations of a mathematician. In place of proof and certainty the historians must put possibility, probability and plausibility. As Colonel A H Burne remarked in explaining his principle of inherent military probability, which he applied to the appreciation of battlefields:

[R]eliable records of an English battle are distressingly meagre. When one has discounted the exaggerations inevitable in a medieval chronicle, the distortions due to misconception, the errors due to absence of maps, and sometimes even deliberate fabrication – there is not much pure grain left. Ancient history, as it is presented in the history books, is a compound of fact and inference or conjecture, and the conjecture will vary with the individual. This is particularly true of battles. My method here is to start with what appear to be undisputed facts, then to place myself in the shoes of each commander in turn, and to ask myself in each case what I would have done...I then compare the resulting action with the existing records to see whether it describes any incompatibility with the accepted facts. If it does not, I then go on to the next debatable or obscure point in the battle and repeat the operation.[3]

The use of such methods can never produce final and perfect conclusions. The evidence of the ground is solid and material, and changes to it can be discovered by unearthing records or consulting settled collective memory. But the significance of the ground is a matter of judgment, based on experience, a notion of human nature, beliefs about behaviour in earlier actions, and other subjective considerations. Judgment can be flawed: in selecting the place where Caesar forded the Thames, Lieutenant-Colonel Burne once nearly drowned a party of military tourists.[4]

Modernists are constitutionally averse to such accidents and adventures; they prefer dull and comforting certainty. Thus, they are strongly inclined to concentrate upon the peripheral military activities, the evolution of theory and doctrine, civil-military relations, strategic planning, and campaign history embellished with big arrows and definite lines on small maps. All this leaves an aching void at the centre of the student of the military art, a hunger for understanding of the most important, decisive and mysterious of phenomena, the clash of forces in the field.

Extreme modernists have taken flight from history as such. They describe themselves as social scientists, intent upon achieving for their comprehension of human behaviour the same degree of precision as claimed by natural scientists and mathematicians. But the claims of the natural scientists to precision cannot be sustained, particularly in the life sciences. In genetics and microbiology, experiments which fail are ignored, provided a certain percentage of the tests are successful. Absolute reliability of results can be achieved only in mathematics, in itself a series of tautologous intellectual games, wholly artificial and unconnected to reality. When applied to reality, especially human activities, mathematical methods consistently fail the practical, demonstrated by the failings of meteorology, econometrics, economics, insurance and the football pools. As in the case of astrology, the paraphernalia of the method and sublime confidence of those who apply it are more striking and impressive than the results. The appearance of precision and the egotistical self-confidence of practitioners appeal to the mentally lazy or those with sterile minds. It is easier to gather figures about human behaviour, feed them into a computer, and garnish the statistics produced by the machine with remarks laudatory of scientific method, than it is to sit and think. Thus, we have attempts to reduce the conduct of war to an "exact science", based upon pure technology and mathematical models of collective behaviour. Previous efforts to understand and predict the nature of war by statistical analysis, engineering paradigms and business administration have produced discouraging results. The theories of Bloch and Angell failed in the real world. The effects of aerial bombardment on civilian populations and war economies were not accurately predicted during the Second World War. The Hamlet Evaluation Scheme applied by the US Army in Vietnam failed. Soviet norms did not apply in Afghanistan.

The desire to know the future is not new, and it would indeed be advantageous to military planning to fulfil it. Wallenstein relied on astrology as an aid to planning his strategy. Military intelligence organs are staffed by practising futurologists. But the current practitioners usually realise that facts can exist only in the past and the present, and not in the third temporal dimension, the future. For practical and historical purposes, the acquisition of facts, of knowledge, is of limited value to the military practitioner or historian.

The serious purpose of military history, accompanying others such as entertainment and propaganda, is the development of wisdom. Wisdom, whether theoretical or practical, does not require precision, as the acquisition and retailing of facts does. Wisdom must take account of the significance of evidence presented, whether in documents, oral statements and other texts, or in the physical characteristics of ground, weapons and other material evidence. This is a matter of interpretation, not mere reading, of a comprehension which is imaginative as well as sceptical. Wisdom produces a state of mind in which ignorance and uncertainty do not automatically inspire panic and intellectual flight from the wood but into the trees of ascertainable facts and doctrinaire orthodoxy.

Military history is organic and diverse. It is premodern, modern and postmodern. Good military history must include an understanding of military operations. Since these are not suitable phenomena for the application of modern intellectual methods, good military history cannot be modern. On reflection, one might conclude that all good military history has been reactionary or postmodern, having bypassed modernity entirely.

Notes

1 Major-General Rupert Smith, *Gulf War: Relations with the Americans*, BCMH Conference on Coalition Warfare, Staff College, Camberley, 21 November 1992.

2 Charles Wells Russell (ed), *Gray Ghost: The Memoirs of Colonel John S. Mosby* (New York: Bantam Books, 1992): 121.

3 Information from conversation with Professor J Wilton-Ely.

4 Lieutenant-Colonel Alfred H Burne, *The Battlefields of England* (London: Methuen, 1951): xi-xii.

Selected bibliography

Adams, Valerie. *The Media and the Falklands Campaign* (London: Macmillan, 1986).

Aldgate, Anthony and Jeffrey Richards. *Britain Can Take It: The British Cinema in the Second World War* (Oxford: Basil Blackwell, 1986).

Barthes, Roland. *Mythologies* (London: Granada, 1973).

Bennett, W Lance and David L Paletz (eds), *Taken By Storm: The Media, Public Opinion, and U.S. Foreign Policy in the Gulf War* (Chicago; London: University of Chicago Press, 1994).

Bond, Brian (ed). *The First World War and British Military History* (Oxford: Clarendon Press, 1991).

Bourne, John. *Britain and the Great War, 1914-1918* (London: Edward Arnold, 1989).

Boyd-Barrett, Oliver and Peter Braham (eds). *Media, Knowledge and Power* (Beckenham: Croom Helm, in association with the Open University, 1987).

Brownlow, Kevin. *The War, the West and the Wilderness* (London: Secker & Warburg, 1979).

Campen, Alan D (ed). *The First Information War* (Fairfax, VA: AFCEA, 1992).

Carruthers, Susan L. *Winning Hearts and Minds: British Governments, the Media and Colonial Counter-Insurgency* (London: Leicester University Press, 1995).

Connaughton, Richard. *Military Intervention in the 1990s: A new logic of war* (London: Routledge, 1992).

Cumings, Bruce. *War and Television* (London: Verso, 1992).

Curran, James and Michael Gurevitch (eds). *Mass Media and Society* (London: Edward Arnold, 1991).

Dawson, Graham. *Soldier Heroes: British adventure, empire and the imagining of masculinity* (London: Routledge, 1994).

Dibbets, Karel and Bert Hogenkamp (eds). *Film and The First World War* (Amsterdam: Amsterdam University Press, 1995).

Forbes, Ian and Mark Hoffman (eds). *Political Theory, International Relations, and the Ethics of Intervention* (London: Macmillan, 1993).

Freedman, Lawrence (ed). *War* (Oxford; New York: Oxford University Press, 1994).

Fussell, Paul. *The Great War and Modern Memory* (Oxford: Oxford University Press, 1975).

Gray, Ann and Jim McGuigan (eds), *Studying Culture: An Introductory Reader* (London: Edward Arnold, 1993).

Harris, Robert. *Gotcha! The Media, the Government and the Falklands Crisis* (London: Faber and Faber, 1983).

Haste, Cate. *Keep the Home Fires Burning: Propaganda in the First World War* (London: Allen Lane, 1977).

Hyams, Jay. *War Movies* (New York: Gallery Books, 1984).

Knightley, Phillip. *The First Casualty. From the Crimea to Vietnam: The War Correspondent as Hero, Propagandist, and Myth Maker* (London: Pan Books, 1975).

Marks Greenfield, Patricia. *Mind and Media: The Effects of Television, Computers and Video Games* (London: Fontana, 1984).

McInnes, Colin and G D Sheffield (eds). *Warfare in the Twentieth Century: Theory and Practice* (London: Unwin Hyman, 1988).

McLaine, Ian. *The Ministry of Morale: Home Front Morale and the Ministry of Information in World War II* (London: George Allen & Unwin, 1979).

McQuail, Denis. *Communication*, second edition (London; New York: Longman, 1984).

Mercer, Derrik, Geoff Mungham and Kevin Williams. *The Fog of War: The Media on the Battlefield* (London: Heinemann, 1987).

Messinger, Gary S. *British propaganda and the state in the First World War* (Manchester: Manchester University Press, 1992).

Miller, David. *Don't Mention the War: Northern Ireland, Propaganda and the Media* (London: Pluto Press, 1994).

Morrison, David E. *Television and the Gulf War* (London: John Libbey, 1992).

Murphy, Robert. *Realism and Tinsel: Cinema and society in Britain 1939-1948* (London: Routledge, 1989).

Pedeltey, Mark. *War Stories: The Culture of Foreign Correspondents* (London: Routledge, 1995).

Pimlott, John and Stephen Badsey (eds). *The Gulf War Assessed*

(London: Arms and Armour Press, 1992).

Reeves, Nicholas. *Official British Film Propaganda During The First World War* (Beckenham: Croom Helm, in association with the Imperial War Museum, 1986).

Richards, Jeffrey and Anthony Aldgate. *Best of British: Cinema and Society 1930-1970* (Oxford: Basil Blackwell, 1983).

Rose, Tania. *Aspects of Political Censorship 1914-18* (Hull: University of Hull Press, 1995).

Rutherford, Andrew. *The Literature of War: Five Studies in Heroic Virtue* (London: Macmillan, 1978).

Sanders, M L and Philip M Taylor. *British Propaganda during the First World War, 1914-18* (London; Basingstoke: Macmillan, 1982).

Schlesinger, Philip. *Putting 'reality' together: BBC news*, second edition (London; New York: Methuen, 1987).

Short K R M (ed). *Film & Radio Propaganda in World War II* (London; Canberra: Croom Helm, 1983).

Stewart, Lieutenant-Colonel Bob. *Broken Lives: A Personal View of the Bosnian Conflict* (London: HarperCollins, 1993).

Taylor, Philip M (ed). *Britain and the Cinema in the Second World War* (London: Macmillan Press, 1988).

Taylor, Philip M. *Munitions of the Mind: War propaganda from the ancient world to the nuclear age* (London: Patrick Stephens, 1990).

——————. *War and the media: Propaganda and persuasion in the Gulf War* (Manchester: Manchester University Press, 1992).

Thompson, Kristin and David Bordwell. *Film History: An Introduction* (New York: McGraw-Hill, 1994).

Thompson, Mark. *Forging War: The Media in Serbia, Croatia and Bosnia-Hercegovina* (London: Article 19, 1994).

Travers, Tim. *The Killing Ground: The British Army, the Western Front and the Emergence of Modern Warfare 1900-1918* (London: Allen & Unwin, 1987).

Virilio, Paul. *War and Cinema: The Logistics of Perception*, translated by Patrick Camiller (London: Verso, 1989).

Woodward, Sandy with Patrick Robinson. *One Hundred Days: The Memoirs of the Falklands Battle Group Commander* (London: HarperCollins, 1992).

Young, Peter R (ed). *Defence and the Media in Time of Limited War* (London: Frank Cass, 1992).

Index